POWERBOAT CARE AND REPAIR

POWERBOAT CARE AND REPAIR

How to Keep Your Outboard, Sterndrive, or Gas-Inboard Boat Alive and Well

Allen Berrien

International Marine / McGraw-Hill
Camden, Maine • New York • Chicago • San Francisco •
Lisbon • London • Madrid • Mexico City • Milan • New Delhi •
San Juan • Seoul • Singapore • Sydney • Toronto

The McGraw-Hill Companies

4 5 6 7 8 9 0 DOC DOC 0 1 0 9 8

An earlier version of this book was published as *Boating Magazine's The Boat Doctor*.

Library of Congress Cataloging-in-Publication Data
Berrien, Allen D.
Powerboat care and repair : how to keep your outboard, sterndrive, or gas-inboard boat alive and well / Allen Berrien.— 1st ed.
p. cm.
Rev. ed. of: Boating magazine's the boat doctor. c1998.
Includes index.
ISBN 0-07-141946-2
1. Boats and boating—Maintenance and repair. 2. Motorboats—Maintenance and repair. I. Berrien, Allen D. Boating magazine's the boat doctor. II. Title.
VM322.B4724 2003
623.8′231′0288—dc21 2003013371

Questions regarding the content of this book should be addressed to
International Marine
P.O. Box 220
Camden, ME 04843
www.internationalmarine.com

Questions regarding the ordering of this book should be addressed to
The McGraw-Hill Companies
Customer Service Department
P.O. Box 547
Blacklick, OH 43004
Retail customers: 1-800-262-4729
Bookstores: 1-800-722-4726

Folio illustrations by Chris Van Dusen, text illustrations by Jim Sollers.
Photograph on page ii courtesy Boston Whaler.
Photographs by the author.

This book is dedicated to my wife, Maggie. You've been my calm in the midst of the howling gale.

It's also dedicated to the howling gale—our four children: Kate, Elizabeth, Heather, and Clay. I love you all.

Contents

Acknowledgments

Writing a book is a lonely enterprise. Yet, in my experience, it's never something that's done alone. I've learned everything I know about boats from a host of people too numerous to mention. There are, however, some who have made such significant contributions that they must be personally acknowledged.

First, I must thank my father and my grandfather who decided that running a boatyard was a nice way to make a living (and a life). As soon as I was old enough to walk, I hung around the family yard.

I owe a special debt of gratitude to Hanford L. "Babe" Botsford, a neighbor, commercial fisherman, boat carpenter, and mentor from as early as I can remember. Besides teaching me about boats, Babe taught me humility, something that all of us need a little of. He used to say, "I taught you everything I know and you still don't know nuthin'."

Thanks also to Fred Bixby, the foreman of the mechanical crew at my family's yard. Fred taught me to be neat, organized, calm, and precise. I've used his lessons for a lot more than mechanical work since he imparted them to me years ago. They've always served me well.

Paul and Skip Birbarie of Birbarie Marine have been generous with their time whenever I've called to pick their brains with outboard-related questions. And that's been a lot.

Bob Crocker of Volvo-Penta North America is a font of sterndrive and inboard engine experience; he has saved my tail more times than I care to mention. He's probably forgotten more about boat engines than I'll ever know. He's also a good man who's smart enough to work for a good company.

I'd be remiss if I neglected to thank Carsten Jenssen of Molasses Hill. Carsten was a mentor, machinery expert, and good friend to me since I was about ten.

I owe special thanks to my patient editors at International Marine, Molly Mulhern, Jonathan Eaton, and Margaret Cook.

Lastly and most significantly, thanks to my mom, Florence, who taught me to read and to love books and words. Due to her diligence, I'll never forget that there's a *rat* in *separate*.

Introduction

We all like to work on our own boats if we can find the time. As Ratty pointed out in *The Wind in the Willows*, "there is nothing—absolutely nothing—half so much worth doing as simply messing about in boats."

There are also sensible, rational reasons for doing your own boat work. For starters of course it saves money. But it pays other dividends as well. Some of these have an even sweeter payback than mere money.

To wit: When you work on your own boat, over time you get to know it better than the mechanic at the boatyard does. This is important for psychological reasons. Most of the machines and tools in our lives are so complex that we can't really relate to them anymore . . . all we can do is stand back in awe and admiration. Most of us haven't a clue how our computers, wireless phones, or cars work. We just pray that they continue to do so.

Boats are still set a bit apart from this new-age state of affairs (you can still mess about with them). Though the engine control systems that monitor and control fuel and spark have gotten away from the ken of a do-it-yourselfer, other systems remain accessible (and serviceable by mere mortals without a closet full of specialized equipment).

Much of the mechanical componentry in even the most modern boat is not that different from the stuff in a boat built forty years ago. Pumps are still pumps, switches are still switches, and so on. You don't need a graduate degree in engineering to do the seasonal maintenance work on your boat. What you need is some time, some tools, and some training.

It's up to you to find the time, if you can. As for the tools, you'll find some suggestions for assembling a suitable tool kit in the last chapter of this book. I also provide tips for buying good-quality tools and some tool-kit development strategies. Here are a couple of examples: I've found that once you've got the basic tools, it pays to buy another more specialized tool each month. You'll soon have a rich assortment of tools at your beck and call. And if you've read this book, you'll know how to use them properly.

You can subsidize the cost of an expensive tool by considering the money it will save you. If you spare yourself a $125 labor bill by doing your own tune-up, you can pretty well justify the one-time expense of a $125 torque wrench to tighten the spark plugs. Once the job is done, you still have a torque wrench in your tool kit (and the ability to save $125 each year).

When it comes to time, tools, and training, it's probably the last item that proves to be the toughest. Take heart, though. Once you've assimilated the resources in this book and used them to point you to further information, you'll be well on your way to becoming a proficient do-it-yourselfer.

This book won't, however, tell you how to do *everything* on your boat. Why not? Because there are some parts of your boat that do call for specialized training and tools to tackle. They're beyond the scope of this book and beyond the capabilities of most do-it-yourself boatowners. (Or the contents of his tool kit.)

Which brings up an important point: Successful do-it-yourselfers know which tasks are beyond them. They stop before they get in over their heads and wisely call in the professionals before they mess things up.

Indeed, you won't be able to do everything. Just the same, you might be surprised at the list of boat tasks you can handle. Virtually all routine seasonal maintenance is within the capabilities of a competent do-it-yourselfer equipped with a modicum of tools.

Even if you don't choose to do much of your own maintenance and troubleshooting, simply understanding your boat's systems has some satisfying benefits. First, when you have to call in the pros, you'll have a better understanding of what they're doing.

Also, if you know your way around your boat's machinery spaces you'll know when something isn't just right. That is, if you get into the habit of making frequent inspections, which I advocate and detail in this book. Consider a hypothetical oil leak that you discover during an engine room check. Even if it isn't something you want to tangle with yourself, noticing it enables you to get a mechanic on the case quickly, before it becomes an expensive problem.

That's a central tenet to a really important aspect of owning a boat that's given short shrift these days—the notion of being a good *ship's husband*. The best boats have someone who all but holds that boat in their heart. I call this person a ship's husband. A good one takes good care of a boat in the traditional sense: making sure that problems and deficiencies are promptly corrected so that the boat is as safe and satisfying as it can possibly be. (I think it's more like the relationship that we have with horses.)

Mechanics—all mechanics—have a much higher regard for customers who do at least some of their own work and keep a clean, orderly engine room. (That's where they work, you know.) I've spent about a quarter century working and playing in a boatyard, and in this book I share some pointers to make your dealings with the boatyard more satisfying and effective.

There's one final benefit that accrues to those who work on their own boats. It's the greatest one of them all: You get to enjoy the satisfaction and pleasure of doing something with your own hands. In this differentiated and specialized society that we've evolved into, many of us work with our heads alone. That leaves heart and hands out of the equation.

Am I suggesting that you'll find happiness and the true meaning of life by working on your own boat?

Well, yes, in a small way I am. Perhaps working on your boat will give you an opportunity to reconnect with something that's important to you as a human being. As Thomas Carlyle (1795–1881) said, "Man is a tool-using animal . . . without tools he is nothing, with tools he is all." I know which I'd rather be.

Warnings

Before we set to work I would like to offer some words of warning. Working on your boat's equipment can be fun and satisfying. Having to make a trip to the emergency room because you got injured, burned, or poisoned is not. So read over these pages and heed the warnings they contain when you work on your boat. Remember—you're going to be depending on this boat you're working on. Shortcuts are not a good idea. If your car lets you down and you have to leave it on the side of the road, you can walk home. That's not true of your boat.

General Dos and Don'ts

Dos

- Enlist the aid of a helper to keep an eye on you, lend you a hand if you have to do any heavy lifting, and summon help if you get into trouble.
- Wear eye protection and other protective clothing systems—gloves, cool suit, etc.—to protect your skin and eyes from flying objects, harmful chemicals, oil and antifreeze, and burns.
- Work neatly and keep your worksite clean. Mop up spills, vacuum or sweep up debris, clean your tools, and put things away when you finish a task.
- Store and dispose of toxic chemicals and materials considerately and safely. We all have to share this planet. If you dump gasoline and other toxics on the ground, shame on you. Most towns have toxic waste drop-off days a couple of times a year and facilities to recycle drain oil. Call your Department of Public Works for details.
- When your boat is stored on land, you'll have to use a ladder to get on board. Make sure you tie the ladder off securely (to a spring-line cleat for example). Don't tie it to something horizontal like a rail; it won't be as secure. Ladders are popular places to get hurt and an unsecured ladder is an accident looking for a place to happen. Don't climb down a ladder carrying a battery, heavy toolbox, or parts. Instead put on a pair of leather work gloves and lower these down with a rope. Make sure no one is standing down there before you "lower away."

Don'ts

- Don't use automotive replacements for marine-specific parts. For example, marine electrical components are shielded so they don't cause sparks. If you use an automotive alternator, distributor, starter motor, or other electrical component on your marine engine, you're compromising your boat's safety, breaking coast guard regulations, and risking forfeiture of your boat's insurance coverage.

Similarly, fuel system components on marine engines are different from their automotive equivalents. If you have to replace a fuel pump, carburetor, or any other fuel system component, make sure you get marine parts, not automotive replacements. Even marine fuel hose is different; it's designated Type A, meaning it's designed to withstand two minutes of fire before the fuel within begins to burn. (There are also alcohol-resistant variants of this product. Since most fuel has some alcohol these days, this is what you should have. Shields Marine Hose makes one called Shields Fire-Acol; for more information, go to the Shields Web site, www.marinehoses.com.)

- Don't perform mechanical work if you're impatient, tired, or in a bad mood. Similarly, if you are under the influence of alcohol or other mind-altering substances, leave the tools in the toolbox and do something safer.
- Don't start a job if you don't have the correct tools, supplies, and knowledge in hand. That way you won't be tempted to take dangerous shortcuts that wind up injuring you or making you perform substandard work.

SPECIFIC WARNINGS

Moving Parts

To winterize some types of engines, you might have to run your boat's engine in gear, when it's on land. That means the propeller will be spinning. This is extremely dangerous. Make sure that you keep yourself and others well clear of the propeller during these steps to prevent nasty injuries. If there's any chance that curious people might come along to take a look, station someone on the ground to keep them from getting near this hazard. If you're working on an outboard or sterndrive-powered boat, it's pretty easy to remove the prop, which lessens the hazard.

Several of the operations in this book require that you work on the engine or the boat's equipment when the engine is running. When you do this, pay careful attention to the moving parts, especially the drive belts and engine accessories, such as the alternator and pumps.

Do not wear loose clothing or jewelry (a short-circuit hazard) when doing these steps, and move carefully. Though you're not likely to be wearing a necktie when you're working on your boat, carefully consider the clothing you do wear. If your shirt cuffs are ragged or loose fitting, roll them up carefully whenever you have to work around machinery that's in operation.

Also, for operations that require you to use test equipment such as timing lights or meters around equipment that's running, be sure to keep the test probes and wire leads clear of the moving parts.

Gasoline and Gasoline Vapors

Gasoline and its vapors are highly explosive. In fact the vapors are the more explosive of the two. These vapors are also heavier than air, so they sink to the bottom of the engine room and bilges. Of course you should run your boat's blowers to ventilate these spaces whenever you prepare to start the engine, but that's not enough. Careful boaters also get down in there and perform a "sniff test" to detect the presence of vapors before starting the engine or other machinery.

Also, you should be particularly careful not to introduce any spark or open flames in these areas. Use explosion-proof flashlights only. If you must use a tool with an open flame, such as a torch, make absolutely certain there is no explosion hazard present.

These rules apply to the engine room of course, but they apply equally to the bilges since the fuel tanks can create a fire hazard here as well. Never smoke in these spaces. If you're a smoker, wait until you're outside and well away from the boat before you light up.

Gasoline is also toxic. If you have to drain any gasoline out of your boat's fuel system for any reason, the safest course of action (provided the fuel is not stale or contaminated) is to use a funnel to pour it directly back into the fuel tank through the deck fill. Don't dump it out on the ground, or pour it down the storm drain.

Toxic Chemicals

In the course of working on your boat, you will have to use many other toxic substances. Solvents, such as carburetor cleaner; ethylene glycol antifreeze; antifouling bottom paint, prep wash, and tie-coat preparations; even many cleaning preparations are toxic. Handle all of these with care.

In the case of the most dangerous of these, you should wear protective gear and clothing when you use them. A breathing respirator with the proper cartridges (usually toxic mists–type), rubber gloves, eye protection, and a disposable cool suit are important components of your tool kit. Don them whenever you're likely to be exposed to dangerous substances.

Ethylene Glycol Antifreeze

This stuff is so insidious it merits its own special warning section. As you might have heard, this toxic antifreeze has a sweet smell that is appealing to pets, wildlife, and even children. Don't under any circumstances leave pans of this chemical around, since these critters might be tempted to take a drink and poison themselves.

Burns and Scalds

Engines get hot in operation. Wear gloves or allow components to cool off thoroughly before you handle them or lean on them.

Liquids such as drain oil and coolant are capable of causing really nasty burns. If you have to work with these while they're hot, make sure you work safely and protect yourself by wearing gloves.

Storage Battery Hazards

There's a lot of energy stored in your boat's battery. Whenever you work on the connections, make it a steadfast rule to use a wrench that's not long enough to touch both terminals at the same time. If you ever accidentally short out a storage battery by touching both terminals with a wrench, the tool will likely weld itself to the terminals and the battery will almost certainly explode, spewing battery acid and bits of battery all over the place.

I've seen this happen just once. That was enough for me. The biggest piece of the battery left over after the explosion was no bigger than my thumb. Fortunately my friend who did this dumb stunt had his face out of the way. He was lucky. Be especially careful whenever you're making connections to charge or provide a "boost" to a storage battery. Sparks are almost always created when these connections are made or broken. Hydrogen from the battery and gasoline vapors, which are often present in the engine room, are both sources of explosion hazards.

Batteries give off explosive hydrogen gas when they're in use and especially when they're being charged (by a battery charger or the engine's alternator). Do not allow any open flames or sparks in their vicinity.

If all that isn't enough, batteries are filled with electrolyte: a strong mixture of sulfuric acid. If this gets on your skin, it will cause serious burns. If it gets on cotton clothing, those clothing articles will disintegrate the next time you wash them. (Now you know why mechanics wear polyester.) Whenever you carry a battery, use an approved carrier or the battery box to do so. Even the outside surfaces of a dry, seemingly clean battery are covered with enough of this chemical to destroy your clothing if not burn your skin.

AC Electrical Shock Hazards

Your boat's AC electrical system can kill you. For safety's sake, even when you're working on the 12-volt DC system, you should make sure that there's no 110-volt AC power present in the boat. You can do this by disconnecting the shore-power cord and shutting off the generator. If there's any chance that some "helpful" person might come along and plug it back in or power up the generator, tag the inlet receptacle and the generator control panel with warning signs that will keep them from doing this.

The reason for this is simple. There are places in your boat's wiring where the AC and DC electrical system are in close proximity to one another, especially at the master control panel. You could be troubleshooting and making measurements with your meter and accidentally stray into the 110-volt AC section of the system.

High-Tension Shock Hazards

Your engine's ignition system is a source of high voltage. Modern engines in particular are capable of providing a much hotter spark than the ignition systems of yore. This is especially dangerous for people with heart trouble, pacemakers, or other types of cardiac implants.

Whenever you are troubleshooting the ignition system, use the approved spark checking tools and techniques outlined in the text of this book. In addition, between measurements, make sure that the key is all the way in the "off" position. If it remains in the "run" position, the ignition system is often still live and capable of delivering a lethal (or at least annoying) jolt.

Fire Danger

Whenever you are working on your boat or its engine, have one of your fire extinguishers (you have at least two on your boat, right?) close at hand. That way, if you start a fire, you won't have to wriggle out of a tight spot and hunt for an extinguisher to deal with it.

1 CLEANING AND EXTERIOR MAINTENANCE

Balanced Cleaning

Everything we do in life has environmental consequences. Think about it. Whether you buy a newspaper, let the dog out, or wash your boat, you have an impact on your environment. Unfortunately, maintaining boats means using a lot of chemicals and pollutants. But it is possible to have clean boats and clean bays. How? By giving some thought to which products we buy, how we use them, and how we dispose of them. It's a matter of balance.

Water: The Universal Solvent

Let's start with the most powerful element in our arsenal of cleaning gear: water. All by itself, water is capable of working wonders. With just a few additives it can clean virtually anything. In fact, many boat cleaning chores can be handled with nothing more than a freshwater rinse. If you do your boating in salt water, you know that you have to wash the boat when you return from an outing. If you're only removing the salt from the hull and superstructure, fresh water alone will often do the job. Hose the boat down, hit it with the mop or sponge, and rinse. Done.

If you've got to get rid of some light-duty soil and grime, use a light-duty cleaner. A couple of capfuls of Murphy Oil Soap or Sudbury Boat Zoap dissolved in a bucket of water will remove most routine dirt from a boat without major environmental consequences.

Stronger than Dirt?

If you automatically drag out the heavy artillery—harsh chemicals and abrasives—for routine cleaning on your boat, you're making a big impact on more than just the environment. You're doing a number on the dirt, the Earth, *and* your boat's finish.

All boats comprise many materials that need to be cleaned. These include gelcoated fiberglass; aluminum, stainless steel, and other metals; fabric; vinyl; glass; teak and other woods; and rubber. Let's take a look at each material and consider its unique cleaning problems.

Gelcoated Fiberglass

Far and away, cleaning gelcoated fiberglass is the main housekeeping chore that most boatowners face. It can be quite a challenge, too.

Gelcoat is catalyzed polyester resin; that is, a plastic. Although it seems like pretty tough stuff, it's not. In fact, it's a real softy. Like all such materials, it contains plasticizers to keep it shiny and supple. (It also contains pigments to give it color and UV resistance.) Over time, these additives are leached out of the chemical matrix and the gelcoat loses its original lively fresh look. On a microscopic level, the plastic becomes brittle and eroded as it ages.

I've seen lots of boats that have weathered so badly that, no matter what their owners do, they can't clean and polish the finish so it stays nice looking. Once a boat's fiberglass hull has weathered, there isn't much you can do except sand the surface and paint it with linear polyurethane.

You can, though, take steps to slow down the rate of deterioration. The three big enemies of gelcoat are UV (ultraviolet) radiation from the sun, industrial smog, and ozone in the atmosphere. The best way to protect your boat from most of these ills is to store it in a shed or snap a cover over it when it's not in use. For most of us, however, those aren't practical options.

Wax: Secret Weapon #1

But all is not lost—especially if you are religious about keeping a good coat of wax on your boat. To a certain extent, when you wax your boat you fill up the interstices of the gelcoat's matrix with wax. Doing so keeps airborne nasties such as sulfur dioxide and ozone from doing as much damage as they would if the boat were not waxed.

Waxing also helps keep dirt from migrating down into the matrix. Sure, your boat will still get dirty. But the dirt on the surface of a waxed boat is just that: surface dirt. A well-waxed boat is much easier to clean than one that's not because wax helps keep dirt from penetrating beneath the surface. If you keep the hull and vertical parts of your boat's superstructure well waxed, you'll be rewarded every time you clean them. For safety's sake, don't wax the decks or other places where you walk or scramble.

Another nice feature of waxing is that it seals your boat's finish and helps retain its plasticizers. These youth-giving components of gelcoat begin to waft away from your boat as soon as it's pulled out of the mold. Anything you can do to slow down the rate of deterioration helps keep the finish young and bright.

The durability of a wax job is in direct proportion to the degree of difficulty applying it. Sorry; easy come, easy go. If it's easy for you to apply it, it's easy for Mother Nature and your cleaning processes to remove it. If you spray it on and buff it off with a paper towel, you can expect the beautiful waxed finish to last about a week.

The most durable and difficult to apply waxes are those that contain a lot of natural wax, particularly carnauba. It's a pain to apply and buff this stuff out, but the reward is a beautiful finish that will last at least half the typical boating season—unless you wash your boat with harsh cleaners that strip the finish.

Low-Impact Cleaning

Stay away from cleaners that contain bleach. Yeah, I know, they're great for removing yellow and brownish stains and black marks on your boat's topsides. But they're hell on the plasticizers in gelcoat. If you use them, your boat will look great right after cleaning it, but it won't stay clean and, worse, it will look old before its time.

Abrasive cleaners, such as scouring cleansers, are just as bad. They'll remove dirt from your boat's skin to beat the band, but they'll also scratch that skin—the gelcoat—in the process. If you could see how abrasives and gelcoat interact on a molecular level, you'd see some pretty rough stuff going on. These products actually cut into the surface and, with each cleaning, remove a bit of that precious gelcoat.

When you consider that your boat probably started its life with only 10 to 20 mils (0.01 to 0.02 inch) of gelcoat covering its fiberglass substrate, it makes sense to protect it against wear. So clean with care.

Solvents are out, too. Although acetone and toluene can remove all sorts of stains, they also absolutely wipe out the plasticizers in the process. You can weather your boat's finish more quickly with solvents than with anything else.

Another problem with solvents is that they dissolve many stains but don't really lift them off the surface. As a result, when you try to remove a stain with a solvent you often get a weaker stain over a larger area. Who needs that?

Secret Weapon #2

Using gentle cleaners—ones that are just strong enough to tackle the dirt but not so strong that they eat your boat—is one of the best ways to conserve your boat's finish. But since I've ruled out using bleach, abrasives, and solvents, you might be wondering what's left.

Obviously, you can safely use soaps and detergents to clean your boat. For normal cleaning of a well-waxed boat, these do a good enough job. But what can you use to tackle those yellow or brownish hull stains typically caused by microorganisms in the water? Fortunately, a cleaning system has become available in the last few years that's much more effective than soap or detergent. These cleansers contain chelating agents, which are especially good for removing difficult stains—even the ones that only bleach was able to tackle in the past.

Chelating agents are pretty amazing chemicals that have an affinity for organic dirt molecules. The agents have special double-ended molecules. One end likes to attach to dirt; the other end is attracted to water. These tricky little molecules worm their way into the chemical matrix of gelcoat. When you rinse your boat off with fresh water, they come out with the dirt in tow.

I know, I know—it sounds too good to be true (it slices, it dices). But unlike the Vegamatic, these compounds actually do work as advertised. Star brite (4041 SW 47th Ave., Fort Lauderdale, FL 33314; 800-327-8583; www.starbrite.com/marine.htm) makes two cleaners with chelating agents—Instant Black Streak Remover and Hull Cleaner. The next time you have to clean stains from your boat's hull, I suggest you give one of these products a try and give the harsher chemicals, such as bleach, abrasives, and solvents, a pass. Your boat's finish will thank you.

Treating and Maintaining Teak

Genuine Burma teak—*Tectona grandis*—is a traditional, hard, and heavy wood that, because of its durability and resistance to rot, has been used in boatbuilding for centuries. There's no doubt about it: Nothing dresses up a plain fiberglass boat like the warmth of teak trim. But with its attendant maintenance, this beautiful wood can be both a blessing and a curse.

Left in its natural state in the marine environment, teak weathers to a silver-gray color that's reminiscent of driftwood. If nothing is done to it, its natural oils do a pretty fair job of protecting it from weathering and checking. But few people like to have their boats trimmed with wood that looks like it washed up on the beach. You have two options for treating teak: varnish or oil.

Varnish

If you are a dab hand with a varnish brush and you've got a good bit of spare time (or money to pay someone else), you can go the varnishing route. Yes, contrary to widespread opinion, teak can be varnished. Its natural oiliness makes the task somewhat more challenging than varnishing mahogany, and not everyone likes the look of varnished teak, but it can be done.

Of course, any varnished wood looks great until it gets scuffed with sand-laden boat shoes. That's not the end of the world, though. You can give the wood a light sanding with 220-grit paper and apply another coat of varnish whenever you like. See what I mean about having time on your hands?

One other drawback to varnished teak is that it's pretty slippery stuff, especially when wet. Therefore, you want to be careful if you've got varnished teak cockpit soles or side deck covering boards. They're not impossible to navigate, but they're certainly not as confidence-inspiring as oiled teak or fiberglass nonskid. Many boaters who varnish their teak put down strips of self-adhesive nonskid to counter this problem. It does kind of spoil the effect of the beautiful expanses of teak, but it might save you a trip to the emergency room.

Oil

By and large, most people choose to go the middle road with teak care: occasional cleaning, sanding, and application of a few coats of oil. Not only is this method less work than varnishing, but oiled teak is more durable and safer to walk on. There is one fly in the ointment, however.

Depending on what cleaning methods you use, you might be removing a little bit of the teak with each cycle of cleaning and oiling. This is particularly true if you use the harsher cleaning methods (which, incidentally, are the most effective).

Everyone has a favorite teak oil preparation. The best bet is to see what other boaters in your area are using. If you like the look of the teak trim on a particular boat, ask the owner what product they use.

Unlike varnish, teak oil is very easy to apply. It's not a surface coat. Whatever you apply soaks into the wood almost immediately. Therefore, you don't have to worry about brush marks or flaws. All you have to do is apply the oil with a cheap throwaway brush. (Make sure it's a bristle or chip brush, not a foam one.)

Apply the oil liberally and allow it to soak in and polymerize before you apply the next coat. With most products you'll get the best results by applying two or three coats.

If you keep after your boat's teak, you won't have to use harsh cleaning systems as often. When the teak starts to look a little thirsty, get out the oil and apply another coat or two.

Unless you're a really careful brush handler, you might want to mask the fiberglass areas adjacent to the teak before you apply the oil. Although you can clean up most brands of oil with a rag, some leave a yellowish stain when they dry on a fiberglass surface. If that's the case with the oil you decide to use, you should definitely use masking tape to keep the oil where it belongs.

As for brands, I've had the best luck with Tip Top Teak oil, but I think most of these preparations are pretty much the same. It's the regular use of them that keeps teak trim looking nice.

Virtually all teak finishes contain tung oil. Star brite, for example, has three kinds of finishes, with varying amounts of tung oil, mildewcide, and UV inhibitor. Star brite's Premium Teak Oil has about three times as much tung oil as their "regular" oil. Their Tropical Formula has, in addition to tung oil, dryers that cause the product to cure, or polymerize, in the teak more than the other two.

Some teak oil preparations give the wood an unpleasant color—usually an orange cast. But whatever you like is right for your boat. That's why I think it pays to look at other people's boats and ask them what they use.

Cleaning Teak

Teak cleaning techniques run the gamut from mild to wild. The lightest duty methods use detergents and surfactants. The next rung of the ladder (in terms of harshness) are bleaching products, most of which contain oxalic acid as the active ingredient. Finally, if you're starting with neglected, badly weathered teak, you're probably going to have to bring out the heavy artillery: acid–caustic cleaners, such as Snappy Teak-Nu. These are two-step liquid preparations. Part A is a very strong acid, usually hydrochloric. Part B is a strong caustic, or base, which is designed to neutralize the acid left over from Part A.

Detergents and Surfactants

These are the safest products to use and most of them work well on all but the most sorely neglected teak trim. Star brite makes two products that are gentle on you, your boat's teak, and the environment. First, you use their Teak Cleaner, which is followed up with their Teak Brightener. The teak cleaner uses surfactants and detergents to clean weathered teak. The teak brightener does just that—restores the brightness to the cleaned wood and prepares it for oiling.

Oxalic Acid–Based Teak Cleaners

Ships' chandleries carry a host of powdered teak cleaners and wood bleaching products that contain oxalic acid as the active ingredient. BoatLIFE's powder formula Teak Brite (BoatLIFE, P.O. Box 71789, 2081 Bridgeview Dr., Charleston, SC 29415-1789; 800-382-9706; www.boatlife.com) is an example of one of these. Using one of these products isn't nearly as dangerous as cleaning your boat's teak with the more caustic two-part cleaners.

Just the same, even these middle-range products are pretty harsh because they contain acid-based bleaching agents. They're also abrasive, so they remove some teak with each use. After you use them, give your boat—especially the teak trim, decks, and topsides—a thorough freshwater rinse to remove all traces of the acid and cleaners.

Caustic Cleaners

If you've decided that your boat's teak needs a heavy-duty cleaning, you're probably going to use Snappy Teak-Nu (www.snappyboatcare.com/teak nu.htm). Let me offer two warnings.

Not only is this stuff hell on the teak, it's also incredibly rough on your skin. It's a two-part system. The first is an acid that tears away the surface of the teak. The second is a strong alkali that neutralizes the acid.

Both components will burn your hands if they're unprotected. And if you have any small cuts, you'll immediately know where they are when this stuff hits them. You *must* wear rubber gloves when using Snappy Teak-Nu. Not the cheapo throwaway plastic painting gloves, either. Bite the bullet and buy a pair of heavy-duty dishwashing gloves (the Playtex brand is good). You need gloves that are strong enough to resist the chemicals and that can get through the entire job without shredding.

Eye protection is a must as well. If you splash either chemical in your eyes, you could be in serious trouble. Before you start the teak cleaning operation, don a pair of goggles.

The second perverse feature of Snappy Teak-Nu is that it has a weird effect on aluminum trim. No matter whether the trim is anodized or not, the chemicals in this product turn aluminum a blackish purple—and the stain cannot be removed . . . ever!

You will use a lot of fresh water to rinse off the chemicals in the course of cleaning the teak, so make sure there is no aluminum trim anywhere the water will run. Any aluminum that's in the water's path will be discolored. Think this through carefully.

Before you start, rig your garden hose and sprayer and run some water on the worksite. Follow the stream all the way overboard. Is there an aluminum bang strip on the side of the boat that the rinse water will dribble over? If so, you will have to remove it or protect it with a taped-on plastic covering.

Covering the trim works well if you do a scrupulous job, but I prefer to simply remove and rebed the trim after the treatment is complete and the boat has been thoroughly rinsed and allowed to dry.

The same goes for any aluminum hatch trim in the cockpit (around the engine hatch, for example) that will be affected by the rinse water. Don't neglect this step—unless you like purplish black streaks on your boat's aluminum trim. I've been tripped up by this staining several times, and I can assure you it's a real bummer.

I hope all of my scary talk about harsh cleaning methods inspires you to try a gentler system on your boat's teak trim. If your boat's exterior teak just needs routine cleaning and brightening, there are easy-to-use products on the market that do an admirable job.

Postcleaning

If you elect to use a harsh cleaner, or even one that's oxalic acid–based, you will wind up with clean, smooth teak, but at a cost. All such products remove the filler in the wood.

Filler is the summer wood, the soft material that fills the spaces between the winter wood—the harder part of the wood's grain. When you remove filler you freshen the look of teak, but you also raise the grain. Strictly speaking, you don't so much raise the grain as lower the spaces between the grain. But the net result is the same—the wood has a ridged, uneven feel and appearance.

To restore teak's smooth surface you must sand it. Sanding evens things up again, but after all of this treatment the wood is smaller in dimension than it was before you started. After a while, you can end up with grab rails that are noticeably smaller than when they were new. Over time, covering boards and other flat teak trim pieces can become as thin as cigar-box wood. Therefore, don't undertake these harsh treatments lightly or more often than necessary.

Sand as little as possible and with a medium grade (180 grit) of sandpaper to retain as much of the teak as you can. A light sanding is all that's necessary; you only want to do enough to level the surface of the wood in preparation for oiling.

Although many people don't bother sanding when they clean teak with the gentler cleaning methods, I think it's a good idea to do so. Of course, the sanding doesn't have to be as heavy duty as when you use strong caustics. All it takes is a gentle touch with 220-grit paper. If you omit this step, the teak won't be smooth and even.

Fabric

Most boats use some "canvas" on board. I put that word in quotes because canvas, strictly speaking, is a material made of cotton, hemp, or flax. For the most part, the canvaslike cockpit covers and Bimini tops on modern boats are made with a Dacron fabric called Sunbrella that has a waterproofing compound soaked into it after it's woven. When the fabric is new, this coating helps to repel dirt as well as water. Unfortunately, though, the water and dirt repellent characteristics are lost over time.

Sunbrella material can be cleaned with almost any gentle soap or detergent (Sudbury Boat Zoap works well). Scrub gently—just hard enough to clean any grime or stains that have settled onto the fabric. Harsh scrubbing or harsh cleaners hasten the loss of Sunbrella's water repellency. In fact, when you scrub it with a scrub brush, you can tear the individual Dacron fibers and give the cloth a fuzzy appearance.

Before the water repellency is lost, it's best to recoat the freshly cleaned and thoroughly dried fabric with Star brite Waterproofing—it contains the same compound that newly minted Sunbrella is treated with when it's manufactured. Of course, nothing lasts forever. Subjected to UV radiation, industrial smog, and ozone, this fabric has a useful life of three to six years depending on the conditions it's subjected to.

Vinyl-Coated Fabric

"Canvas" items that are made from vinyl-coated fabric are particularly easy to damage with harsh cleaners. No matter how tempting it might be, don't use household cleanser on vinyl-coated fabric. You'll not only remove the stain, you'll hasten the weathering of the vinyl coating. Before you know it, the coating will start to shred and fall off the fabric substrate that supports it.

When you stow cover parts that are made of this material, it's better to roll them up rather than fold them. You'll lessen the stress on the coating material and make it last longer. Star brite makes a product called Vinyl Shampoo that is quite effective at removing stains and yet is pretty gentle on the vulnerable vinyl coating. They also make a product called Vinyl Polish that cleans and helps reseal the pores in aged vinyl.

One more thing you might try: Apply a protectant such as Armorall to keep the plasticizers intact in the vinyl coating of these parts.

Time takes its toll on vinyl-coated fabric, just as it does on Sunbrella. As a general rule, vinyl doesn't hold up nearly as well as Sunbrella, and darker, more strongly pigmented colors of either material are more vulnerable to degradation than the lighter whites and grays.

Clear Vinyl

The so-called isinglass panels on side curtains, which aren't isinglass at all, are made of clear vinyl. They are subjected to all sorts of insults in the marine environment.

First, they're easily scratched. Carelessly cleaning even small salt spots can scratch the smooth surface. Before cleaning them, rinse them well with water. Then, clean with a gentle soap solution and a sponge. Finally, generously rinse them again afterward. If you've gotten all the abrasive salt crystals off and have rinsed the cleaning agents thoroughly, you can then safely wipe the vinyl with a synthetic chamois. (Don't use paper towels; they scratch and cause hazing.)

As with vinyl-coated fabric, if these clear curtains need to be removed for stowage, they should be rolled, not folded.

Second, clear vinyl is prone to getting cloudy spots. The spots are caused by two different mechanisms. Abrasion causes white discolorations. You can carefully polish out this minor hazing with a mildly abrasive agent such as Star brite Scratch Remover/Restorer; then protect it by applying their Plastic Polish.

If the vinyl isn't scratched, a simple application of the polish can help make it easy to clean and longer lasting. The polish aids in retaining the plasticizers in the vinyl. Once the plasticizers are lost, the vinyl's life is all but over.

Yellow or brownish discoloration on clear vinyl can't be cleaned up. This is a sign of burning and usually happens where the vinyl comes in contact with the metal frame that supports the top. The sun heats the metal and the metal burns the vinyl.

You can prevent the burning by slipping short lengths of pipe insulation over the frame wherever it contacts the clear vinyl. (Pipe insulation is that gray foam with a slit down one side that's placed over hot-water pipes in unheated basements.) If pipe insulation looks too tacky for you, Star brite makes small molded plastic standoffs to accomplish the same job. They're called Window Savers.

Glass

When it comes to cleaning glass on board a boat, you first must determine if the "glass" is really glass. Most clear hatches, for example, are made of acrylic. Don't subject acrylic to harsh cleaners or scrub brushes; they'll scratch it. Acrylic is tougher than Plexiglas, but you can still scratch it with careless cleaning.

If you have any plastic windows—acrylic or Plexiglas—that are scratched, you can polish them with the two Star brite products mentioned above for treating clear vinyl. But an ounce of prevention is worth a pound of cure. Save the rough cleaning methods and compounds for tougher jobs.

To clean "real" glass, first rinse it off with fresh water and then clean it in the conventional way with Windex or another ammonia-based window cleaning product. Or, you can clean it the way I do, which yields better, more streak-free results.

After rinsing off the salt, toss a few capfuls of vinegar in a bowl of water. Swab the windows with a paper towel dipped in this solution and make sure to get the edges and corners thoroughly. Then, polish and dry the windows with wadded newspaper. The printer's ink in the paper is a very fine abrasive. It polishes the glass to a cleaner, more sparkling appearance than anything else you've ever used for window cleaning.

Rubber

Rubber and plastic parts on a boat can be kept young looking by regular applications of a protectant such as Armorall or 303 Aerospace Protectant. Ultraviolet radiation from the sun is one of the worst enemies of plastic and rubber; both of these products contain UV protection. They also help retain the plasticizers that keep these materials from getting brittle and weatherworn.

Metal Hardware

Most metal hardware on modern boats is stainless steel or treated aluminum (powder coated or anodized). The care and feeding of these materials is quite simple. Rinse off with water after you get in from an outing and dry with a synthetic chamois.

Stainless steel can be prone to weak rust spots on its surface. If wiping the hardware with a chamois after you rinse it doesn't keep these superficial spots at bay, you can easily polish them out. I like to use Nev-R-Dull, which is a cotton wadding that's impregnated with metal polish. It does smell a bit, and you should be sure to wash your hands after you use it because the polish contains strong chemicals.

There are other effective metal polishes on the market but the first thing you have to do when you use them is find a rag. Since Nev-R-Dull is an impregnated wadding, the rag is already furnished.

Preventing Mildew

Mildew never sleeps. It takes three things to start a mildew colony: darkness, warmth, and moisture. There's actually a fourth component required—mildew spores—but since they're found almost everywhere on the planet, I don't count them.

Like the fire triangle we all learned about in grade school—the one that said you need three things to sustain a fire: fuel, oxygen, and heat—if you take away any one of these elements, mildew can't thrive. For my money, the key to preventing mildew is to remember the mnemonic *COLD*—that is, keep things Clean, Open, Loose, and Dry. Here are some tips for keeping a mildew colony from setting up home on your boat.

- Even the light and drying action from a single light bulb can be effective in stopping mildew—just be sure that a light bulb can be safely left burning in a mildew-prone spot. (You don't want to start a fire.)
- Small 110-volt heating elements, such as the Golden Rod, can be installed in mildew-prone lockers to keep foul-weather gear and other clothing from becoming infested.
- Common sense goes a long way toward preventing mildew. When you're going to be off the boat for any length of time, tip the bunk cushions up on their edges and leave lockers and stowage spaces open.
- Mildew that has already colonized a nonporous surface (such as gelcoated fiberglass) can be cleaned with some chlorine bleach that's cut with an equal volume of water. You'll not only clean the surface, you'll also kill all the mildew spores that are colonizing the areas it touches. Of course, they'll be back again, but if you keep things lighted, dry, and aired out, they won't thrive the way they would otherwise.
- Hang some of Star brite's MDG Mildew Control Bags inside the boat, especially in mildew-prone spaces such as lockers. These have a time-release chemical that's activated by humidity. When the humidity increases, so does the release of the gas. The bags are nontoxic to humans and pets, unlike the old, formaldehyde-based mildew control products. Each bag provides six months of protection for a 300-cubic-foot space.
- If your boat's storage areas aren't well vented, install some small ventilation plates such as the ones made by Perko. They're available in louvered and slotted styles, in round, square, and rectangular shapes. With a half dozen or so of these on your interior and cockpit lockers, you can foster airflow and lessen the likelihood of mildew.
- Don't put foul-weather gear and sea boots away when they're wet. Rinse them off and leave them hanging in the sun until they're bone dry.
- When you stow gear, don't wudge it up or pack it too tightly. Let air circulate around and through it as much as possible.
- Install a few rainproof deck ventilators like the ones made by Nicro. The solar-powered ones are particularly neat. Whenever the sun shines, a small fan pulls air through the boat.
- When you clean your boat, wipe mildew-prone surfaces with apple cider vinegar. This makes it tough for mildew spores to recolonize.
- Clean the bilges with Sudbury's Automatic Bilge Cleaner. Rinse well after cleaning, and then scrub with a diluted solution of chlorine bleach.

It *is* possible to have a clean boat and a clean environment. If we all use a little common sense when we buy cleaning products, carefully follow their directions, and dispose of the products properly, we'll keep our boats looking great without killing the planet.

Questions and Answers

Question: I recently purchased a used 278 XCL Chaparral. What can I do to keep the black paint that's around the exterior metal windshield frame from peeling?

Answer: According to Chaparral, since your boat's windshield frame is black, it's definitely painted instead of powder-coated. Use an acrylic spray paint and compatible primer on the areas where the paint has failed. Whatever you do, don't use sandpaper to prepare the surface—it will leave scratches that will show through the new paint. Instead, use a coarse grade of bronze wool. Mask the glass with masking tape and paper to keep overspray from spoiling it. Also, be sure to use fine-grade bronze wool lightly between primer and paint coats. (By the way, never use steel wool on a boat—it leaves rust marks anyplace its fur falls.)

Question: I recently purchased a used sedan-bridge cruiser. The head compartment, which is lined with fiberglass, smells very strongly of toilet chemicals. I have removed the toilet and the holding tank, yet the odor persists. The compartment is very poorly ventilated. Has the odor from the chemicals permeated into the fiberglass? What can I do to remove the odor?
Answer: Have you checked the hoses that connect the toilet and holding tank? After a time, most waste hoses become permeated. If you wipe the outside of the hose with a clean rag and can then smell the toilet chemical's bouquet on the rag, the hose must be replaced.

Make sure you use sanitation hose. I like the stuff made by Raritan, but other MSD manufacturers also make suitable hose. If indeed the odor has permeated the gelcoated fiberglass—which I doubt—all is not lost. You can clean and neutralize the smell, but it will take some work. The best product for this disinfecting and odor-destroying job is Soft Scrub or any other similar paste-formula, chlorine bleach–fortified cleanser.

Using one of these products will dull the highly polished gelcoat surface somewhat, but it should eliminate the smell. Use it on all surfaces in the compartment except the mirror and portlights. If there's any teak trim in the compartment, sand and oil it.

Also remove the shower curtain, lay it out flat, and clean it thoroughly. If it still reeks, replace it with a new one. (Of course, then the head will smell like a new shower curtain, which is nothing to write home about either.) Any privacy curtains will have to be removed and laundered.

Bit by bit, all of these actions will remove the odor from the head compartment. Next, you need to develop a strategy to keep it from returning. Here are some pointers: Leave the head door wide open when you're not using the boat, refrain from using the head more than necessary, empty the holding tank promptly after each outing, flush the holding tank and hoses frequently (don't leave holding tanks partially full for long periods of time), and don't use more toilet chemical than needed.

Question: I have a Bayliner 21.5 Ciera Sunbridge in brand-new condition. The boat has been used for less than ten hours. The rest of the time, it's been covered up.

Most boats have a chalklike finish, especially on the top deck surfaces. On my boat, I've been fighting this by color sanding with 1,200-grit paper, white rubbing compound, and black ebony waxing with a professional polishing machine.

I can never get an automotive-type finish with a good reflection. Am I fighting a losing battle? Just how good a finish can I expect?
Answer: For starters, I don't believe in waxing decks. It makes them too slippery. The chalky appearance might not look too good, but it's a heck of a lot safer.

The reflectivity of a gelcoated fiberglass surface ultimately depends on the tooling that was used to mold the part. How highly polished was it? After the part is molded, you can compound and polish 'til the cows come home, but there's only so much you can do.

Even if the mold was perfectly micropolished, a painted surface will always be capable of outshining a molded, gelcoat-finished part. You really can't expect to get the ultimate automotive finish that you crave. My eight-year-old car has a metallic finish that still shines better than most new boats—and it's only been waxed about four times. Part of that auto finish you describe comes from the clear coats that are used on cars these days.

That's why many expensive fiberglass boats are painted with Awlgrip, Imron, and other linear polyurethane paints. When properly applied, these have higher gloss than polished gelcoat and can be topped with a compatible clear coat for even greater depth.

If you're really nuts for a high-gloss shine, consider having your boat painted. It's expensive, though. If your boat is really in perfect condition, expect to pay around $3,500 for a linear polyurethane paint job. If it's not perfect the price will be somewhat higher. (Surface preparation is a large part of the job. All scratches, "ratbites," and other cosmetic flaws have to be filled and sanded before priming and painting.)

You can pick from dozens of colors, including metallics. This is not a job for a do-it-yourselfer; it calls for professional spray equipment and safety gear.

Question: Several of the boats at my marina, including mine (a 31-foot Silverton), have water-spotted windows. None of us can figure out how to get rid of these spots. We've tried glass cleaner, mineral deposit remover, alcohol, vinegar, etc. Nothing seems to work.

I've heard about a product that's supposed to take these spots off like magic. I need your help tracking it down.

Answer: You might be able to remove the spots by cleaning the windows with Lime Buster, a product made by Whink Products Company (1901 15th Ave., P.O. Box 230, Eldora, IA 50627; 800-247-5102; www.whink.com).

Since Lime Buster has an acid formulation that can attack anodized aluminum trim and other finishes, be sure you continuously flush the work area and everything "downstream" with plenty of fresh water as you work. Apply Lime Buster with a damp sponge. Scrub the deposits off the glass and then rinse the surface thoroughly with fresh water.

Whink also makes an even stronger acid cleaner called Rust Stain Remover that, although faster than Lime Buster, is even more likely to mess up anodized aluminum trim. If it's used carelessly, Rust Stain Remover will actually etch the glass and leave a hazed finish that can't be restored. Therefore, I'd stick with Lime Buster to remove mineral deposits, salt spots, or other window glass flaws.

Most water contains minerals that leave deposits that actually etch the surface of glass. In the process, microcraters are formed in the glass—and you can't clean them with anything because there's nothing to remove. Theoretically, you could start with the finest wet or dry sanding that would level the surface and eliminate the pits, then follow up with lighter abrasives until the surface was perfect.

Good luck. Glass is very hard stuff; it's not nearly as easy to compound as softer materials such as gelcoat. You would be signing on for a huge job and I think the results would be worse than the spots you have now. When you're done, chances are you'll be left with very fine scratches or "hazing."

Lots of boatowners who have Dacron "canvas" window covers have the same problem you're experiencing. To avoid it, chamois the windows dry after you wash the boat to take away the etching opportunity. If your local rain is acidic, you might not be able to prevent this from happening, unless your boat has window covers.

Question: When vinyl letters are removed, is there any product to use, other than compound, to remove the glue residue?

Answer: There's no need to get out rubbing compound to deal with this stuff. In fact, it does more harm than good. What you want is a solvent. 3M, the leading maker of tape and other sticky stuff, also makes the best stuff to remove their residues. It's called 3M Adhesive Remover, and it's most often sold in 16-ounce cans.

Like all powerful solvents, this stuff has nasty vapors. Use it in the open air, stand upwind, and wear rubber gloves to protect your skin. If you have to use it in a poorly vented area, work quickly and use a respirator with toxic mists cartridges.

Allow the adhesive remover to soak in to the old glue for a few moments, then wipe off the residue with a solvent-soaked rag.

2 BOTTOM PAINTING

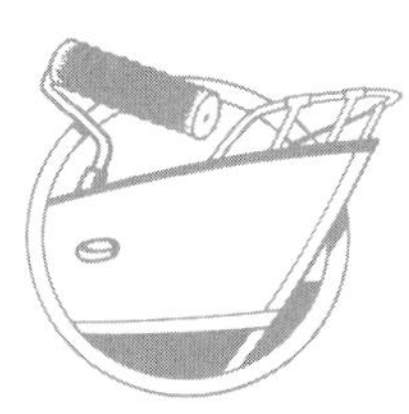

Overview

Most boatowners have to use antifouling paint on the bottoms of their boats. If you keep a boat in salt water without it, the bottom will soon host a multitude of critters such as barnacles, sea squirts, and other things that only a marine biologist could identify. All of these freeloaders serve to slow a boat down, often dramatically. The only answer, besides keeping the boat out of the water most of the time, is to apply antifouling paint.

In fresh water, the flora and fauna are different but the effect is almost the same. Depending on local laws and conventions, you might need antifouling paint if you use your boat on a lake or river.

Of course, if you keep your boat on a trailer or in rack storage when it's not in use, you can easily get by without antifouling paint, even in salt water. Since this stuff is toxic, I recommend that you skip it if you possibly can. Even if your boat stays in the water for a week at a time, the bottom can be easily scrubbed or pressure-washed when you haul out the boat, especially in fresh water.

Bottom paint can be applied quickly, but if you want a smooth finish you'll have to take more time. However, this is time well spent. If the bottom is bumpy or lumpy, your boat won't be as fast as it could be and it will consume more fuel.

Some elementary knowledge about how fiberglass boats are constructed will help you better understand how to get first-rate results when you paint your boat's bottom. As you might already know, your boat's hull was built from the outside in. It was constructed in a female mold and the first thing to go in there was the exterior gelcoat. After the sprayed-in gelcoat cured, the fiberglass cloth and resin were laminated into the inside to make the boat's structural substrate. (Gelcoat itself has virtually no strength.)

Before applying the gelcoat, the builder carefully inspected this highly polished mold for defects, dust, and scratches. Once the mold got a clean bill of health, a liberal coat of a special wax known as mold release agent was applied and smoothly buffed out.

Inspecting and waxing the mold are critical steps in determining a boat's final appearance. Any bits of dirt or dust will appear as defects in the finished surface. Naturally, builders rarely achieve perfection. They work in environments that are as clean and dust-free as possible, but we're not talking about microprocessor factories here. (However, unlike semiconductors, small flaws *can* be patched after a boat is completed.)

Remember that mold release agent I mentioned? It is definitely a mixed blessing. Although it allows a boat to be released from the mold—because nothing sticks to it—it also wreaks havoc with bottom paint application because, you guessed it, nothing sticks to it.

Because most of you are painting boats that already have bottom paint on them, I'm going to address that situation first (see pages 15–16.) For those of you who are lucky enough to own brand-new boats, I'll walk you through the process of de-waxing a new bottom (see pages 16–18).

Bottom Paint Technologies

Before you visit your local ship's store to buy bottom paint, it really pays to learn about the different kinds of paints that are available today. Each of the major marine paint manufacturers offers a few different "families" of paint; your choice will depend on how much money you want to spend, how much effectiveness you want, and what type of boating you do. The paint you choose can even be influenced by how fast your boat goes. For example, certain rosin-based "soft copper" bottom paints only work reliably on boats that move at displacement hull speeds.

Copolymer Paints

These are the most costly bottom paints. They are ablative, which means that they are designed to wear off in use; that is, whenever your boat moves, the paint leaches off into the water. In fact, when your boat sits still in moving water—when you're moored in a current, for example—the same thing happens. Ablative paints go dormant over the lay-up season. Then when your boat is launched in the springtime, any paint that remains on the bottom swings back into action.

International Paint Company pioneered this type of paint about fifteen years ago. Their premium copolymer paint is called Micron Ultima and it costs a bundle. I've gotten good results with copolymers by applying three coats of paint. Depending on how much you use your boat, where it's moored, and how warm the water is, three coats might last two full seasons or longer.

One nice feature of this type of paint is that you still have antifouling protection in place as long as there's paint on the boat's bottom. When you apply three coats, the first coat—called a "signal coat"—is in a contrasting color to the two coats that go over it. When the signal coat begins to be exposed, its different color "signals" you that most of the paint has disappeared. Then it's time to think about repainting.

Conventional Bottom Paint

The next notch down in the bottom paint hierarchy is conventional bottom paint. Most of these are either modified epoxy systems or vinyl-based systems.

Modified Epoxy Bottom Paints

Modified epoxy bottom paints strike a nice balance between cost, ease of application, and effectiveness. The most popular of these seems to be the ubiquitous Fiberglass Bottomkote family of paints from Interlux. Unlike the copolymer paints, the vehicles of these paints do not leach off the bottom of the boat. Only the toxic, active ingredients—the biocide—leach out as the paint's effectiveness deteriorates, so you will have to scrape or sand the leftover paint off the boat's bottom every few seasons.

Vinyl-Based Bottom Paints

Like the modified epoxy paint formulations, vinyl-based antifouling products occupy the vast middle ground of the paint world. They cost less than the copolymers and they work quite effectively for high-speed (that is, faster than sailboats) boats. They do, though, build up over the years. Thus they also require that the boat be periodically scraped clean.

Whether you choose modified epoxy or vinyl-based is mostly a matter of personal preference and availability. You also have to take into consideration what you've used in the past. As a rule, vinyl-based paints contain solvents that are too "hot" to be applied over existing paint other than vinyl-based. For example, if you apply a coat of vinyl-based paint over a bottom that was previously painted with Fiberglass Bottomkote, the old paint will be attacked by the solvents in the new.

Low-Cost Bottom Paint

At the bottom of the bottom paint hierarchy, you'll find the paint that I used to call soft copper when I worked in the boatyard. These are often rosin-based and typically use cuprous oxide as the biocide. They don't have a very heavy load of biocide, which means they're the least effective antifouling bottom paint.

These paints are mostly used for workboats, barges, pile drivers, and boats belonging to really thrifty owners. If they're applied to boats that move any faster than displacement hull speeds, they erode quickly and, even if they stay in place, are not very effective at forestalling bottom growth.

They do have one overwhelming advantage: They cost a fraction of the price of the premium paints. That's why they're popular with people who own workboats.

Painting and Masking Pointers

After you've prepared your boat's bottom using the instructions presented here, you're going to have to use masking tape to keep the paint where you want it and ensure a clean sharp edge at the waterline.

First, a warning: All masking tape is not created equal. If you use the bargain basement stuff, you'll be well on your way to getting a bargain basement bottom painting job. If you can justify the expense, buy one of the better grades such as 3M's Fine Line tape. True, it costs over $6 a roll. That may be hard to justify when you can get something that looks like masking tape for as little as 69¢ at the local True Value store. Believe me, though, the good tape is worth the extra expense. It handles better, can be "bent" to follow the curved areas of the waterline, and tears off easily and neatly. Cheap masking tape is really freezer wrapping tape. It yields a miserable edge and makes for extra work that will cost you more in time than you'll save in money.

I like using ¾-inch wide tape. It's especially nice if your boat's waterline follows any difficult contours. If there are no tricky curves, you can get some added security by using 1-inch wide tape.

Start at the bow and anchor the tape to the boat's hull by pressing the first section down firmly with your fingertips. Pull a foot or two of tape off the roll and bring that section down against the hull, eyeballing along its length to make sure it's going to adhere where you want it to.

Once you're satisfied with the tape's position, press it down against the hull. Before going on to the next section, press the lower edge down tightly with your fingertips. If you neglect this step, the tie-coat (a strong chemical formulation that, when applied to the bottom of a brand-new boat, actually dissolves the gelcoat a little) and/or bottom paint will creep underneath the tape and leave you with a less-than-crisp edge on your finished job. (The same thing might happen if you use brand X tape, even if you do press it down securely.)

Masking tape can be tricky to work with because it can't bend around the twisty parts. When you have to follow a difficult contour—at the boat's stem for example, or where a lifting strake runs through the area you're masking—tear off a batch of short pieces (2 or 3 inches long). Use each piece to make part of the necessary bend and, when you're done, make sure you press them all down firmly to ensure solid adhesion and a clean, crisp line in your finished paintwork.

Bottom Paint Pointers

I reckon I've probably painted eight or ten miles worth of boats' bottoms. And I've undoubtedly made every mistake in the book. In the interest of saving you from repeating all of them, I offer the following tips and tricks.

The most important thing to remember about antifouling paint is that it can't keep barnacles and slime off your boat if it's sitting in the can. Put another way, you've got to apply a liberal coat (or two) to achieve the effectiveness you're paying for. And pay you do; bottom paint doesn't come cheap. So be sure to lay it on generously. I use a roller to apply it and make sure I "charge" the roller well with paint. You get the best results if you apply the paint's "guts," not just the color.

Before you take the lid off the paint can, make sure to have it freshly shaken upside down for at least five minutes (ten is better). If you don't do this, the paint's biocide—the guts I referred to above—will remain in the bottom of the can where they've settled since it was manufactured and packaged. That's the stuff you paid dearly for; you want to make sure it gets applied.

While the paint is shaking, ask for a paint stirring stick, too. Each time you refill the roller tray, give the paint in the can a good stirring first. The active ingredients are heavy metals and they settle out very quickly. Remember, the protection doesn't work if it doesn't make it onto the boat.

If I know I'm going to use the entire contents of the can immediately, I like to use a sharp screwdriver to cut a few holes in the groove around the circumference of the top. The holes allow the paint that normally gloms up the groove to drip back down in the can, saving you some paint, money, and mess. However, if you're going to save the balance of the paint for next year, the holes might compromise the airtight seal of the can and allow the contents to dry out and become unusable.

Try to stay relaxed when you're applying bottom paint and work as neatly as you can—cleaning up bottom paint is no fun, and drips and spills are expensive. For this reason, after filling the roller tray, it's a good idea to put the can with the balance of the paint somewhere you won't trip over it or step in it. (I've done that more than once.)

Now it's time to paint. Charge the roller with a good load of paint and blot it by rolling on the roller tray's corrugated ribs one or two times. The roller should still be loaded with as much paint as it can carry without dripping (too much).

Roll on paint horizontally along the waterline first and don't roll out the paint too thinly. If you do, holidays (sparsely covered spots) will begin to appear. Before that happens, put another load of paint on the roller. Don't be satisfied by a coating that's just barely thick enough to achieve the desired color. What you want is a generous coat that's several mils thick. The color won't scare the barnacles away. Only a good coat of paint will.

With some paints—especially vinyl formulations—it's best to pull off the masking tape as soon as you've rolled the edge. By rolling, say, a 9-inch wide strip along the waterline, you'll be hard pressed to run over that wide a boundary and mess things up. Next to 9 inches, what's another ¾ inch (the masking tape's width) of protection?

After you've coated the waterline, continue to paint the rest of the boat's bottom. Roll downward from the already-painted area but, again, stop before the coat you're applying becomes thin. I usually roll down these few feet, and then start another stripe down from the waterline.

I proceed in this way until I've finished one side of the boat, then make another pass of vertical stripes. Usually these two passes of stripes get me down to the bottom of the boat's bottom. This is an important area to pay attention to, so get down there and thoroughly paint the boat's forefoot from stem to stern. If you miss any spots here, your boat will wind up with a beard growing along its forefoot—definitely not cool.

After you've painted the other side of the boat the same way, it's time to use your throwaway brush to get all the spots that a roller can't adequately coat. On inboard-powered boats, these include running strakes, through-hull fittings, propeller pockets (especially where the shaft[s] exit), trim tab hinges, propshafts, and the hubs of the propellers. And speaking of propellers, I don't bother painting any more than the hubs because the paint will quickly fly off the working surfaces of the propeller blades anyway.

If you own a sterndrive-powered boat, you'll need to paint all those areas except the running gear. Don't paint any area of the sterndrive or its attendant hardware (trim hoses, props, etc.). Doing so is a sure invitation to galvanic corrosion, also known as electrolysis. If you apply copper bottom paint to any portion of your aluminum sterndrive, it will probably be eaten for breakfast by this malady. Stay away.

There are sterndrive-safe paints out there, though I haven't found them to be particularly effective. Most of these are TBT (tributyltin) formulations that are highly toxic (more so than regular antifouling paint). Therefore, TBT-based products are sold only to licensed applicators. "Civilians" can't buy them for do-it-yourself application.

In my experience, I've found it better to leave the drive unpainted and keep after any growth that appears by scrubbing it off with a scrub brush before it gets to the barnacle stage.

When you've finished painting the hull, pull off the masking tape as soon as you can, especially if you're using a vinyl-formula paint. If allowed to dry partway, vinyl paint will sometimes shear off as you remove the masking tape. The best way to avoid this is to pull off the tape as you paint.

Cleanup

After touching up the running gear and other tricky bits, you're ready to clean things up. (Don't forget to install sacrificial zinc anodes. I tell you how on page 18.) Here are some tips to make cleanup as easy as possible.

Prop the roller tray on top of the open can of bottom paint and use your throwaway brush to squeegee the bulk of the residual paint back into the can. When the tray is clean, brush the paint out of the rim of the can and seal it tightly. Rap the lid down with a hammer to keep the remaining paint fresh. Then, clean the worksite, making sure to collect all the masking tape, empty cans, throwaway brushes, and the like.

If you followed my suggestions and wore protective gear, you shouldn't have splattered too much paint, but even so, it's inevitable that you'll have gotten some paint on yourself. I used to clean bottom paint off my skin by rubbing with a thinner- or acetone-soaked rag. That was in the bad old days. Now we know better—solvents are definitely hazardous to your health. (They might be hazardous to your reproductive health as well.)

Happily, I've discovered an excellent way to remove even the most stubborn bottom paint without harsh solvents. All you need is some Go-Jo or similar mechanic's hand cleaner cream and a handful or two of fine sawdust. The best sawdust for this is the stuff that collects under a table saw. Ask someone at the boatyard if you can scoop a coffee can's worth from the carpenter shop.

Apply a generous dollop of Go-Jo to your hands and, once you've rubbed it in well, grab a fistful of sawdust. Rub your hands together with the hand cleaner–sawdust mixture. For the first minute or so, nothing will happen. Then, all of a sudden, the paint will begin to slide off.

Keep going, concentrating on your fingernails and any other areas that still have bottom paint spots. Wipe your hands with a clean rag or rinse them with water. If any paint remains, repeat the hand cleaner and sawdust treatment. Voilà! Clean hands without harsh solvents.

Details, Details

Don't forget that there are going to be some spots that you can't paint because of the boat's cradle, poppets, or the rollers on your trailer. If the boatyard is going to launch your boat, leave the yard crew enough leftover tie-coat components and bottom paint to complete these areas.

Also leave the crew a disposable paint pot to mix the tie-coat in, a couple of good size throwaway brushes, and some prep-wash. And always let the office or the yard crew know that you're expecting the blank spots to be touched up before the boat is splashed.

Repainting Fiberglass Boat Bottoms

Preparation is everything. Assuming that your boat's bottom was pressure washed or scrubbed when it was hauled out, all the algae, slime, and barnacles should be long gone. If not, you're going to have to wet it down and scrub the bottom with a scrub brush or 3M Scotch Brite pad to get rid of the old slime.

Barnacles are best removed by flicking them off with a putty knife. This removes the shells but, unfortunately, often leaves behind the little disks of the tenacious glue that they adhere with. Get rid of these by sanding with coarse (80-grit) sandpaper. It's worth taking the time to get them off. If you don't, there's no way you'll wind up with a smooth, fast, and fuel-efficient bottom. Be sure, however, that you confine your sanding to the barnacle attachment sites. Don't chew up your boat's precious gelcoat in the process.

When the bottom is clean, scrub the waterline with some soap and water and rinse it off well when you're done. Rinsing well is important. If any soap residue remains, the masking tape will not stick. Wipe the surface dry if you plan on masking and painting immediately. To ensure that it's completely dry—which it must be to paint—go get a cup of coffee after you wipe things off.

Preparing the previously painted surface is pretty simple. Unless the bottom paint is falling off in large areas, you just need to knock off the loose stuff with a piece of 120-grit sandpaper. (Before you do this, don the protective gear described below.)

Some folks like to use a scraper, but I reserve this tool for bottoms that I'm going to strip completely. If any painted areas have failed down to the gelcoat, gently clean them with water and a Scotch Brite pad. Then you can follow the instructions for new work outlined next. Only the failed areas need to be treated with tie-coat.

Whether you scrape or sand, you must protect yourself against the toxic dust from the antifouling paint. Wear a toxic dust–compatible mask to avoid breathing nasty bottom paint dust that is loaded with heavy metals and other toxic substances. You should also wear a form-fitting pair of goggles to protect your eyes, a disposable Tyvek "cool suit" coverall, and rubber gloves. If you've never seen a cool suit, you should get acquainted. It's a one-piece coverall that costs less than $20 and is rugged enough to get you through a season's worth of dirty work before it begins to disintegrate and needs to be discarded. As the name suggests, a cool suit is more comfortable to wear than a conventional coverall. When you've finished sanding or scraping, clean yourself carefully before you eat or drink.

Bottom Painting a Brand-New Boat

If you recall, I talked about mold release agent (wax) at the beginning of this chapter. As I said there, every trace of this wax must be removed for bottom paint to adhere. There are two ways to accomplish this removal operation.

The first method—dewaxing and sanding—we're going to dismiss right out of hand, even though it works well. Indeed, it works well if you get all the wax off and roughen up the gelcoat enough to remove the shine and get a "toothy" frosted appearance, but unfortunately, doing so fosters an even bigger problem.

Have you heard of boatpox? There's a lot of confusion about this strange blistering phenomenon that crops up on fiberglass boat bottoms. One thing is certain: The likelihood of your boat being afflicted with this malady is greatly increased if you sand down its gelcoat. So forget about sanding new gelcoat. (See pages 18–20 for a complete discussion of boatpox.)

Instead, I suggest that you dewax and tie-coat. Then, following the manufacturer's instructions, apply the antifouling paint over the tie-coat. This usually has to occur within a specified amount of time to ensure good adhesion. If you dewax properly and follow the manufacturer's directions, the tie-coat performs a neat trick: It chemically locks the bottom paint and the gelcoat to each other for keeps.

Each of the major antifouling bottom paint suppliers makes a tie-coat system to use with their products. A word of warning: Tie-coat and bottom painting systems are not like a Chinese restaurant menu. Don't be tempted to pick one from column A and one from column B. Mixing and matching different brands of paints is ill advised. If you choose to use Interlux bottom paint, stick with that company's tie-coat as well.

No matter which bottom paint system you decide to use, you must thoroughly dewax your boat's bottom before tie-coating. If you slip up on this step, your time and money are essentially squandered. You won't even know you have a problem until you haul the boat out of the water at the end of the season. The heartbreaking thing about this is that the paint will adhere until the boat is launched. But shortly thereafter, the paint will probably begin to fail and fall off your boat's bottom in big patches.

The tricky thing about dewaxing is that you're removing something that you can't see. To be certain that you've done a good job, be at least twice as diligent as you think is necessary. Miss a few square inches and guess what? Bye-bye paint (on that portion of the boat).

So be sure to do a good job. Here's how.

Though you can use a generic solvent, such as pure toluene, for dewaxing, I think it's best to choose the prep-wash solvent that's made by the manufacturer of your antifouling paint and tie-coat. That means if you're using Interlux's system, you will dewax the bottom with Solvent Wash 202 prep wash before applying their Primocon tie-coat system.

No matter what brand you use, there are some universal rules to follow for successful dewaxing.

- Collect some clean rags or disposable wiping towels that don't disintegrate when wet, and a can of your prep-wash solvent.
- For respiratory protection, work outdoors or in a well-ventilated space. Make sure there's no risk of spark or open flame (needless to say, smoking is out). Wear a respirator and make sure it's fitted with the appropriate toxic mists cartridges. A paper dust mask is not a respirator; it offers no protection against solvent fumes.
- Protect your skin against the prep wash by wearing a disposable Tyvek cool suit. Finish off your ensemble with protective goggles, gloves, and a paint hat.
- To ensure good paint adhesion, it's most important to dewax above the waterline. Remove the wax at least half an inch above the upper limit of your bottom painting area. (Later, after the bottom paint has dried, you can go back and carefully hand-wax the boot top area right down to the paint.)
- When you dewax, you must repeatedly turn the rag over and unfold and refold it to expose a fresh surface. Keep it generously flooded with solvent and, once you've used all the fresh surfaces, toss it aside and take up a fresh one to continue the procedure.
- If you're too stingy with the rags or the solvent, you will just push the wax around and fail to remove it completely. (And I've already warned you of the dire consequences that result from that mistake.)
- Do the entire job in one sitting so you can be absolutely sure you haven't missed any spots. Once you're done, allow the solvent to evaporate from the rags, then dunk them in a pail of water before disposing of them to lessen the likelihood of spontaneous combustion.

Tie-Coat Time

Once you've masked the upper edge of the area to be coated, it's time to prepare your tie-coat.

Put your protective clothing back on before you begin to mix the tie-coat. (If you splash some of this on your clothing, you'll be left with a stain that can't be removed.) Don't forget the respirator. Don the goggles, too, because you definitely don't want to splash any of this stuff in your eyes.

Mix the preparation according to the directions on the containers. I use a disposable paint pot to mix it in, then, once it's mixed, I pour it into a roller tray for application. The resulting preparation will be pretty runny stuff.

You'll obtain the best results by rolling the tie-coat on rather than brushing. However, use a throwaway brush for the tricky areas that can't be reached with a roller: hull strakes, propeller pockets, and the like. Don't use the foam brushes—they disintegrate after a little while. Most boatyards sell inexpensive (less than $2) bristle brushes that are known as "chip brushes." They're what I prefer to use.

What you're shooting for when you apply the tie-coat is a smooth finish—any leftover lumps will be "telegraphed" through the bottom paint coats. As mentioned before, a lumpy bottom costs your boat speed and efficiency, so it's worth taking the time to get it right.

Don't bother applying the tie-coat to your boat's trim tabs, running gear, or through-hull fittings (metal or plastic). It only works on gelcoated fiberglass. These other areas should just be cleaned and sanded before you apply bottom paint.

Speaking of bottom paint, you should have it ready because, in most cases, it must be applied over the tie-coat within a specific time frame. Even if you're allowed to apply the paint on a subsequent day, I advise you to get it done in one push so you don't have to remove the masking tape and apply it anew another day.

Conventional crepe-paper masking tape causes

all sorts of troubles if it's left on overnight. It pulls moisture out of the air and, the following day, when you try to remove it, you'll likely find it welded in place. Then you have to use 3M Adhesive Remover or lighter fluid to get it off, both of which can mess up your paint work. (The Fine Line tape from 3M is not as problematic as the conventional crepe-paper-type, and can usually abide being left in place for a couple of days and nights—another point in its favor.) But still, I strongly advise you just charge through the whole job in one day if at all possible.

Zinc Time

Once you've properly coated the bottom with fresh antifouling paint, your boat is almost ready to be launched. All that remains is to get the zincs in order.

Depending on what kind of power your boat has, you might have anywhere from one to six (or more) zincs. Regardless of the number, there are some fundamental rules to follow that will let your boat's sacrificial anodes do the best job protecting your boat's underwater hardware that they can.

Conductivity Is Key

The first thing to remember is that zincs are electrical components and, like all electrical components, they require good clean connections. So after you've undone the mounting hardware and removed last year's zincs, you want to get the zinc mounting sites clean, shiny, and bright. Here's how.

Get a piece of coarse emery cloth or some 80-grit sandpaper. Thoroughly rough up the areas where the zincs attach (there's often a bit of corrosion residue in these spots). Make sure you remove every trace of corrosion—don't quit until the metal looks brand new.

Zincs are attached with stainless steel machine screws that thread into the mounting site (sterndrives and outboard zincs) or the other half of the zinc anodes (shaft and rudder zincs for inboard-powered boats). Over the course of a season, this mounting hardware is inclined to loosen. There is, however, a way to keep that from happening; I call it two-stage tightening. Here's how it's done.

Start by mounting the zincs and tightening the mounting hardware securely. Most people stop here, which is why so many zinc anodes get loose during the boating season. Now, go one step further by sharply rapping the zincs with a hammer. With rudder zincs, trim tab zincs, and ones that are mounted on outboard and sterndrive gearcases, hit the mounting screws squarely. Shaft zincs on inboard-powered boats shouldn't be hit on the screw head. Instead, smack them midway between the screw heads from both sides.

There's no need to pound away here; a couple of sharp raps will do the trick. This process tightens the zincs and allows the mounting hardware to become a bit loose in the process. Now you can do the final tightening that will allow your zincs to hang on securely for the entire season.

Retighten them—tightly—with an Allen wrench or screwdriver (depending on what type of mounting hardware they have). There you have it. You've tightened your boat's zincs for keeps. Trust me—they aren't going anywhere now.

Boatpox

Earlier, I mentioned that if you sand your boat's gelcoat you will increase its likelihood of getting a case of boatpox. What is it? What causes it? And what's the best treatment if your boat becomes afflicted? Read on.

The technical name for this malady is osmotic blistering, which refers to the fact that the blisters are created due to osmotic pressure. If your science is a bit weak, osmosis is the diffusion of chemicals through a semipermeable membrane.

In a case of boatpox, the semipermeable membrane is your boat's gelcoat. Seawater is driven to diffuse through the gelcoat by the varying chemical concentration inside and outside of the gelcoat. There is a higher chemical concentration under your boat's gelcoat than there is outside of it (in the sea). The chemical concentration under the gelcoat is caused by leftover unreacted chemicals from the manufacture of your boat.

Since it's the difference in chemical concentration that drives the mechanism that creates the blistering, the likelihood of blistering is greater for boats that are immersed in fresh water. (Fresh water is more chemically pure than salt water, which makes the difference in chemical concentration more extreme.)

Over time, your boat's gelcoat becomes plasticized (softened), which makes it easier for the diffusion of water molecules through it. So all else being equal, the longer your boat is kept in the water the more likely it is that blisters will crop up in its underwater surfaces.

Higher temperatures also increase the potential difference that drives boatpox, so if your boat lives in warm water it's more at risk of getting a crop of pox.

The Cure

So what do you do if your boat's bottom has blisters when it's hauled out of the water? The most effective cure consists of three steps: cleaning out or excavating the blisters, filling them in with epoxy filler, and applying a barrier coat over the bottom to reduce the likelihood of it happening again. (This barrier coat should not be confused with the tie-coat that ensures bottom paint adhesion to new boat bottoms.)

Excavating Blisters

If your boat only has a few blisters, you might be able to clean them by grinding them out with the tip of a grinding bit in a Dremel Moto-Tool. The problem with this procedure is that it only takes care of the blisters that you can see. It's possible that there's another whole crop of them waiting to strike sometime in the not-too-distant future. In fact, as a rule, blisters begin to disappear almost immediately after a boat is hauled out of the water. When this happens, the blisters haven't really gone away, they've just "deflated." If you don't eliminate all of them, both the ones you can see and the ones you can't, they'll be back soon after the boat goes back in the water.

I've found an excavation technique that not only takes care of today's blisters, but also exposes the ones lurking under the surface. That technique is sandblasting.

Sandblasting works great for excavating boatpox-plagued gelcoat because it vibrates the unsupported gelcoat and "de-roofs" any hidden blisters. Then the blast of air and sand clears away the compromised gelcoat. But I only recommend this technique with some very important reservations.

First, unless you're a professional sandblaster, don't tackle this project by yourself. Do not run down to the local rental center, outfit yourself, and start blasting. You can do way more damage to your boat than it's already suffering from. Even a professional sandblaster might not be able to do this job without damaging the fiberglass substrate underneath the infested gelcoat.

That's why gelcoat sandblasting should only be done by someone who has done it before and knows the potential pitfalls and dangers. Fiberglass is different from steel surfaces: It's important to use low blasting pressure, a shallow angle of attack, and a not-too-aggressive cutting medium.

Finally, when the sandblasting is done, thoroughly rinse off the bottom of the boat with pure fresh water. Allow it to dry completely, which might take anywhere from a few days to a month or more. Pump the bilges and sponge them dry because moisture can work its way through from the inside of the boat too.

There's a good way to periodically check the progress of the laminate drying process. Cut out a half dozen 6-inch squares of clear plastic and tightly tape them down on various parts of the boat's bottom. Make sure you get a tight seal around all four edges so they are sealed down airtight to the boat's bottom. Every couple of days, peel up the squares, inspect their undersides for the presence of condensed water, and replace them with new squares. Once no more water condenses underneath your squares for a few days, you can safely assume that the laminate and the remaining gelcoat have thoroughly dried.

This last step is critically important. If the laminate has water trapped inside and you apply your epoxy and barrier coats, you will have set yourself up for a repeat performance of the boatpox show.

Gougeon Brothers—the makers of West System epoxy products—have published a useful 52-page booklet on boatpox repair and prevention procedures. It sells for $3. (Their address is 100 Patterson Ave, P.O. Box 908, Bay City, MI 48707-0908; 989-684-6881; www.gougeon.com.) Ask for part #002-650.

Filling Blisters

This second step of the boatpox cure is within the capabilities of a competent do-it-yourselfer. You must use an epoxy-based filler, though. If you use a polyester-based medium, it will only be a matter of time before the boatpox returns. And, after you've finished this job, you definitely won't want to go through it again.

You can mix up your own filler with a high-quality epoxy resin such as West System Epoxy and a suitable filler. Gougeon Brothers makes both of these products and their use is described in the booklet mentioned above. However, most people repairing boatpox go an easier route.

They use a premade filler specifically engineered for boatpox repairs. Interlux makes a family of products called Interprotect for dealing with boatpox (International Paint, 2270 Morris Ave., Union, NJ 07083; 908-686-1300; www.yachtpaint.com/usa). (By the way, this company's Web site is a veritable cornucopia of bottom painting, boatpox remediating, and general pleasureboat finishing advice. It's worth a visit if you have any questions or confusion on these topics.)

Don't apply any more filler than necessary to fill in the excavated blisters. These are all epoxy-based and when they cure they're as hard as rock. You don't want to have to do any unnecessary sanding to get the bottom smooth.

The Barrier Coat

After you've filled in the old blisters and faired the bottom, you're ready for the final step: applying an epoxy-based barrier coat to guard against future migrations of boatpox-causing water through the remaining gelcoat.

International Paint's Interprotect family of products also includes a barrier coat. Follow the directions on the packaging and, once it's applied, you're ready to apply a couple of coats of antifouling bottom paint.

After you've cleaned up around the boat, tightly sealed any containers of unused paints and potions, and made yourself presentable, you're done. Don't forget to set aside some supplies and materials if the boatyard crew is going to have to paint the spots you couldn't get because they were under the cradle or poppets. If you've completed all the on-land chores outlined in chapter 8, Commissioning, your boat is all set to be put in the water.

Questions and Answers

Question: I have a Sea Ray 180 BR with a 4.3-liter MerCruiser drive. I keep the boat in a river most of the time, except to haul it out once every month or so to clean the accumulated grunge off the bottom. Should I apply bottom paint, or will this bimonthly maintenance suffice? I should add that, once the boat is out of the water, it usually stays out for a week or two.

Answer: If you haul out regularly and scrub the boat and sterndrive thoroughly, you might be able to get away with the system you're using. Might. It depends on the water where you keep the boat.

Is it moored in the tidal portion of the river, in salty or brackish water? If so, you have to contend with saltwater critters and slime, which are more troublesome than their freshwater counterparts.

When salt water warms up to a certain temperature, barnacles spawn and you get what's called a barnacle "set." That's a zillion baby barnacles swimming around looking for a nice landing spot. Within a week or two, they glue themselves to their starter-home sites, harden up, and begin to grow into full-fledged barnacles. If you don't scrub the boat's bottom and sterndrive clean before they finish this project, you're going to have a dandy crop of barnacles to deal with. (Before they secrete their miracle glue, they can be brushed off with a scrub brush. Afterward—well, you know.)

Therefore, if you're not sure you can keep ahead of the barnacles and slime, it might take a load off your mind to apply antifouling paint. Since you mention that the boat sometimes stays out of the water for a week or two, you'll get the best performance by using copolymer paint. (Copolymer paint remains fresh and ready to work between immersions. Conventional antifouling paints lose their potency when out of the water.)

Over time, this type of paint wears away like a bar of soap. Therefore, several coats (usually three) are applied and then, as the paint wears, fresh biocide is continually exposed. Unlike regular paint, this stuff is "good to the last drop."

Question: I recently purchased a Winner 2280 Sport Cuddy with a 225 hp outboard. The boat was always trailered and therefore never had the bottom painted. Is there any way to determine where the waterline is without putting the boat in the water, marking the waterline, and then taking it back out?
Answer: Oh, I suppose if you found a similarly powered and equipped Winner 2280, you could take a series of offset measurements and notes (from a dinghy alongside). But you'll get much better results by launching *your* boat, letting it sit in the water for a while, then hauling it back out. Before you do this, make sure you've got the boat loaded up with fuel and all the gear you're ever likely to ask it to carry.

You'll have to leave it in the water long enough to allow a "scum line" to form where the boat is immersed. It's like a bathtub ring, so dirty water works best.

After you've hauled your scum-lined boat, use a permanent marker to make tick marks every foot or so. You'll want the bottom paint to come up at least an inch or so higher than the scum line when you've finished. That way, the boat will have antifouling protection in the splash zone and won't grow a green beard.

If this boat has never had bottom paint, you will need to dewax the bottom and use a tie-coat under the antifouling paint. Check the label of your bottom paint for specific details.

Question: I have had a problem with my 1988 MerCruiser sterndrive. The sterndrive became pitted over the past four seasons when I had it docked. This spring I sanded, primed, and spray-painted (using Mercury Black Max paint) the areas that were pitted. Both the primer and paint were for marine use and I followed the instructions. Finally, I applied a coat of clear coat to prevent the growth of algae and zebra mussels.

This fall when I took the boat out of the water, all of the spots that I had sanded and repainted were bare aluminum and the paint had come off. Did I do something wrong and what can I do to prevent this problem from recurring when I repaint my sterndrive in the spring?
Answer: As you've discovered, it's not easy to properly repaint a sterndrive. Simply scratching the failed spots with some sandpaper, then priming and painting rarely works for long. MerCruiser publishes a technical information sheet titled "How to Correctly Repaint a MerCruiser Sterndrive" (write to request this document from MerCruiser; Attn: Consumer Affairs, 3003 N. Perkins Rd., Stillwater, OK 74075-2299; 405-743-6566; www.mercurymarine.com). The sheet includes surface preparation and recoating guidelines. Part numbers and quantities of the required Pittsburgh Paint Company products—including a special converter-primer—are also listed.

The whole operation is very fussy and requires professional tools and knowledge. For example, the two-part epoxy paint must be applied with a spray gun. If you so much as touch the prepared surface, the paint might fail to adhere. (A spot of oil from one of your fingertips can spoil the adhesion.)

Even if you follow the recommended procedures, you might still wind up with paint failure. The culprit is electrolysis. If your boat has an electrolysis problem, any paint you apply will be blown off the drive in short order. Before you start any kind of running gear repainting job, you should always make sure this isn't the root cause of the problem.

Be sure all wiring connections are clean and solid. Pay particular attention to the battery cable ends—at the batteries, of course—but don't forget the other ends, too. The battery should be clean and you should make sure you're not using a nonmarine battery charger. (Using one of these could irretrievably damage your sterndrive in a matter of days.)

3 TROUBLESHOOTING GASOLINE-FUELED INBOARDS AND STERNDRIVES

THE BIG THREE

Remember the fire triangle mentioned in chapter 1: It takes three things to sustain a fire: fuel, oxygen, and heat. There's a similar trio that you have to learn if you're going to troubleshoot gasoline-fueled engines. To start and run successfully, they require fuel, ignition, and compression. Take away any one of these and, like a fire with a missing ingredient, the engine stumbles and fails.

When you troubleshoot an engine that won't go, your mission is to check for the presence of the necessary items, find which one is missing, and figure out how to restore it so you can get the engine back in business.

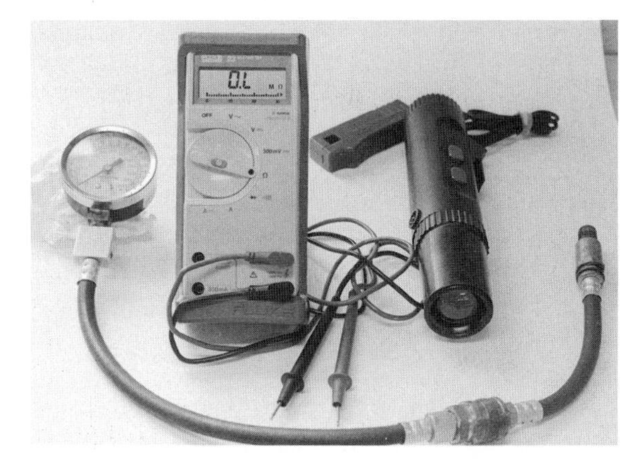

An assortment of measuring tools for boat troubleshooting. From left to right: compression gauge, digital multimeter, and timing light. Note that the timing light is a self-powered one, so there are no power leads to hook it up to 12-volt DC.

Fuel

It stands to reason that your boat's engine won't operate without gasoline. It isn't enough to simply have an adequate supply in the tank, even though that's the first thing you should check when an engine won't run. Nope, engines are sort of fussy about the way their gasoline is served; it has to be supplied in extremely small, bite-size pieces. It's the job of the carburetor (or fuel-injection system on the newer engines) to prepare the fuel.

When gasoline is introduced into an engine, it's said to be atomized and, although the droplets of fuel that are sprayed in are a lot larger than atoms, they're still small. Their small size allows them to enter the cylinder quickly and burn in a smooth, powerful pulse of energy.

The fuel system components of a typical gasoline engine installation include the tank, antisiphon valve, fuel lines, primary filter–water separator, fuel pump, and carburetor (or fuel injection pump and injectors). In some instances, there's also a small secondary filter built into the inlet fitting in the carburetor body.

Any one of these components can cause a fuel system problem, as can the quality of the fuel itself. If it's stale or contaminated with water, the engine will die or run poorly.

Ignition System

This system comprises all the components that provide the spark that gets things going in your engine. A good supply of atomized fuel won't do anything if it doesn't receive a nice hot spark at just the right moment.

Like any electrical component in the bilges of a boat, marine engine ignition systems have a rough life. Engine room environmental conditions range from cool and dank to hot and laden with ozone. These conditions take a toll on wiring connections, relays and other switches, and the electrical and electronic components that make up the ignition system.

But by far the biggest cause of trouble in this system is neglect. If you follow the maintenance steps outlined in this book, chances are you'll never even need to refer to this chapter because you will have nipped any potential troublemakers in the bud before they've had a chance to ruin your day.

Compression

An internal combustion engine works sort of like an air compressor or pump in that it has tightly fitted pistons that move up and down in the cylinders. When a piston moves up to the top of the cylinder with the valves closed (more on these details later), the air above the piston is squeezed. When air is squeezed or compressed, it heats up.

A word to the wise: Many newly minted troubleshooters like to test a balky engine for compression when it won't go. Although compression *is* one of the three items needed to make an engine run, it's the least likely cause of engine failure. Unless something dramatic and catastrophic happens inside your engine (like a hole in the top of a piston or a failed head gasket), chances are the problem lies in the fuel or ignition systems.

So unless you heard a bad noise or have other reasons to suspect a compression failure, save the compression test for last. That's because as a rule, compression is something that an engine loses over time as its precisely fitted parts begin to wear out. Pistons and piston rings get sloppy and the valves and valve seats are gradually burned and eroded. Compression testing is also more of a pain than checking for spark or fuel.

Even so, checking your engine's compression at the end of each season is a useful survey tool; doing so will enable you to document the gradual wear that's taking place. (I'll tell you how to make a compression check later in this chapter.) The results of the test will give you a good idea when an overhaul or repowering is going to be needed and let you budget for it.

WHAT *IS* A FOUR-CYCLE ENGINE, ANYWAY?

You might have heard your inboard or sterndrive engine referred to as a four-cycle engine. Your car also has a four-cycle engine. Most outboard motors have traditionally been two cycle, but many of the newer ones are four cycle. The designation *four cycle* refers to the fact that, for each firing of a particular spark plug, the piston in that cylinder goes up and down two times. (Each up or down travel of a piston counts as a cycle.) Here's a blow-by-blow description (pun intended) of these cycles. Remember that, although we're only considering what's going on in one cylinder, these events are happening continuously and sequentially in all of the engine's cylinders whenever it's running.

One more thing you need to know: Intake and exhaust valves, which are spring-loaded, act just like their name. They open and close at specific times to let atomized fuel and air into the cylinder (intake valves) and to let the spent exhaust gases back out (exhaust valves). Don't fret about them, though—you're not going to be doing any work on them. Now on with the show.

Intake Stroke

This is the beginning of the action. When things start out, the piston in our cylinder is at the top of its travel, a position known as top dead center (TDC).

The exhaust valve is closed and the intake valve has opened as the piston begins to move downward

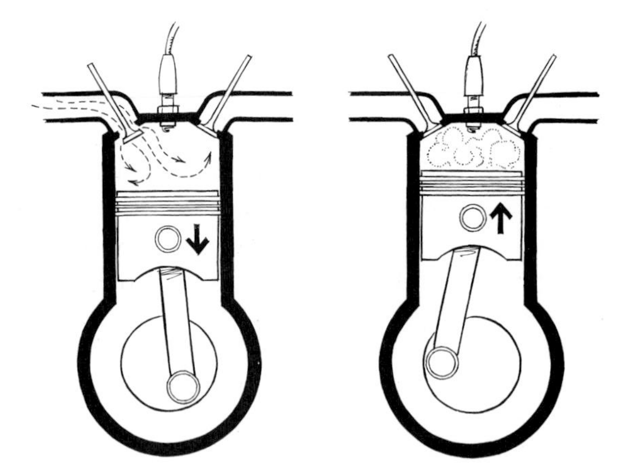

Intake stroke: The intake valve is open, and the downrushing piston sucks in a charge of fuel and air.

Compression stroke: Both valves are closed, and the piston is moving up, compressing the fuel-air charge.

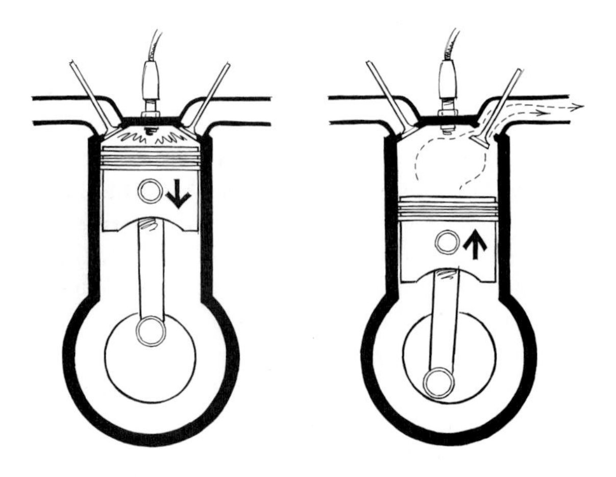

Power stroke: The spark plug has fired, igniting the fuel. The controlled explosion forces the piston down and allows the engine to do useful work.

Exhaust stroke: The exhaust valve is open, and the uprushing piston evacuates the spent exhaust gases.

in the cylinder. With the intake valve open, the downrushing piston sucks a charge of atomized fuel (fuel-air mixture) from the carburetor through the intake manifold into the cylinder. By the time the piston reaches the bottom of its travel—you guessed it, bottom dead center—there's enough fuel and air in the cylinder to set the stage for combustion.

Compression Stroke

Before the piston starts to go back up again for this cycle, the valve gear in the cylinder tightly closes the intake valve. Needless to say, this and all the other operations necessary to make our engine run are happening very quickly.

With both valves at the top of our cylinder shut tight, the piston compresses the fuel-air mixture as it travels back up toward TDC. A few thousandths of a second before the piston gets back to TDC, the ignition system sends a strong jolt of high-energy electricity to the spark plug in the cylinder. This creates a fat, blue spark and starts the conflagration that makes powerboating possible.

Power Stroke

Now that the piston is at the top of its travel, a wildfire is raging in the tightly confined space at the top of the cylinder, and the real action begins.

With both valves in the cylinder tightly shut, the pressure wave produced by the tightly confined explosion in the top of our cylinder has nowhere to go. Something has to give, and it does. The only part that's free to move is the piston. The extreme pressure drives it back down toward the bottom of its travel. The push exerted against the top of the piston is converted by the crankshaft into the rotary motion that spins the crankshaft (and ultimately the boat's propeller).

Exhaust Stroke

Now that our cylinder has finished its work for the time being (meaning the next few thousandths of a second), it's time for a bit of housecleaning. The cylinder is loaded with what's left over after the power stroke—spent exhaust gases.

That's what the exhaust stroke is for. With the piston at the bottom of its travel, the exhaust valve opens and provides a path for these gases to be expelled. The piston—which by now is zooming back up toward the top of the cylinder—pushes the spent gases and heat out through the open exhaust valve. These gases are ducted out through the exhaust manifold so they can be expelled overboard through your boat's exhaust system.

No Rest for the Weary

In a nutshell, that's what your four-cycle engine does when it's operating. Sounds pretty simple, right? Of course, there's this to ponder: When your boat's engine is running at wide-open throttle, say 4,400 rpm, this entire sequence of events is happening about 36 times per second in each of its cylinders. Pretty wild, eh?

Troubleshooting Your Boat's Engine

If you go down to your boat one fine day and the engine either fails to crank (it might click a little) or cranks over but won't start, it's time to walk through a troubleshooting routine. Let's start with an engine that won't crank.

Engine Won't Crank Over

If your engine greets you with a big fat nothing or a few wimpy clicks when you turn the key, you don't need to start checking for fuel, ignition, or compression problems. Your problem is in the battery or starting system.

First, make sure you've got the engine control set to neutral. Almost all marine engines have start-in-neutral safety switches to keep you from firing up the engine in gear with its sometimes surprising consequences. Typically, these switches are mounted in the control or at the transmission (in the case of most inboards). They are often very fussy and, if you don't have the engine exactly in neutral, they will keep the engine from cranking.

So start by wiggling the shift control at the helm and trying again. Sometimes that's all it takes to get the engine to crank.

Next, using an ohmmeter, check to see if the safety switch is defective or misadjusted. (Refer to chapter 5 for information about how to conduct such a continuity test.) Remember: Before you test this switch with your ohmmeter, make sure the main battery switch is shut off.

Most neutral safety switches close the circuit only when the engine is in neutral. They're typically mounted on an adjustable bracket, so check to make sure it's positioned to work as intended—that is, only when the engine is shifted into neutral.

The next thing to check is the battery's state of charge. Refer to chapter 5 if necessary, and use your voltmeter to measure the open circuit voltage at the positive and negative terminals. The open circuit voltage should measure at least 12.5 volts, though that indicates a partially discharged battery. If it's really up to snuff, you should expect to get a reading of 12.7 volts or better.

If your voltage testing indicates that the battery needs charging, go ahead and do so. But once it's charged, you're not out of the woods yet. If the battery was low, you have to figure out why it got that way. Most likely, something is wrong with the charging system. (Unless, of course, you discover that you left something on the last time you used the boat and, in your absence, the current drain killed the battery.) See pages 26–34 for details on troubleshooting your charging system.

If the voltage reading indicates that the battery has a good charge, the next thing to check are its terminals. Are they dirty or corroded? (Surely you periodically inspect and clean them, so that couldn't be the problem.) On the off chance you haven't cleaned the terminals or aren't familiar with the procedure, here's the routine:

1. Start by shutting off the battery switch. Before you use a wrench to disconnect the battery terminal clamps, think safety. Make sure you pick a wrench that isn't long enough to touch both

terminals at the same time. (If it does, it can short out the battery, which will probably explode in your face.)

2. Loosen the nut that secures the clamp and wiggle the terminal back and forth before you try to lift it off the battery post. If it won't wiggle or lift off, spread the jaws a bit with a screwdriver. Don't lever the terminal off the post—doing so can break the seal around the battery post and ruin the battery. (As with the wrench, make sure the screwdriver you choose is too short to make a short circuit across the battery terminals.)
3. When you've removed one terminal, use the female end of your battery cleaning tool to wire brush the battery's terminal post until it's clean and bright.
4. Uncap the tool, exposing the male brush inside, which is used to clean the inside contact surfaces of the terminal at the end of the battery cable. Clean this surface until it's shiny and bright, then replace the clamp, tighten it securely, and spray on some battery terminal protectant. (Some folks prefer to smear some Vaseline on. This works well, but I think it's kind of messy.)
5. Repeat the disassembly, cleaning, and reassembly procedure with the other terminal. If the terminals or the posts on the battery were corroded, you might very well have solved the no-cranking problem already. Turn on the battery switch, ventilate the engine room until you're sure it's clear of explosive gasoline vapors, and try starting the engine again.

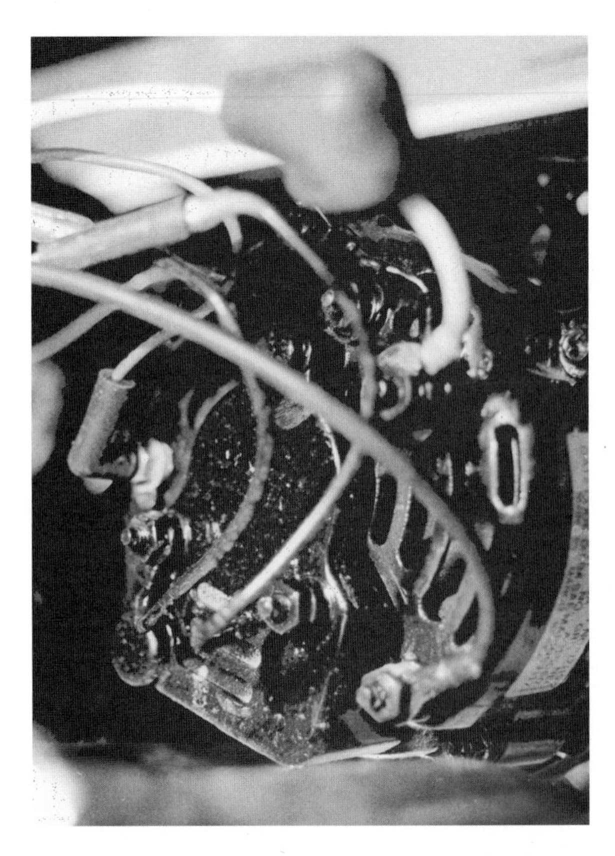

Connections on the back of an alternator. Note that the protective rubber boot of the output lead has been pushed back to provide access to this connection.

Troubleshooting the Charging System

Begin by checking the alternator drive belt to make sure it's not missing, loose, shiny, or cracked. If you find any of these faults, you must renew the belt and check its tension before you head out on the water. Refer to chapter 8 for details on getting the alternator drive belt tension correct.

Next, disconnect the battery or shut off the vapor-proof switch. Then carefully inspect the connections on the back of the alternator to make sure they're clean, shiny, and bright. To avoid mixing up these connections, make a diagram outlining them or, better yet, just take one of them off at a time for cleaning and replace it before you remove the next one. After cleaning and reinstalling them, apply a coat of Liquid Electric Tape to seal them from corrosion and keep them reliable.

Safe Battery Boosting

I'm tempted to leave this section blank because, strictly speaking, there is no safe way to use jumper cables to start a gasoline-fueled inboard or sterndrive engine. Even using jumper cables on a car is

TROUBLESHOOTING CHART

Engine Doesn't Crank Over When Key Is Turned

Is shift lever in neutral? ▶ ▼ Yes, still won't crank	No, put lever in neutral
Is neutral safety switch misadjusted? ▶ ▼ No, still won't crank	Yes, adjust as needed
Is neutral safety switch defective? ▶ ▼ No, still won't crank	Check with ohmmeter, replace if defective
Is battery discharged? ▶ ▼ No, still won't crank	Yes, charge battery and check charging system
Are the cable connections corroded or dirty? ▶ ▼ No, still won't crank	Yes, clean connections
Is the key switch defective? ▶	Check with ohmmeter; replace if necessary

Engine Cranks But Fails To Start

Are the spark plugs wet with fuel? ▶ ▼ If dry, proceed to fuel system troubleshooting	Yes, proceed to ignition system troubleshooting

Fuel System Troubleshooting

Is gas tank empty? ▶ ▼ No, still won't start	Yes, fill tank
Is primary fuel filter clogged with debris? ▶ ▼ No, still won't start	Yes, renew filter; check for water
Is secondary fuel filter clogged with debris? ▶ ▼ No, still won't start	Yes, renew filter
Is antisiphon valve defective? ▶ ▼ No, still won't start	Yes, inspect/replace if necessary
Is fuel pump defective? ▶	Yes, inspect/replace if necessary

Ignition System Troubleshooting

Spark test with timing light ▶ No cylinders firing, check voltage to coil with ignition on, test with voltmeter	Some cylinders firing, replace distributor cap and rotor

a dangerous operation. The battery can explode if the cables are hooked up incorrectly, and there are always some sparks when you hook up the last cable connection from the booster battery to the dead battery.

In a car, the sparks are rarely a problem because the battery is in a well-ventilated space. A battery in a boat, on the other hand, is not; it's in an engine room. If there are any gasoline vapors present, just hooking up the jumper cables can cause an explosion—even if you don't mix up the connections.

Before you hook up jumper cables or a battery charger, which can also cause sparks, make sure the engine room is completely vented and that there are no explosive gasoline vapors. If you use jumper cables, here's the safe sequence for making the connections.

1. Start with the red (positive) cable. Hook up one end to the positive terminal of the battery that will be giving the boost, then hook up the other end to the positive terminal of the dead battery.
2. Now make the negative connections. Use the black cable and, again, connect the clamp to the battery giving the boost (the negative terminal this time).
3. Connect the other end of the black cable to the engine block where the moving drive belts won't foul it when you start the engine.
4. Provided there are no gasoline vapors present, you're almost ready to twist the key and start the engine. (Make sure the cables won't be fouled by the drive belts and other moving parts.) If your booster battery is in another boat, you may want to have its engine running for this operation.
5. Now crank the disabled engine. Once the engine catches and begins to run, disconnect the cables in the reverse order from the way you hooked them up. Again, mind the moving parts.
6. Don't shut off the engine and don't throw off the docklines and head out just yet. First, you must check the charging system to make sure it's working properly. If it isn't, you need to fix it before you go out.

Inspecting the Charging System

When your boat's battery is low, get your voltmeter out and make sure the charge system is functioning properly. Set it to measure the lowest range of DC volts that's 15 volts or above. Now bring the engine up to a fast idle, say 1,500 rpm, and leave it running at that rate. Hook up the test leads to the negative and positive terminals of the battery.

You should get a reading of at least 14 volts, which indicates that the alternator is charging the battery. Now switch on every DC-powered piece of equipment on the boat: Open the faucets, flip on all the lights inside and out, the navigation electronics, and anything else that you can. The idea is to subject the charging system to a substantial load.

If the alternator and voltage regulator are in good trim, the measured voltage at the battery should not drop by more than one volt. If it does, and the drive belt and wiring connections passed muster, you should shut things down, remove the alternator, and deliver it to an auto electric shop for reworking.

The problem with the alternator might be something as minor as a bad rectifier assembly or voltage regulator. In a modern alternator, however, both of these components are located inside the alternator housing, which means that the alternator still must be removed for servicing.

The reason I advocate repairing rather than replacing your alternator is that the original alternator on a marine engine is a shielded marine unit. The ones at the auto parts store are not. Don't substitute an automotive unit because its unshielded construction will generate sparks that are an explosion hazard in your boat's engine room. (The same is true for all electrical components on marine engines: distributor, starter motor, and the like.)

Engine Cranks, but Won't Start

When your engine cranks over but doesn't start and run successfully, brush off your fuel, ignition, and compression troubleshooting skills. If the engine doesn't start within ten seconds or so, don't continue cranking it—you'll just kill the battery and have two problems to deal with instead of one.

Testing for Fuel Delivery

I know this is silly, but sometimes we overlook the most obvious cause of poor fuel delivery. That is, taking a look in the fuel tank.

Is there anything in there? If not, you've solved the problem. Fill up the tank.

But fuel problems aren't always that easy. If an empty tank isn't your problem, you need to find out if the fuel system is delivering any fuel to the engine's cylinders. The easiest way to do this is to remove a spark plug.

If you've cranked the engine for ten seconds and it hasn't fired up, the spark plugs should be damp and smell like gasoline. If they aren't, that means that no gasoline is making it into the cylinders. There might be a problem with the fuel filter(s), carburetor, fuel lines, antisiphon valve, or fuel pump (in that order of likelihood). If you suspect that a clogged filter might be the source of your engine's problems, refer to chapter 8, which discusses how to inspect and service fuel filters.

Note: Many of the newest marine engines have electronic fuel injection and a fuel problem might be electrical in origin. Consult your owner's manual to find out if there are any critical fuses, or places that you can test for voltage to troubleshoot your boat's system.

Many marine engines have a secondary particle filter where the steel fuel line enters the carburetor. This filter is often neglected and, when it gets clogged, it will bring things to an abrupt halt. Consult your engine manual to find out if your engine's carburetor is so equipped. It's not easy to change this filter but here are some helpful tips.

1. Turn off the battery switch or disconnect the battery. Then gather up the necessary tools. You will need a line wrench sized to fit the fitting at the carburetor end of the steel fuel line. Don't attempt to unhook this connection with a conventional open-end wrench. If you do, you'll most likely round off the flats on the fitting and make the entire fuel line assembly unusable. You will also need a larger, open-end (or adjustable) wrench to hold the fitting that this small inverted flare fitting is threaded into at the carburetor.
2. Hold the large fitting with the large wrench and use the line wrench to "shock" the small fitting loose. Once it spins freely, back this fitting out the rest of the way. (Sometimes you'll encounter a little pressure in the fuel line at this point.) Now tuck a clean rag underneath and pull back on the steel line just far enough to allow the end of it to clear the recess it enters. (If your engine has a metal clamp and bolt holding the hard steel fuel line to the engine block or cylinder head, undo this clamp first or you won't be able to unhook the fuel line without damaging or bending it.)
3. Once you've maneuvered the fuel line out of the way, use the open-end wrench to remove the larger fitting that's threaded into the carburetor body. The filter you seek is installed inside this large nut. Replace the filter with a new one (which will set you back less than $5) and replace the nut in the carburetor body. You will have to install a new sealing washer under this nut before you reinstall it. If the filter doesn't include this part, make sure you get it while you're at the parts counter. Tighten the nut with the new filter in it securely. Don't put so much force on it, though, that you strip the threads in the carburetor body.
4. Now maneuver the end of the steel fuel line back into its recess and carefully start the inverted flare fitting back into its threads by hand. Don't use a wrench to tighten this part until you're absolutely positive that it's not cross-threaded. The easiest way to do this is to spin it in by hand or put very little force on the line wrench to tighten it.
5. If it takes more than a minimum of effort, stop tightening, back it out, and try bending the line a bit so it enters squarely. Once you've succeeded in getting it in without cross-threading, tighten it securely with your line wrench. *Warning:* This

is an inverted flare fitting. As mentioned in chapter 6, it shouldn't be tightened too tightly. Once the fittings are made up snugly, tighten it about another 1/8 of a turn.

Whenever you disturb this connection, you will have to immediately check for leaks when you start the engine. But before starting the engine, remove any gasoline-soaked rags from the engine room, leave the compartment wide open so it can ventilate thoroughly, run the blower for ten minutes, and check for gasoline vapors. Here's how to check the connection for leaks.

Start by washing your hands, so they're not polluted with the smell of gasoline. Now start the engine. Then run a clean rag around the connection and give the rag a sniff. If you smell any gasoline on the rag, the connection has a leak. Stop the engine immediately and correct the problem.

Most gasoline-fueled boats have an antisiphon valve (a small plumbing device) installed where the fuel line attaches to the fuel tank. The valve is a safety device. Inside it is a small, spring-loaded ball that serves as a check valve. If the engine's fuel pump is working properly and is sucking on the fuel in the line, the ball in this valve is pulled off its seat and allows fuel to flow. If, on the other hand, the fuel line is somehow disconnected or broken, the lack of suction forces the spring to snap the ball back down securely on its seat, thereby keeping the entire contents of the tank from siphoning out into the boat's bilges. (However, the fuel in the line will probably drain out.)

Once in a while, one of these antisiphon valves gets corroded or sticks for some other reason. If that happens, the fuel pump won't be able to draw a supply of fuel from the tank to the engine. This doesn't happen very often, but if you've checked everything else in the fuel system you might want to disassemble the fuel line connection at the tank and remove the antisiphon valve for testing.

After removing the valve, blow into it from the fuel tank side—you should be able to push the ball off the spring and blow air through this component. If it seems to take a lot of pressure, go to the parts counter and try the same routine with a replacement unit. If the one from your boat seems balkier, ante up the $8 or so that a new antisiphon valve costs and install it in lieu of the questionable one.

Don't forget to make sure that the threads are clean and coated with a smear of Teflon thread paste when you reinstall the valve. Because it has a pipe thread, it requires a good tightening to effect a proper seal. Like any disturbed fitting in your boat's fuel system, you must remember to check for fuel leaks after this task is completed. Follow the procedure outlined above.

There's one other fuel system component that can fail and cause your engine to be fuel deprived: the fuel pump. Truth be told, fuel pump failures are pretty rare. But, if you've checked everything else and can't find a problem, you can do a rough test of the fuel pump. Note that I said "rough test." To fully check a fuel pump it's necessary to check it for fuel delivery pressure using a special gauge. You're not likely to have or be able to get access to one of these. But here's the rough test procedure.

1. You will absolutely have to have a line wrench in the correct size for the fittings on the hard steel line between your engine's fuel pump and its carburetor. If you try to undo this connection with a conventional open-end wrench, you'll almost certainly ruin the fittings that are permanently attached to this line. (As mentioned earlier, some engines have a metal clamp and bolt holding the hard steel fuel line to the engine block or cylinder head. If your engine is so equipped, undo this clamp first or you won't be able to unhook the fuel line without damaging or bending it.)
2. Make sure the battery switch is turned off. Now use the line wrench to disconnect the fitting at the carburetor end of the hard steel fuel line leading from the fuel pump. After you've backed out the fitting all the way, pull the line back out of out the recess it was threaded into and carefully maneuver it over a shallow, disposable aluminum loaf pan. You might have to bend the sides of the pan down a bit to get it to fit in the confined

space under the end of the fuel line. Once you've done this, hold a clean rag loosely over the end of the line so any fuel coming out won't spurt.

3. Have your helper crank the engine. Within a few seconds, fuel should begin to spurt from the end of the fuel line into your pan. If it does, tell your helper to stop cranking the engine. If it doesn't, let the starter crank for another five seconds or so. If the rest of the fuel system has checked out OK, but no fuel appears at the end of the line after eight or ten seconds of cranking, the fuel pump isn't working.

Replacing a fuel pump is not too onerous a chore. Make sure you get the replacement pump from your marine engine dealer's stock and not an auto parts store—a marine fuel pump is specially designed not to leak if the pump diaphragm is ruptured. Install the new pump with a fresh gasket and be sure to reattach the clear plastic sight tube that leads up the base of the carburetor.

You might have to reuse the adaptor fittings that are threaded into the fuel pump's body. If you do, make sure you clean off their threads with a wire brush and apply a smear of Teflon thread paste to them before threading them into the fuel pump body. These are pipe fittings, so they need stronger tightening than the inverted flare fittings, but don't overdo it either. Keep the tightening force commensurate with the size of the fittings. Otherwise you will probably crack the body of the fuel pump or gall the threads of the connection.

Once the adaptor fittings have been installed, follow the recommendations given above for tightening inverted flare fittings (snugged up, then tightened ⅛ of a turn). Then, after ventilating the engine room by running the blower for ten minutes, sniff for gasoline vapors. If none are present, go ahead and start the engine, immediately checking for leaks as described earlier.

If you're not absolutely sure whether fuel is making it to the carburetor, there's another easy test of the fuel system on carbureted engines. If you shut off the battery switch, remove the engine's flame arrester, and hold the choke butterfly open, you can peer down in the carburetor throat with an explosion-proof flashlight. While you're doing this, have a helper push the throttle all the way forward. If you hear and see a spritz of fuel being delivered by the carburetor's accelerator pump, the fuel system is probably not the source of your engine's starting difficulties. It's time to move on to the spark show.

Testing for Spark

Perhaps you're old enough to remember the old trick of checking for spark by holding a spark plug against the engine block with a screwdriver while you crank the engine. You do? Well, try to forget it.

That is a dangerous practice because modern ignition systems can give you a memorable shock. It can also be an expensive practice because it can damage sensitive components in some modern ignition systems. Even worse, you don't really learn much, since even a weak ignition system can jump a small air gap outside of the combustion chamber. (It's also an explosion hazard.)

The safest procedure is to hook up a timing light to one of the spark plug leads, carefully route the cables so they won't get caught by the engine's moving parts (such as the drive belts), and have your helper crank the engine over. If the timing light flashes, there's spark inside that wire.

When you've checked for spark on the first cylinder, have your helper shut the ignition key all the

Timing light attached to a spark plug lead. The contacts here are carbon and will crack if they're handled carelessly.

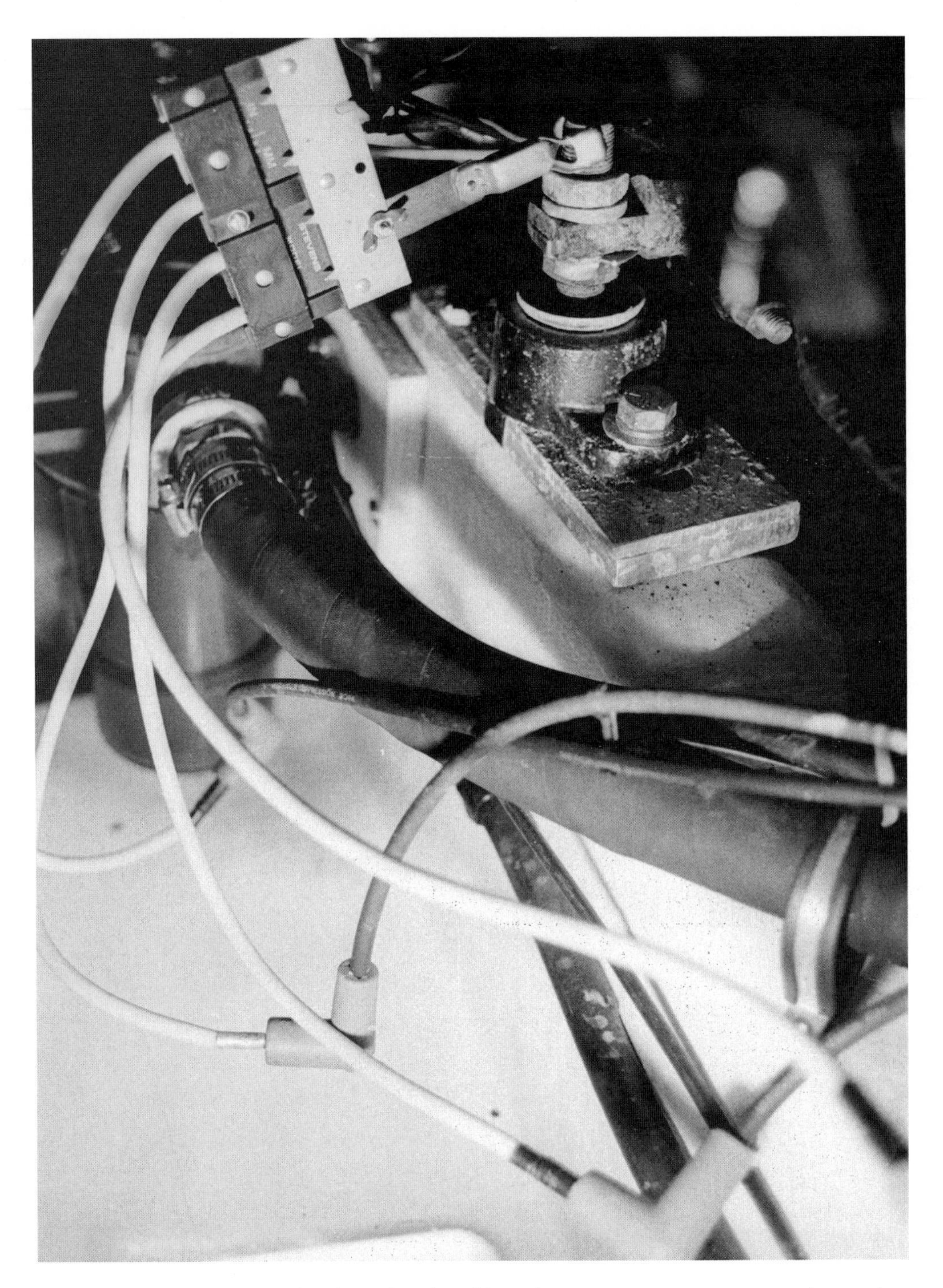

Air-gap spark checker in use. Before this tool can be safely used in an engine room, you must make sure there are no explosive gasoline vapors present.

way off and pocket the key (to avoid surprises). Repeat the test, checking each wire in turn. Again route the wires out of harm's way. If some of them show a spark, but others don't, your problem is almost certainly the distributor cap or the rotor (or both).

If there's no evidence of any spark anywhere, the problem could be the cap and rotor or the ignition coil. Before you go off half-cocked and buy a new coil, use your voltmeter to test for the presence of 12 volts at the primary connections on the ignition coil. These terminals are marked positive (+) and negative (−); attach the positive and negative terminals of the meter to them.

If you don't measure battery voltage (or somewhat less) at the positive and negative terminals on the coil when the key is in the "run" position (not the spring-loaded "start" position), your problem is probably in the key switch or the wiring that connects it to the coil. Shut off all the power to the system and perform continuity tests of the key switch and its associated wiring with your ohmmeter. Refer to chapter 5 for particulars on continuity testing.

The timing light spark test doesn't tell you exactly how strong the spark is; it just gives you an indication of whether spark is present at all. If you want to quantify the spark, you'll need another tool: an air-gap spark checker.

Warning: Using this type of checker creates open sparks. Before you use it in the engine room, be absolutely certain there are no explosive gasoline vapors. Run the bilge blower for ten minutes and get down low in the engine room to sniff for gasoline vapors. If none are present, it should be safe to use the air-gap spark checker.

This device works much like the old spark plug against the block test, except that it's safer for the

Spark plug removed from an inboard engine for inspection. Looking at the plugs can tell you a lot about the health of an engine and the quality of the fuel it's burning: Light tan or gray deposits are indicative of a well-tuned engine on a diet of high-quality fuel.

operator. It also gives more meaningful results because it forces the ignition system's spark to jump a much larger gap. Mine (shown on page 32) is the model S-48H, made by Stevens Instrument Company (111 E. Greenwood Ave., Waukegan, IL 60087; 847-336-9375; www.stevensinstrument.com). It lists for $39.13 plus shipping.

Depending on what type of ignition system your engine has, the spark checker should be set to a gap between ¼ inch and ½ inch. You can find this specification by asking the mechanics at the boatyard or consulting the engine manual. If you still can't find it, a good rule of thumb is that a conventional battery–coil ignition system should be able to jump a ¼-inch gap. Some magneto capacitor discharge ignition systems are much more potent. The spark with some of these systems is capable of jumping a gap as large as a ½ inch.

It helps to have the checker in a shady spot when you crank the engine. Make sure the wires won't be entangled in the moving belts at the front of the engine. When you crank the engine, look for a hot, fat, blue spark at each position on the checker.

If your engine has good spark and a ready supply of fuel to its cylinders, there are two possibilities. The spark plugs are fouled, eroded, or otherwise no good, or the engine doesn't have enough compression to start and run. Since a compression fault is rarely the problem, most likely the spark plugs need to be replaced.

I've found a useful series of color illustrations showing various types of spark plug problems. The Web address is www.gnttype.org/techarea/engine/plugs.html.

Spark plugs don't cost much. If you suspect them, gap and install a new set. (You'll find pointers for replacing spark plugs in chapter 4.) The only difference is that your sterndrive or inboard engine has cast-iron, not aluminum, cylinder heads, so you don't have to worry about stripping or cross-threading the threaded holes. Spin the new spark plugs in by hand and then give them a good grunt with your spark plug wrench to make sure they're tightly installed. Don't forget to set the replacement plugs to the correct electrode gap and tighten the terminals on their tops with a pair of pliers before you install them.

Compression Testing

If your testing indicates that the engine has fuel and spark reaching its cylinders and the spark plugs are in good shape, but it still won't start, the only remaining cause is a lack of compression.

To perform a compression test you'll need a compression gauge, a spark plug wrench, a squirt can of motor oil, some clean rags, and a pad and pencil.

Before testing, you must disable the ignition system. If your engine has a conventional coil and battery ignition system, remove the high-tension lead between the ignition coil and the center contact of the distributor. For safety's sake, don't just unhook one end; remove the high-tension lead completely.

If you've got an engine with electronic ignition, check with your engine manufacturer or local mechanic for instructions about this step; the procedure might be different and you don't want to risk damaging the system by doing something wrong.

Once the ignition system is disabled, use your spark plug wrench to remove all of the spark plugs. Wipe the plug holes clean with a rag and make sure no debris falls into the cylinders.

Screw the compression tester into the number-one cylinder, then set the throttle wide open to allow as much air as possible to enter the engine. Since the engine is cold, the automatic choke butterflies will probably be closed. If they are, hold them open with a screwdriver to allow maximum airflow and an accurate compression reading.

Now have your helper crank the engine while you observe the gauge. The reading should come up pretty quickly—usually within two or three revolutions of the engine. At this point it won't go any higher. Tell your helper to stop cranking the engine and remove the key (to avoid surprises).

Jot the compression figure down on your pad, remove the tester from the cylinder, release the reading on the gauge, and move it to the next spark plug hole. Repeat the test and jot down the reading. Test all the cylinders in the same fashion.

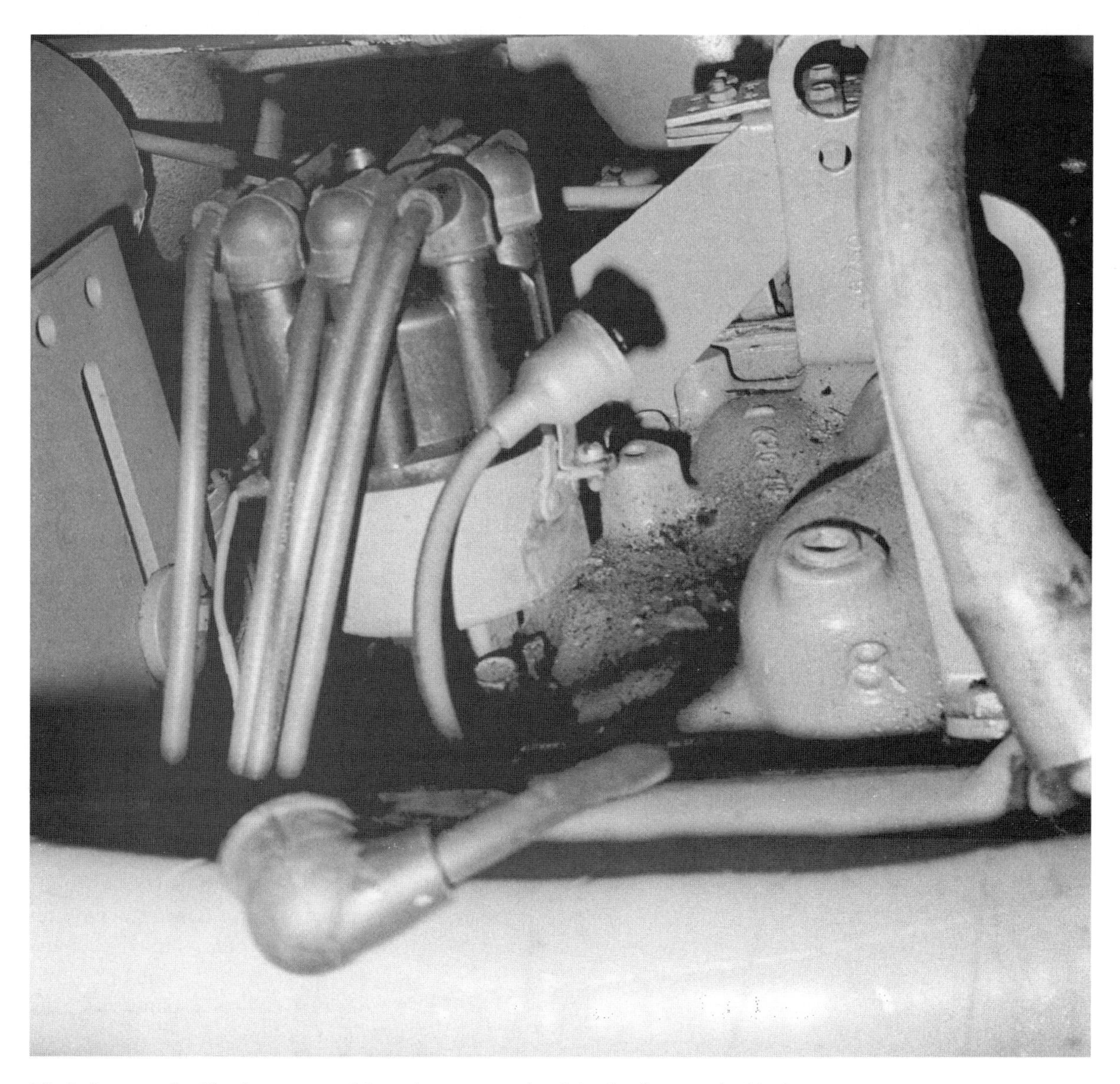

The high-tension lead has been removed from the ignition coil and the distributor to disable the ignition system.

Compression Analysis

The compression should come up quickly if your engine is in good shape. If it took more than five seconds of cranking to build up to its maximum value, you can suspect that the piston rings are worn.

If the reading on a particular cylinder never comes up, the head gasket might be at fault, the pistons and rings might be worn, or the valves and valve seats might be worn or burned. If a pair of adjacent cylinders have low readings, the problem is almost certainly a blown head gasket.

Here's a neat trick to further test any suspect cylinders after you've taken all your readings. Using a pump-type oil can, introduce a couple of squirts of

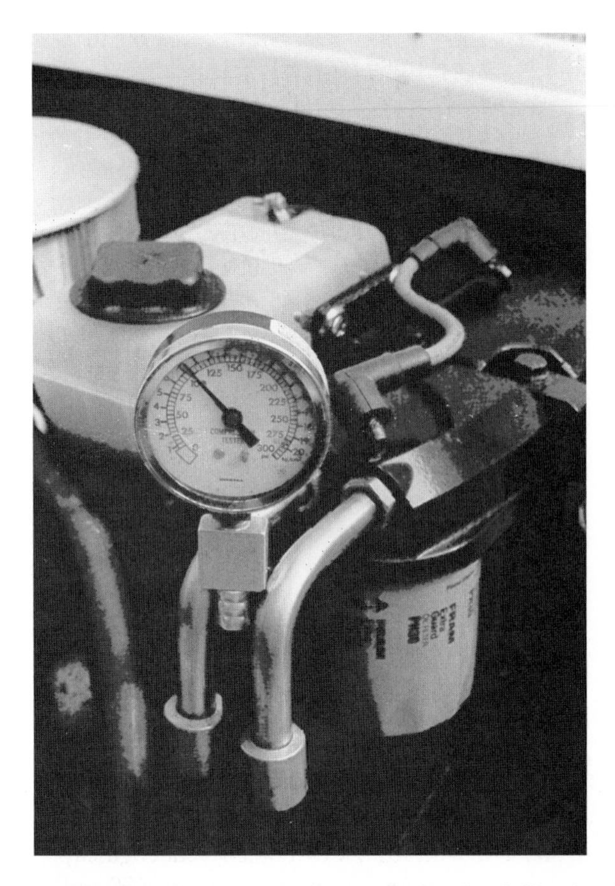

Compression tester in use. Make sure the throttle is held wide open when you crank the engine for this test. This cylinder's compression is about 100 pounds per square inch.

motor oil into the questionable cylinder and repeat the compression test.

If the reading on that cylinder comes up, at least temporarily, that points to worn pistons and rings. If the reading stays just the same, even after you've spritzed in the oil, the problem is probably a head gasket or valves.

When you've finished the compression test, reinstall the spark plugs and plug wires. As I mentioned, a compression test at the end of each season is a good survey tool to track the engine's gradual wear.

If your engine is ever unwilling to start, remember the big three: fuel, ignition, and compression. (And carry a spare set of spark plugs.) Methodical troubleshooting is the best way to work yourself out of trouble. Clear your mind of preconceived notions and check the simplest stuff first. (Like the fuel level in the tank.) Most problems wind up having simple causes. Troubleshooters who sniff up every blind alley on their way to the cause of the problem usually find that the clue that should have tipped them off to the ultimate problem was readily apparent from the start.

Questions and Answers

Question: This will be my third season with my used 31-foot Sea Ray Sundancer. The boat weighs 10,500 pounds, has a beam of 11 feet, 11 inches, and is powered by a pair of Borg-Warner V-drive–equipped 260-horsepower MerCruiser inboards.

Depending on water and weather conditions, my boat does 27 to 31 mph at a 3,000 rpm cruise. With the throttles wide open, the rpm goes to 3,900. Is that correct?

What size props (diameter and pitch) should this boat have? Will the engines be damaged with low rpm?

The V-drives have kept me on the edge of my seat trying to maintain them. The first year, the starboard transmission housing exploded, leaving parts all over the bilge. The next year, even with careful attention, the clutches in the port transmission burned out. Is there some recognized problem with these V-drives?

The boat seemed to be in good shape with only 200 hours on the engines when I bought it.

Answer: According to Sea Ray, your boat left the factory with 17-by-15-inch three-bladed props with medium cup. There's an easy way to make sure that your boat still has the original wheels: Look at them. (Almost all inboard propellers are stamped with two numbers—the first is the diameter and the second is the pitch.)

If your boat's props have been painted, you'll need a scraper and a wire brush to first scratch the old paint off. There are two places to look on the propeller for its dimensions: on the body of the propeller hub between the blades, or on the hub's aft face. The latter spot is often underneath the propeller nuts so, if you don't find the numbers on the side of the hub, you'll have to remove the propeller nuts.

To do this, you will need a pair of pliers, two large adjustable wrenches, and a block of wood that's large enough to wedge between a propeller blade and the bottom of your boat's hull. Use your pliers to remove the cotter pin, then put the wrenches on the two nuts. Loosen the aft one (it's usually thinner and is called the locknut) while you hold the forward one with a strain in the opposite direction of rotation. Once you break the nuts free of each other, spin off the locknut.

Now place your block of wood securely between a propeller blade and the hull so that it will resist the loosening action of your wrench on the other nut (called the propnut). Apply steady pressure on the wrench to loosen it. Don't worry about the prop falling off; it's been pressed onto the tapered end of the shaft by the nuts. Spin the propnut off by hand and read the numbers stamped into the aft end of the propeller hub.

When you've finished, reverse the procedure, moving the block of wood around to the other side of the propeller blade to allow you to securely tighten the propnut. Make it really tight. Once the propnut is tight, remove the block of wood, spin the locknut on by hand, and lock the two nuts together with your pair of wrenches working in opposite directions. (Be careful not to loosen the propnut when you do this step.) Replace the cotter pin with a fresh one. The cotter pin should be made from the stainless steel if the shaft is stainless or Monel. If the shaft and nuts are brass or bronze, use a brass cotter pin.

Sea Ray sent me a performance chart that they prepared when they tested this model with the same power package. Their chart shows a 3,000 rpm cruising speed of just under 27 mph and a WOT speed of 37 mph at 4,000 rpm.

MerCruiser's WOT rpm recommendation for these engines is 4,200 to 4,600. At 3,900, your boat's engines are definitely overloaded or over-wheeled. (For that matter, so was Sea Ray's identically powered test boat that only turned up to 4,000.)

Do you think your boat has lost weight since it was delivered? Be honest here. More likely you've loaded it down like a beast of burden—as we're all wont to do—further increasing the engine loading. If you've installed lots of additional gear and you like to cruise with water toys, inflatable dinghy, outboard, hibachi, and lots of friends on board, it's no wonder you've had V-drive problems.

There's no such thing as a free lunch. Loading a boat down with fuel, gear, or people will always bring WOT rpm down. One way or another, you have to cut down the load on these engines. You have two choices: Reduce the boat's weight or reduce the propeller loading (by reducing diameter, pitch, or cupping). If you can't cut back on the weight, you have to cut back on the propeller size.

Your boat is a special case. Ordinarily, I would reduce propeller pitch. But your props are already pretty low in pitch. For this reason, I think the most sensible way for you to proceed is to have an inch of diameter trimmed from the propellers by a qualified propeller shop.

If the wheels were noncupped, that would typically produce an rpm increase of around 300. Since your props will lose their cupping as well as the inch of diameter when they are trimmed, your engine rpm will probably jump a bit more—perhaps 400 turns. That's because the cupped edges will be cut away when the diameter is reduced.

Trouble is, according to the propeller expert at my local marine machinist, a 17-inch diameter prop comes from a different raw casting than a 16-incher. As a result, the hub dimensions, blade thickness, etc., will all be less than optimal with the trimming I suggested.

So, if the new props seem to correct the overloading, I would optimize the drive train by ordering a new pair of 16-inch noncupped wheels. (Use the old, modified ones as a set of spares.)

If the rpm jumps a bit too much with the cut down wheels, order the new props with a light or medium cup, depending on the wide-open throttle rpm. Your marine machinist should be able to counsel you on this so you wind up with a pair of props that, as Goldilocks would say, will be "just right."

If you get the prop loading down as I suggest, and your V-drives are in good shape now, you shouldn't have any more trouble with them. When loaded properly, these Borg-Warner units serve reliably. For what it's worth, I don't think either MerCruiser or Borg-Warner would give you any warranty coverage.

Your engines will also be a lot happier once these changes are made. Their lot in life (and their life) will be dramatically improved after you've eased their load. This kind of duty often causes a domino effect. The overworked V-drives' overheated oil lends its heat to the engine's already overloaded cooling system—and that's too many "overs" for any piece of machinery to abide.

Question: When I go over 3,000 rpm in my Chaparral 234 with a 1993 MerCruiser 5.7-liter Alpha One sterndrive, the temperature goes up. If I continue up to wide-open throttle, the temperature goes up from 160° to 195°. I've tested this many times. The engine turns 4,000 rpm at wide-open throttle. I'm concerned about whether I can operate the engine like that or is there something wrong with it?

Answer: Your engine has a 143° thermostat. Depending on the ambient water temperature where you run the boat, operating temperature should range from 145° to 175°. If your engine is getting up to 195°, that's a problem.

You could have a restriction on the inlet or the discharge side of the cooling water system. I assume you've checked to make sure there isn't a plastic bag draped over the raw-water inlet on the sterndrive. These cause more cooling problems than anything else you can think of.

Barnacles also cause their share of overheating problems, especially toward the end of the season. Sterndrives have small openings cast in the gearcase housing to admit water. If these are choked with barnacles or other marine growth, the engine will overheat, especially at high rpm.

How's the flexible impeller in your engine's water pump? Depending on operating conditions, these can last anywhere from about three years down to around three minutes. If you've ever maneuvered your boat in shallow, sandy, or silty water, the pump housing and impeller could have been scored. This can easily reduce efficiency enough to account for the overheating.

Your boat is also overpropped, which overloads the engine and worsens any overheating tendencies. You should reduce propeller pitch by at least 1 inch (2 would be better). MerCruiser would like to see your engine turning 4,200 to 4,400 rpm at wide-open throttle. Two inches of pitch reduction would bring your WOT rpm right up to the top end of that range. (If your boat's bottom was slimy, rough, dirty, or covered with barnacles, your propeller might be just right. Try it next spring with a fresh, clean bottom.)

A final possibility is that the temperature gauge itself is wrong. Electrical gauges sometimes are. To keep them honest, most mechanics keep a mechanical temperature gauge and sender in their toolbox. If you can lay your hands on one of these, remove the electric gauge's sender unit and thread the mechanical one in its place. Then check the engine's operating temperature. If it is indeed going above 175°, you definitely have an overheating problem.

Question: I have a nineteen-year-old maxicube cruiser that has propeller problems. When I bought the boat last winter, it had a 16-by-16-inch cupped propeller. With that prop, the engine doesn't quite reach 4,000 rpm at wide-open throttle. My cruising rpm is about 3,300. I've been told that this is putting too much strain on the prop, which is why I keep spinning drive hubs. (I've spun the hub several times.)

The local shop recommended I prop it to turn between 4,400 to 4,600 rpm at wide-open throttle. I've tried a 15¼-by-15-inch prop and a 16-by-14-inch one. Both gave me a WOT rpm in the recommended range, but I had to run the engine at 3,700 to 3,900 rpm to stay on plane. According to the boatbuilder, the 15¼-by-15-inch prop is the one that came with the boat originally.

The engine is a 260 hp, 350 cid MerCruiser sterndrive. The drive has the designation 1.50R stamped on its side. I assume that refers to the gear ratio. I have trim tabs also. According to the shop,

I've been using a "Black Max"-style prop. Any recommendations?
Answer: If the engine is only getting up to 4,000 rpm at wide-open throttle, it's definitely overloaded. You don't mention how the two other props you tried worked out, other than to say that they got the rpm up into the recommended WOT range.

I would go with the 16-by-14-inch prop. Unless you have to, you shouldn't give away any diameter, because diameter affects how much effort a prop can deliver to the water. Working all by itself (no twin), your engine has its work cut out for it. You would be cutting down its ability to do that work if you reduced prop diameter.

On the other hand, reducing the pitch from 16 to 14 inches will let your engine deliver all the power it's capable of without laboring as it is now. As a rule of thumb, an inch of pitch reduction corresponds to an increase in rpm of 150 to 200. As a result, changing to a 14-inch pitch wheel should let your engine get up into the middle of its recommended WOT rpm range. Don't delay; do it today.

Since the prop loading will be markedly reduced, swapping propellers should also eliminate your hub spinning problems.

Question: I have a 1988 Four Winns with a 260 hp Cobra sterndrive. She runs fine at all speeds in forward gear. However, after I shift into reverse it feels like she's choking out. If I attempt to give her gas, she stalls. It's as if some of the cylinders actually quit. I'm at a loss.
Answer: Good job describing the symptoms. Your problem sounds like a textbook case of an ESA (electronic shift assist) system problem.

This is a system that intentionally raises hell with the engine's dwell setting while a shift is being effected. That reduces drivetrain strain because the engine is "stumbling" and doesn't develop much horsepower.

Your engine's ESA is not restoring the dwell setting to normal when it's supposed to. You need to take the boat to an authorized OMC sterndrive dealer and have the shift cable readjusted. That will probably fix the problem. If not, the dealer will be able to figure out what's needed.

4 THE CARE AND FEEDING OF OUTBOARDS

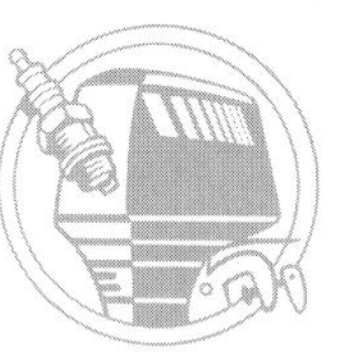

Outboards: An Overview

In the old days, outboard motors had a reputation for being temperamental beasts. They were hard to start, hard to keep going and, worst of all, tricky to work on.

I spent my wonder years at the family boatyard, which is right across the harbor from the municipal launching ramp. During the summer it was typical to see folks come down, launch their outboard-powered boats, and spend the next hour messing around with them. The kids would get bored and start fighting, the moms would roll their eyes, and the dads would (usually unsuccessfully) tinker with their cranky engines.

Funny thing was, the people who had the least trouble with their outboards were the ones who used them all the time: marine contractors, commercial fishermen, and the like. In those days, that's what outboards thrived on. Run 'em hard and run 'em often; then they would perform reliably. The occasional user, on the other hand, had to settle for less than reliable performance.

No wonder. For starters, those outboards of yore ran on a mixture of 1 part oil to every 24 parts of gasoline—a pretty rich diet. In conjunction with the marginal magnetos that passed for outboard ignition systems back then, those rich mixtures meant that the spark plugs were always on the ragged edge of fouling.

Thankfully, times have changed, and so have the reputations of outboard motors. Many of the newest outboards on the market don't use any oil mixed with the fuel at all—they have four-cycle power plants. Because they use straight gasoline for fuel, they run much cleaner. All else being equal, this makes them more reliable.

They also run more quietly. Those factors make them a better choice on two pollution-fighting fronts: conventional and sonic pollution. My guess is that the days of the two-cycle outboard are numbered. Thankfully, these too have gotten much cleaner over the last few decades, but they're still pretty dirty machines. I think that the planet and, specifically, the waterways and oceans aren't big enough to absorb an infinite amount of pollution.

Just the same, most of the outboards in use today are still two-cycle models. The typical ignition system used these days delivers a spark that's three times "hotter" than the old magneto systems could put out. When you combine that hot spark with a fuel-oil ratio that's typically four times leaner than it was in the bad old days, you've got the formula for a much more reliable outboard. Just about as reliable, in fact, as other types of marine engines. Witness the number of people who go offshore—way offshore—with outboard-powered boats. You wouldn't have done that with a circa 1960 outboard (or even a pair of them).

There was another problem going offshore with the old outboards—you couldn't have carried enough fuel to get back home. Talk about gas hogs! They were notoriously thirsty. (They would pass anything but a gas dock.) The old 40-horse models used to snarf up more fuel than today's 90-horse models. (My family had a Hunt 14, an early deep-V boat with the first three-cylinder engine Evinrude ever made. At wide-open throttle, the engine consumed almost a gallon of fuel per mile—quite an appetite.)

Although efficiency and reliability have gotten a lot better, even modern outboards need some attention and maintenance to run happily. With today's ignition systems, tune-ups in the conventional sense of the word have become passé. In the springtime, you set the gap on a new set of spark plugs (except in the case of center-firing ones; these don't even need gapping) and spin them in.

Still, these motors need to be lubricated and their filters must be kept clean. But these are simple chores that can be accomplished by mere mortals with a normal complement of shade tree mechanic's tools.

How to Keep an Outboard Motor Happy

There are a few things you can do to keep your outboard motor humming along nicely. The tasks are not particularly complicated, nor do they cost a whole bunch of money. But they pay big dividends in reliability and trouble-free performance. Not only that, doing it yourself also saves money.

Dietary Considerations

Gasoline

No marine engine likes to be fed a diet of stale fuel. But outboards in particular will simply not stand for it. Last year's gas? Forget it, unless it was stabilized (and bring spare plugs and a wrench, even if it was). Last month's gas? Maybe. (Bring along the plugs and wrench to be safe.)

By the way, if you have to dispose of some stale gasoline, don't dump it on the ground or pour it into a storm drain. If you do, it's going to wind up in the waterway that you and your children use for swimming. Instead, ask the crew at your boatyard if they can dump it into one of their machines. Since these things are run nearly constantly, they can abide stale fuel better than your persnickety outboard motor can.

Buy top-quality, branded fuel with the octane rating specified in the owner's manual. If you trailer your boat, don't be tempted to fill up at the brand X station on the way to the launching ramp. The cheap gas you buy there might have some water in it and, even if it doesn't, you're taking a chance on quality. You might be able to get away with this stuff with your car, but not with an outboard. In most cases, the problems with off-brand fuel aren't as dramatic as an engine that fails to start or run properly. They're more insidious and stretched out over time.

Cheap gas in an outboard causes combustion chamber deposits, often mistakenly called carbon deposits. (Actually, some are and some aren't.) Over time, these deposits can raise hob with your engine and, in some cases, the engine has to be disassembled to really clean them out. Who needs that kind of aggravation? (To say nothing of the expense.) There are treatments that you can add to the fuel to help the engine consume these deposits. See your dealer if you suspect that your engine needs this treatment, or do it as a preventive measure each season. Don't use any additives that aren't sourced by your engine's manufacturer.

Two-Cycle Oil

The same can be said for off-brand two-cycle oil. If your engine was manufactured in the last ten years or so, the owner's manual will specify oil certified as TCW-3 to be either mixed in with the gas or put in the VRO (variable-ratio oiling) tank in the case of engines equipped with this feature. The TCW-3 designation is awarded to oils that successfully survive a series of chemical tests and some actual operational tests in outboard motors. (See the Q&A on pages 51–52 for more information about the TCW-3 designation.)

Strictly speaking, that means you can buy your two-cycle oil at Wal-Mart and your engine will run happily. Well, maybe.

Some oils that receive the TCW-3 designation will successfully pass the testing procedures and yet, over time, will foul your engine with unwanted combustion chamber deposits.

Whether this happens to your engine depends on what oil you use and, to a large extent, on how you run your engine. I might sound like a fuddy-duddy here, but when it comes to my outboards, I don't take chances. I spend the extra money and buy the oil that's recommended (and branded) by my engine's manufacturer.

Admittedly, this is a more expensive way to go, but I feel that the peace of mind it gives me is worth the price. After all, how much do you really spend on oil when compared with the cost of a disassembly and decarbonization job? By the way, if you buy the oil in case lots at your dealership you can probably get a pretty friendly price, even on the factory-branded stuff.

Fuel-Oil Ratios

Aluminum, which is what outboard motor pistons and engine blocks are cast from, is susceptible to galling. This refers to destruction of the smoothly-machined surfaces. It's caused by friction. When galling occurs, say in the cylinder walls and/or piston skirts of an outboard motor, metal is removed and these parts are usually ruined. In extreme cases the engine can even seize up. Clearly, this is something you don't want going on inside your boat's engine.

It's amazing how little oil is needed to keep this dreaded condition from occurring. Years ago, we had a 25-horsepower outboard on a workboat in the boatyard. Someone once refilled the fuel tank and forgot to add the requisite pint of two-cycle oil.

Care to guess how long that engine ran under heavy-duty workboat conditions? Would you believe three or four hours, most of it at wide-open throttle pushing big boats around? That surprised me. When it finally seized up, we refilled the tank (and added oil this time) and the engine had come unstuck in the interim. We were lucky, though.

We never did remove the side covers and check things out. We were too busy launching boats. We just put the engine back into service and put another couple hundred hours of the same kind of duty on it. That's pretty amazing when you consider that for several hours that engine ran just fine with a fuel-oil ratio somewhere around 500:1. (All that was left was the residual oil from the remaining gas before the fill-up.)

The modern VRO-equipped outboards run with oil ratios that range from 50:1 at wide-open throttle to about 75:1 at idle rpm. Outboards with nonoiling VRO systems use a 50:1 fuel-oil ratio. To certify their products for use at this ratio, the engine manufacturers conduct torture tests of extra-tight engines with oil ratios far leaner (typically 150:1 in the case of a 50:1 engine).

Think of it—150:1. That's hardly any oil. Yet somehow these test engines survive this procedure. Of course, you shouldn't try this on your engine. Too little oil can cause galling and even a seized engine.

Too much oil can cause problems as well. This is more of a problem with small engines—the ones with portable tanks. What happens is that, each time your 6-gallon tank is "empty," it still has as much as a gallon of fuel-oil mixture in it. You add the dose of oil recommended for 6 gallons of gas and then pump in 5 or 5½ gallons. Over time (with each fill-up), you steadily increase the ratio of oil to gasoline. Eventually, your engine is running on such a rich mixture that it becomes more susceptible to spark plug fouling and unreliable operation.

To keep this from happening, limit the amount of oil you add. If the tank is still ⅙ full, keep ⅙ of the dose of oil in the can. You can save these partly used cans and then, using a funnel, collect them. At that rate, you'll have a "free" dose of oil at every sixth fill-up. You'll also save your engine from having to run on a diet of too much oil.

This is less of an issue on boats with permanently installed tanks. In fact, most of these boats have larger, VRO-equipped engines that eliminate the problem anyway. But if you have a straight-ratio-oiled engine, pay attention to how much oil you add at fill-up time. Your engine will appreciate it and reward you with less smoke and pollution, fewer cases of spark plug fouling, and more reliable service.

Long-Term Survival Strategies

Today's outboards are not only a lot more complex than lawnmower engines, they also cost a lot more. In fact, the most expensive outboard on the market sells for more than the least expensive car! Think about that for a moment. With an investment like that, it clearly behooves an outboard owner to take good care of this costly piece of machinery. What you need are some long-term survival strategies.

Aluminum and Salt Water

Outboards are mostly made of aluminum. This is a wonderful metal but . . . aluminum and salt water are like oil and water—they don't mix. When they do, the result is corrosion. For an outboard motor, this is the beginning of the end.

Outboard manufacturers take great pains to keep these incompatible elements apart. To a large measure, they succeed. It's up to you, though, to make sure their efforts aren't wasted. You must keep the designed-in safeguards in place and doing their jobs.

Anticorrosion Paint Systems

If you bothered to read the literature when you bought your outboard, you'd know that the engine manufacturer devoted a lot of attention to the paint. If you think this is a matter of cosmetics, you've got another think coming.

Sure, a smooth, pretty paint job looks nice on an outboard. But first and foremost, it's there for protection. Some of the paint systems used today include twenty or more steps. The top coats (the ones you can see) are there to look nice. But all the stuff underneath that pretty finish is applied to protect the engine's aluminum castings from the ravages of corrosion.

This protection begins to break down as soon as you scratch the paint. So the first step in conserving your engine's finish and forestalling corrosion is taking care around the engine, especially when you're docking your boat. Do things slowly and avoid backing into pilings, bulkheads, and other boats.

The same holds true for the portions of your engine that are below the waterline. Your engine's gearcase isn't a depth-sounder. Pay attention when you're navigating in shallow water, especially if the bottom is sandy or rocky.

If, despite your best efforts, you do get a "ratbite" in the engine's finish, don't wait until the end of the season to repair it.

Once the finish is breached, corrosion begins immediately. And corrosion never sleeps—especially around salt water. What starts out as a small scratch quickly becomes a blistering wound in the paint if it's not attended to right away.

Once you've scratched the paint down to bare metal, you'll never be able to re-create the factory finish with its myriad priming, washing, and painting steps. But you can rough up the site of the repair, spray on some good-quality primer, then blow on a few mist coats of factory-supplied engine enamel. Your engine will appreciate it if you do.

Galvanic Corrosion Protection Devices

There's a second type of corrosion that outboard motors are susceptible to—galvanic corrosion, commonly known as electrolysis. It's an insidious process. Thankfully, there are four things you can do to keep it from ruining your engine.

First, keep your engine tilted up out of the water when you're not using it.

Second, repair any scratches in your engine's finish right away.

Third, make sure your boat's wiring is clean and solid. All connections and cables should be clean, tight, and dry. The tops of the batteries should be kept clean. Following these rules will go a long way toward keeping electrolysis at bay (much of chapter 5 is devoted to this topic).

The fourth defense is to offer a sacrifice to the electrolysis gods—sacrificial anodes or zincs.

Your engine manufacturer has most likely furnished a handful of these specially designed anodes in below-the-waterline locations. The idea here is simple: When dissimilar metals are dunked in water and a small current is leaked between or amongst them, the less-noble metal (galvanically speaking) is sacrificed. The zinc alloy that the anodes are made of is less noble than the aluminum alloy your outboard is made from. If there is any galvanic current flowing (and there almost always is), the inexpensive zinc anode gets consumed in lieu of your expensive outboard motor.

These zincs need a little attention in order to do their job. First, make sure they're there. They should be solidly attached to a clean mounting site, and not covered with any kind of paint or wax.

Periodically inspect the zincs to make sure they haven't eroded too much. At a certain point in the erosion process, the mounting holes start to enlarge. Then the zinc may simply fall off. Obviously, once that happens your engine no longer has any protection.

When you replace the zinc anodes, make sure that the gearcase is clean and shiny where they mount. Use sandpaper or emery cloth for this. Don't remove any paint or primer except where the anode contacts the gearcase, though. If there are any toothed star washers that are to be installed underneath, make sure to hang on to these and put them in place. The teeth on a star washer bite into the zinc and the gearcase, ensuring a good electrical contact between the two, which enables the zinc anode to do its very important job.

The last point—paint and wax—is sort of a no-brainer. You should never apply antifouling bottom paint or wax to your outboard motor's gearcase. Bottom paint, especially, is strictly forbidden. Virtually all antifouling bottom paints use various heavy metals as active ingredients, so applying any of them essentially turns your engine into an electrolysis farm. They also electrically isolate the zinc from the water so it can't work properly.

Corrosion: An Inside Job, Too

We've established that your outboard motor got a fancy, multistep, anticorrosion finish on its outside. The same kind of attention was also lavished on the parts you can't see. Waterways, the inside of the powerhead, and even the inside of the exhaust housing and gearcase were protected when your engine was manufactured.

You can't see these areas, and you certainly can't refinish them. But there is something you can do to help retain the protection they afford. It's called flushing the engine out with fresh water, and all outboard motors that are operated in salt water should be flushed whenever possible after use.

You will need to buy the appropriate flush adaptor from your engine dealer. Follow the instructions on the package, hooking up the flush adaptor to a freshwater source with a garden hose.

When you flush out the engine, fresh water circulates throughout the entire engine: the waterways, the powerhead, and the exhaust housing. To be most effective, run the inlet water supply at a moderate rate and flush the engine for at least five minutes to achieve the maximum circulation of fresh water throughout.

If you haul your boat out of the water on a trailer, or it goes into rack storage when it's not in use, you can and should flush it after each use. Obviously, if you keep your boat in the water, that may not be practical. If that's the case, at least make sure you flush it out at the end of the season.

Hands Off!

If your engine's powerhead needs to be disassembled for a rebuild or decarbonizing job, you should steer clear. You lack three important components that are needed to tackle a major teardown job like this: shop manuals, special tools, and factory training.

Sure, you can buy a shop manual; in fact, I urge you to do so, just to gain a better understanding of how your engine goes about its business. But special tools—now there's a different kettle of fish. It's not unusual for the special tools that are custom-made for one particular model of outboard engine to cost over $1,000. They're hard to get and, more important, they're hard to use. And to make the best use of these special tools, you also need factory training. Don't underestimate its importance.

Back in the 1970s when I was a newly minted Evinrude Service Master, I came back from my two weeks of factory training fancying myself to be an outboard mechanic. In a sense I was. But my first season of real-world outboard repair duty was very humbling. Even with all the special tools on the wall and the factory training under my belt, outboard motor repair was a rugged row to hoe. Eventually I got the hang of it and got pretty good, if I may say so myself.

But it took time. I messed up a lot in the beginning. You want to do major work on your own engine? Forget it; leave it to the pros.

If your engine lives in salt water, you could spend a few months just learning how to remove seized-in-place stainless steel fasteners from aluminum castings. Have you ever tried using a smoke wrench? That's what outboard mechanics call the propane or acetylene torch that they use to heat bolts up to get them loosened without snapping. No one at the school taught me how to use one of these. They didn't need to; all the engines in the school were brand new and got taken apart and reassembled on a daily basis.

And then there's the art of properly torquing the myriad bolts that hold together a complex outboard motor assembly, such as a powerhead. It goes far beyond merely having a torque wrench, which, of course, you must. If you get it wrong, the finished engine will promptly spin a bearing, seize up, get warped castings, or otherwise self-destruct. So trust me when I tell you that you don't want to do major work on your outboard. Consider it to be a can of worms that's better opened only by trained professionals.

That said, what about that minor work? Read on. The following sections detail the operations that *can* be handled by mere mortals.

Do-It-Yourself?

When I was a youngster, outboard motors weren't much more complicated than lawnmower engines. Things have changed, though, and today's outboards are definitely not lawnmower engines.

Today's outboards have computerized electronic ignitions, complex shifting mechanisms, you name it. (Some even have electronic fuel injection.) But that's not all bad news for the ardent do-it-yourselfer. At the same time that outboards have grown more sophisticated, they've gotten much more reliable. Although your engine's ignition system is complex, chances are that, with periodic spark plug replacements, it will run without a hitch for the life of the engine. On the other hand, if it does crap out, you aren't going to be able to troubleshoot the problem without the specialized training and expensive test equipment discussed above.

There isn't much routine maintenance that needs to be performed on a modern outboard. At the end of the season, you need to winterize it, change the gear oil, and grease the linkages, as outlined in chapter 7. These tasks are much the same on even the most modern engines. Depending on the quality of the fuel you buy and the number of hours you run the engine, you'll also have to change the fuel filters occasionally. In the springtime, your engine will need a minimal tune-up when you commission the boat, and that's about the extent of it. See chapter 8 for more information on commissioning your outboard.

All of the above-mentioned tasks can be done by a competent do-it-yourselfer with a modest assortment of mechanic's tools. If you're an above-average shade tree mechanic, you can probably also handle carburetor overhauls and water pump rebuilds, which typically come up every two or three years.

Replacing Spark Plugs

This simple operation comprises a large part of the springtime commissioning operation for an outboard motor owner. Depending on your engine, you might have center-fire spark plugs or the more old-fashioned side-electrode types. Center-firing models do not have an adjustable electrode that must be set to the correct gap before they can be installed. If you have these types of plugs, you can ignore the section on setting spark plug gap. (Don't skip tightening the terminals at the top of the plugs, though.)

Removing Spark Plugs

You will need a spark plug socket, a clean rag, a pair of pliers, and a gap-setting tool (unless your engine uses center-fire plugs).

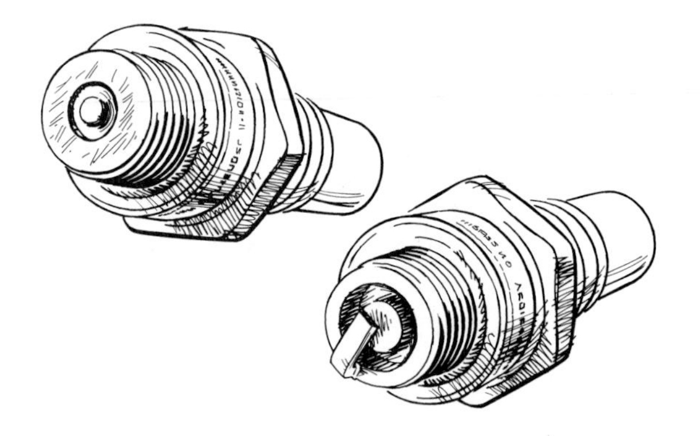

Spark plugs. Left: Center-fire design. Right: Conventional side-electrode type.

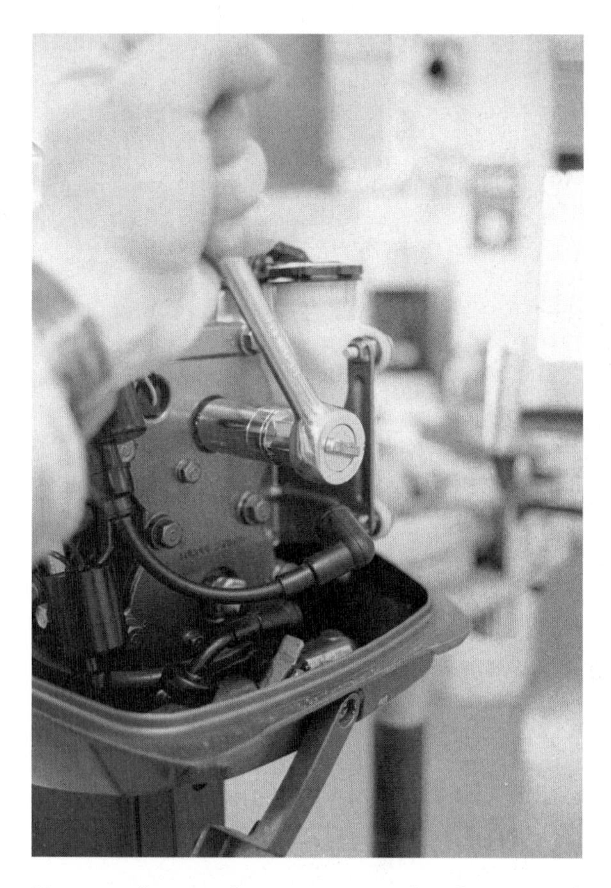

Using a socket wrench to remove an outboard motor spark plug. Make sure the socket is securely seated on the spark plug body before you shock it loose with the wrench.

In most cases, you can't remove the plugs with a conventional wrench because the cylinder-head water cover interferes and won't let you get the wrench down to the flats at the base of the plug. That's why you will want to use a socket wrench with a deep socket for this chore. (If you have one of the special spark plug sockets with a rubber plug-gripping insert, that's nice, but not absolutely necessary.)

The first step is to remove the spark plug wires. *Warning:* Pull on the boots, not the wires. It's best to twist the boots as you remove them, so you don't detach the metal connector inside that contacts the top of the spark plug. (These sometimes get corroded and stuck to the top of the spark plugs.)

After you've removed the first wire, secure its end underneath the hardware or mark it so you can be sure that you will reattach it to the correct plug after you've replaced them. Since most modern outboards have separate ignition coils mounted adjacent to the spark plugs they fire, it's not that easy to mix them up.

After all of the wires are off, get your spark plug wrench out and start removing the plugs. With the wrench in place, it's easiest to loosen the plugs by sharply "shocking" the wrench with one hand while you securely hold the wrench down solidly on the plug with the other hand. When the plug is shocked loose, spin it out the rest of the way by hand.

Now take a clean rag and carefully clean around the spark plug mounting holes. Don't allow any debris or lint to enter the cylinders. Once this is done you can start unwrapping the new plugs and preparing them for installation.

Gap-Setting and Installing Plugs

If your engine uses side-electrode plugs, you will have to look up the electrode gap setting—it's usually found in the engine owner's manual. If not, the outboard mechanics where you bought your engine can tell you what it should be.

You'll need a gapping tool for this operation. The wire type is the best, though in a pinch you can use a feeler gauge. Select the wire or feeler gauge that corresponds to the correct gap and try to slide it

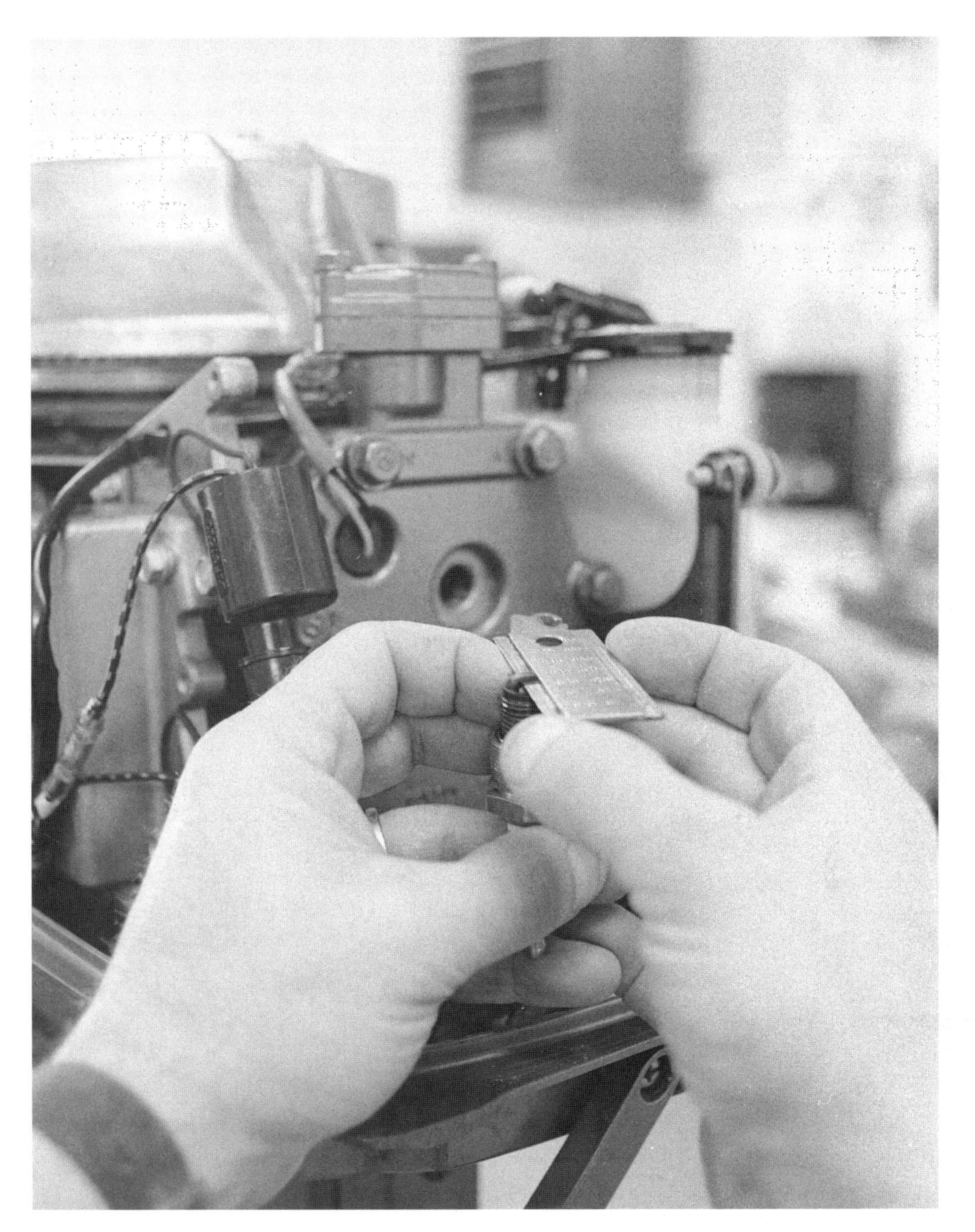

Using a spark plug gap checker. If the gap is too narrow, bend the electrode out; if it's too tight, rap it on a hard surface to close it up a bit.

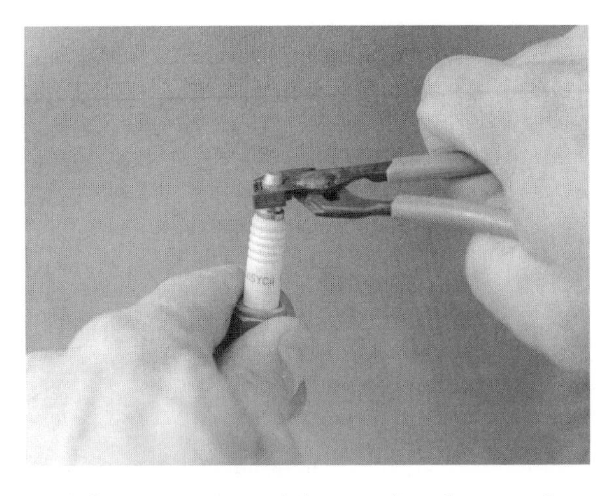

Don't forget to use a pair of pliers to tighten the terminals on top of the spark plugs before you install them in your boat's engine.

between the center and side electrodes. If it won't fit, use the electrode bending fixture that's built into the tool to gently bend the side electrode out a bit.

Once you think you've bent the electrode out far enough, you can recheck it with the appropriate feeler gauge. If you've bent it out too far, gently rap the bottom of the plug on a hard surface to bend it back in. Then recheck it. When you get it right, the gauge will just barely slide between the two electrodes.

After you've set the gap on all the spark plugs, you must tighten the contact post on the top of each one.

Use a pair of pliers or Vise-Grips for this job, and make sure you tighten them securely. Sometimes, one will be missing. If that's the case, look in the "empty" spark plug packages—it's bound to turn up. (They sometimes vibrate off in shipping.) Make sure the ribbed end of this threaded piece is against the top of the plug.

Winding Spark Plugs Into Place

Don't pick up your spark plug wrench yet. To avoid cross-threaded holes in the cylinder head, install the plugs by hand and run them in by hand until they seat in the cylinder head. If they don't run in smoothly, stop, back the plug out, clean the threads and the hole with your clean rag, and try again. Don't cross-thread them.

The steel threads on the spark plugs are much harder than an aluminum cylinder head. If you force a spark plug in when it's cross-threaded, you'll ruin the cylinder head. (By the way, don't let anyone tell you that you can fix this problem with a Heli-Coil threaded insert. In my experience, these don't work well in aluminum heads.)

Once you've successfully spun them all in place until they've seated, get your spark plug wrench out. If you have a torque wrench, by all means use it. The recommended torque for spark plugs in an aluminum cylinder head is 18 to 20 foot-pounds.

If you don't have a torque wrench, tighten each plug about ⅛ of a turn after it's seated. Do not tighten them any more than this, or you will probably destroy the threads in the cylinder head.

Finish the job by reinstalling the spark plug wires. If you've got some OMC Triple Guard or other marine grease, pack a little bit inside each boot before you install it on the plug. This keeps the spring contact in the boot from corroding and seizing onto the terminal atop the spark plug. Twist the boots back and forth as you push them on. Make sure you put each high-tension lead on the correct spark plug.

All owners of outboard-powered boats should make it a point to carry a set of spare spark plugs (pregapped), a clean rag, and a spark plug wrench on their boats at all times. As I've mentioned before, if you don't carry anything else in the way of spares, make sure you bring these along.

If your engine lets you down, nine times out of ten, fresh plugs will solve the problem. If they don't, another good place to look is the fuel filter (or filters).

Fuel Filter Maintenance

Most properly rigged outboard boats have two fuel filters. There should be a primary fuel filter–water separator mounted somewhere along the supply line leading from the tank and a built-in secondary or trash filter underneath the cowl of the engine.

The primary filter is not standard equipment. It's typically installed by the commissioning dealer, the boatbuilder, or the owner. If your boat doesn't have one, I'd suggest you add one pronto. Why? Because the under-cowl filter that your outboard manufacturer supplied isn't worth the powder to blow it to hell.

When it comes to separating water, the trash filter has a capacity of about a half teaspoon. If there's any more water than that, it overwhelms the filter and gets passed along the line to the carburetor(s). Once that happens, the party's over.

On the other hand, a primary filter-separator can usually accommodate a quarter cup or more of water before it's full. Since most of them have clear plastic sediment bowls, it's easy to see if any water is collecting in there. That way you can often do something about it before it makes its way to the engine. (See chapter 8 for instructions on how to clean the primary filter-separator and replace its filter element.)

Even though the trash filter is almost useless, since you've got one, you might as well know how to clean it. Here's how.

Most of these consist of a simple plastic container with inlet and outlet fittings. Trace the fuel line from the connector on the engine's cowl. The first place it goes is this filter.

To service it, get a clean rag and a small gasoline-proof container to empty the filter into. Once you've

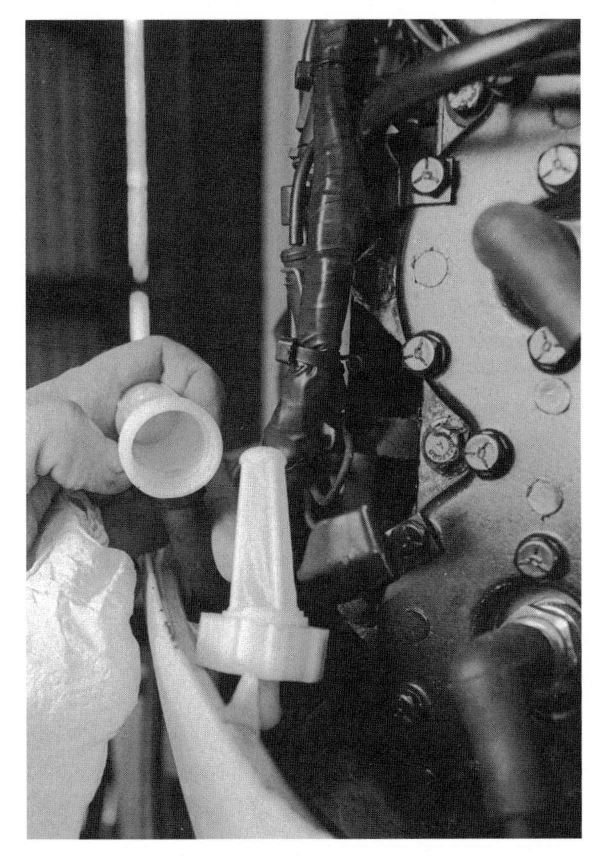

Secondary fuel filter on an outboard motor. Inspect the nylon mesh filter for trash, and survey the contents of the filter "bowl" for water.

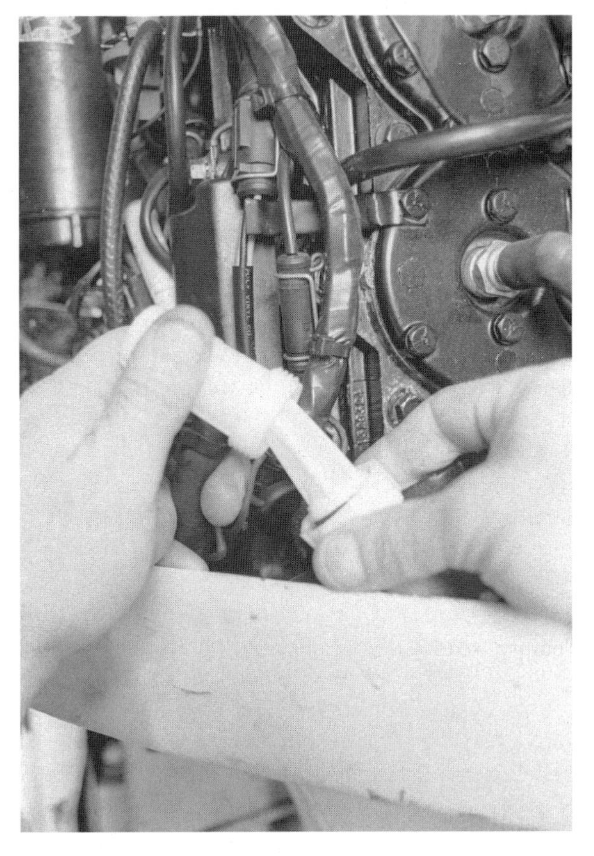

Reassembling the secondary fuel filter on an outboard motor. Don't forget to check carefully for leaks when you start the engine after completing any fuel system work.

located it, unscrew the top of this little filter and dump the filter "bowl" into your container. Look for rust flakes or any other sort of trash on the nylon mesh of the filter. Rap the screen on a hard surface and blow it out with compressed air to clean it. Then with a fresh, lint-free rag, wipe out the inside of the filter body.

When everything is neat and clean, carefully screw the filter assembly back together snugly. Now use a clean rag to wipe any traces of gasoline from the outside of the filter to make it easier to check for leaks, which you must do.

Before you start the engine, pump the fuel primer bulb to fill the system and check for leaks. The best way to do this is to wash your hands and safely dispose of the rag. Get rid of the smell of gasoline from your hands and then, after you pump the primer, use a fresh rag to wipe around the connections and the threaded portion of the filter. Then give the rag a sniff. If you smell any gas, recheck your work, find the leak, correct it, and retest for leaks.

Troubleshooting Your Outboard Motor

Most of today's outboard motors are two-cycle engines, which means that, unlike inboards and sterndrives, the spark plug fires every time the piston comes up to the top of its travel. Just the same, these engines have a lot in common with the four-cycle engines that we considered in the previous chapter. And, of course, four-cycle outboards are coming onto the boating scene with a vengeance.

Whether two cycle or four, troubleshooting outboards is basically the same: If your engine doesn't have fuel, ignition, and compression, it isn't going to start and run successfully. The techniques I outlined in chapter 3 are the same ones you should follow to get a balky outboard back in service.

Be glad that you're able to use the current generation of outboard motors. They're the best ones ever. But, like their ancestors, they still thrive on being used often and hard. This is especially true of the two-cycle models. Intermittent operation and poor quality fuel are their Waterloo. So get out there as often as you can, use good-quality fuel and name-brand two-cycle oil, and carry a spare set of pre-gapped spark plugs and a plug wrench. Those are the keys to successful outboard-powered boating.

Questions and Answers

Question: I own a 15-foot Tide Craft with a 70 hp Nissan motor on it. When I put the boat in a turn, the motor revs up. Or is it cavitation? The motor is mounted with the cavitation plate ¾ inch above the bottom of the boat. Is this correct?

Would a Doel-Fin help this problem? Will lowering the motor slow my speed down? At the elevation I live (5,235 feet), it does 31 mph. Any answers?

Answer: Cavitation is caused by the explosion of small air bubbles on the drawing (front) side of a

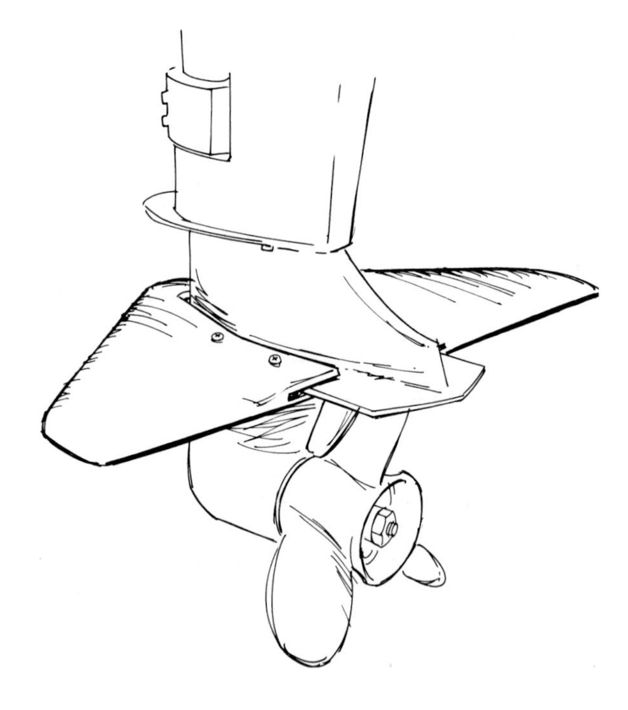

Planing fin, such as the Doel-Fin, installed on an outboard motor. These are also available for sterndrive applications.

propeller. In sustained or severe cases of true cavitation, the propeller blades will be pitted or eroded; it's a destructive process.

The air doesn't come from the surface—it's "boiled" out of the water. (The lower the pressure the lower the boiling point. This is the same reason why water boils at a lower temperature the higher above sea level you go.) The front side of a propeller is an area of very low pressure.

What you're experiencing is almost certainly not cavitation, but ventilation (which is often mistakenly referred to as cavitation). It's an annoying phenomenon, but provided the engine doesn't exceed its maximum rpm limit, it won't cause any damage. Strictly speaking, the thing we call a cavitation plate would be better termed an antiventilation plate.

I have a couple of questions for you. First, is your boat fitted with a tachometer? If so, how high is the engine revving up when the problem occurs? Does it exceed the manufacturer's recommended maximum rpm? (Look in your engine owner's manual for this figure.)

Second, if your engine is equipped with power trim, are you in the habit of trimming the engine in (down) before putting the boat into a tight turn? You should be. If you leave the engine trimmed out during high-speed maneuvering, ventilation is much more likely to occur. Trimming in allows the boat to corner more confidently with greater control.

A Doel-Fin, which is a planing fin (sort of an extra-large aftermarket cavitation plate), will probably not do anything to ameliorate your problem. Mounting the engine lower on the boat's transom will probably help but will also reduce your boat's top speed somewhat.

Question: I own a Rosborough RF-18 Lobster Boat. Over the past few years, 2 to 3 inches of play has developed in the steering system. Is there any way I can eliminate this play without taking the apparatus (cables, ends) all apart? It is the standard Teleflex steering, not hydraulic.
Answer: According to the people at Teleflex, most likely you've worn out the gears in the steering gearbox. This is not made to be overhauled and must be replaced as an assembly. Depending on where you shop, and whether you have the Big-T steerer or the Saf-T model, you can expect to pay $50 to $188 for the replacement. (The Big-T assembly costs more.)

Question: I have a 1979 90 hp Mercury outboard with power trim on my 16-foot Mark Twain ski boat. I'm having problems with the trim motor not starting when I push the button. It will click once when it wants to start, but then goes dead.

I had it checked and was told the brushes are fine. The mechanic said there was a dead spot in the housing around the brushes; he took it apart, cleaned it with some sandpaper, and gave it back to me. It worked at the shop and it continues to work sometimes. When it does go out, I can bump the motor while pushing the button and it will start. Is there a fix for this problem?
Answer: Do you have this problem in both directions or only when you run it up? The reason I ask is that this tilt system uses a solenoid for the up direction but not for the down. If you're having trouble running it up, you should check the solenoid. If it falters in both directions, the solenoid is probably OK.

Another possible cause is a fault in the switch at the helm. However if tapping the motor makes it work, that's less likely to be the cause.

Sounds to me like you probably have a dead spot in the motor's commutator. You can check for this by testing the motor with an ohmmeter. Disconnect the motor leads and attach the meter leads to them. As you rotate the motor, the resistance indicated by the meter should go up and down, but it should never go to a particularly high resistance. If it does, that indicates an open winding.

If the commutator is bad, there's nothing you can do except replace the motor.

Question: I have a 1989 Sea Ray 180 Bowrider with a 1989 135 hp Mercury outboard engine. I bought the boat new. I've been told to only use Mercury engine oil because it has an ingredient called TCW-3. For the last four years, I've used Castrol two-cycle oil and have not experienced any problems. A mechanic has told me I must use TCW-3 oil or I will burn up my engine. Is that true? Can I find an additive to mix in with my existing oil? Can I continue using the Castrol oil?

Answer: I think you're a bit confused about the TCW-3 designation. It's a rating, not an additive. You do not have to use Mercury-brand oil; you can use any two-cycle oil that carries the TCW-3 rating (most of the outboard oil you'll find on the shelves these days is).

The designation should be on the label. If it isn't, the oil you're using is not intended for use in an outboard at all; it's probably for chainsaws and two-cycle lawnmowers. (TCW stands for two cycle, water cooled.)

There is a big difference between TCW-2 and TCW-3. TCW-3 oil was developed about a decade ago when oxygenated fuel was introduced. Some boaters were running into engine troubles by burning 87-octane gasoline in big outboards, such as yours. Oxygenated fuel has adulterants. The TCW-2 oil wasn't lubricious enough to prevent powerhead damage. In some cases, it was being washed right off the cylinder walls in these engines.

If you have any doubts about the gas you're using (you probably should these days), use TCW-3 oil even in engines that don't call for it. It's worth the extra expense.

Make sure the oil you're buying is certified TCW-3 by the National Marine Manufacturers Association (NMMA). To receive this certification, the oil company submits a sample of the oil to NMMA, which then sends it to one of five testing labs that they use for certifying oil. The oil is subjected to a battery of five laboratory analysis checks. In addition an accelerated wear operational test is performed on actual engines.

Question: I have a boat powered by a 1991 Evinrude 60. The engine won't go over 2,500 rpm, which means the SLOW circuit function must be on. What can I do to reset this circuit?

Answer: The SLOW (Speed Limiting Overheat Warning) system has been a little problematic on some of the three-cylinder Evinrudes such as yours.

First, use Thermomelt Stiks to make sure that the engine isn't overheating. Thermomelt Stiks, made by La-Co, look like crayons and are available from most outboard mechanics. There's a low-temperature stick that should melt when it's held against the engine's water cover on the cylinder head, and a high-temperature stick that should not melt.

If the engine is overheating, the problem is probably a result of a tired water pump or clogging in the waterways or thermostat housing.

Thermomelt Stik being used to check the operating temperature of an outboard motor. The high-temperature stick should not melt when it's held against the cylinder-head water cover.

Maybe, though, your engine is running at a good temperature and the SLOW circuitry in the power pack is just fine, but the SLOW function is being triggered in error.

Check the temperature sensor switch for the system—it should have a tan-and-blue wire. Some of these engines, though, have a sensor switch with a solid tan wire that switches on at too low a temperature (203°F). The part number for the correct switch—with the tan-and-blue wire—is 584589. It sells for $32.17 and triggers the system at approximately 240°F.

There's also a possibility that a slug of air is getting trapped in the engine's cooling system. This sometimes happens when an engine operates in aerated water, such as in pontoon boat applications. If this is the problem, your dealer needs to relocate the water pump indicator T to a location higher in the block, allowing the air to bleed out through the indicator port in the engine's cowl.

This is detailed in a service bulletin that your dealer should have on hand. Since it involves drilling and tapping the engine block, it's not a do-it-yourself operation.

5 WIRING AND ELECTROLYSIS

Electrical Overview

When electricity first made its way on board boats—around the turn of the last century—it proved to be both a blessing and a curse. The simple truth is electricity doesn't do so well in the marine environment.

To be sure, things have gotten better since those early days; at least we don't have wiring that's insulated with hemp and gutta-percha anymore. But even with the modern thermoplastics, we still have to make connections. Like a chain that's only as strong as its weakest link, these connections furnish more than their fair share of troubles.

To control electricity and get it to do our bidding on our boats, we have to take great pains to keep it

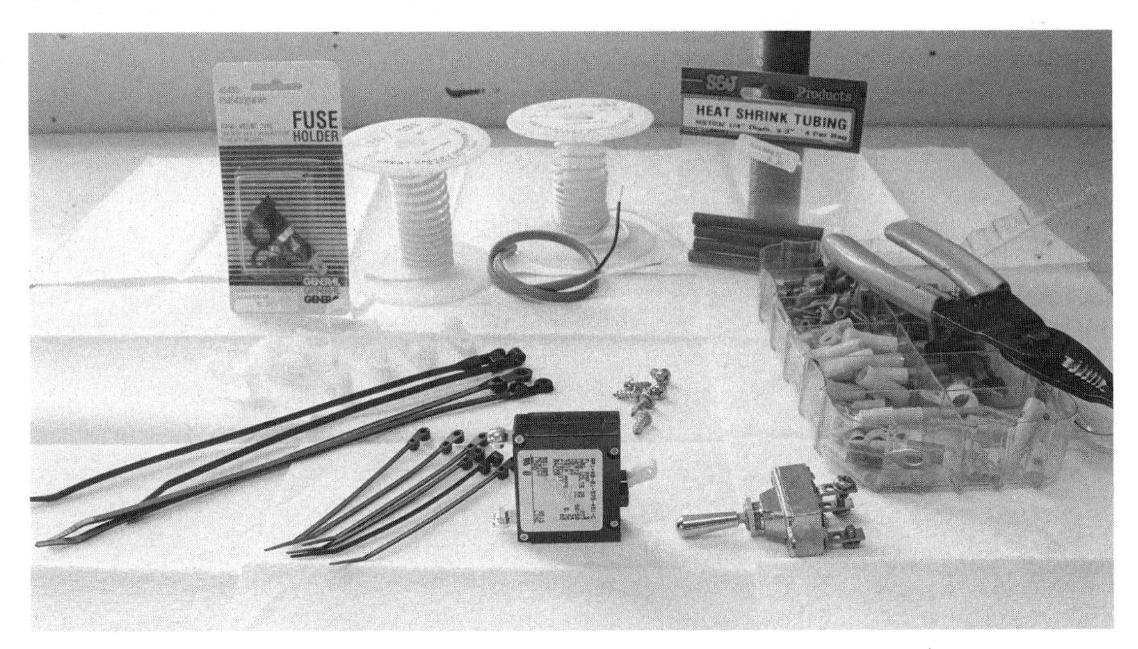

Tools and supplies for making and securing boat wiring and connections. Clockwise from bottom: switch, magnetic circuit breaker, ty-wraps, nylon wire clips, fuse holder, wire, heat-shrink tubing, connectors, and crimping pliers. Stainless steel screws in center.

in its place. For the most part this is not an issue of safety; most of the wiring that runs in the damper areas of boats contains low voltage. (You're not that likely to get a life-threatening shock from a 12-volt circuit.)

Just the same, many portions of your boat's low-voltage DC wiring system are in close proximity to the 110-volt AC wiring. Therefore, whenever you are troubleshooting the DC system, make sure that you've disabled the shore power and the AC generator and marked the inlet receptacle and the generator control panel so that no one will power it up. When you work behind the master panel in particular, make sure you know which system you're working on. They are isolated from one another, but not by much.

The discussion that follows pertains to the DC wiring in your boat. I'll have a little to say about AC wiring later in the chapter but, for the most part, I don't recommend getting involved in your boat's AC wiring system. It can kill you and is best handled by the pros.

The problems with boat wiring are reliability and electrolysis. Poorly made connections corrode and fail quickly in a damp environment. Once corrosion rears its ugly head, the equipment that's fed by these circuits works intermittently, if at all.

In this chapter I'm going to show you how you can make (and maintain) solid, reliable wiring and connections in your boat. I'll also provide information on electrolysis, a widely misunderstood phenomenon that's always looking for a free lunch (of your boat's underwater hardware). Later, I'll debunk a lot of the misplaced thinking that surrounds this bugaboo, and tell you how to keep it at bay.

Some Definitions

Voltage is a measure of the pressure of a supply of electricity. All by itself, voltage doesn't mean much. The amount of work that can be done also depends on current.

Current is the volume of electricity supplied by a source. It's expressed in amperes; typically known as amps. As I said, voltage doesn't mean much. For example, if you connect eight flashlight cells in series (one after another, positive to negative), you get a 12-volt battery. If you try to crank your engine over with that battery, you'll quickly discover that it comes up short. The missing ingredient is current. A starter motor draws a minimum of 150 to 200 amperes of current and our hitched-up team of flashlight cells can't deliver more than about one amp.

Resistance is the restriction that an electrical device presents in a circuit. Not only do electrical devices—such as pumps and starter motors—have resistance, wiring and switches do, too. (In fact, only superconductors have virtually no resistance and, so far, these aren't being used in boats.) Resistance is measured and expressed in a unit called ohms.

There's no need to go into a detailed description of Ohm's law (formulated in the nineteenth century by Georg Ohm, a German physicist). You just need to know that the greater the resistance in a circuit, the less current flows, if the voltage remains the same. Conversely, if the resistance drops and the voltage remains constant, the current will increase.

If the resistance drops down to near zero ohms, the current increases to the maximum that can be supplied by the source. For example, that's what happens if you accidentally drop a wrench on your boat's battery so that it touches both terminals at once (don't try this). The current increases so much that the battery explodes. This is called a short circuit. Unless the battery posts have rubber covers, there's nothing to protect your battery against having dumb things like this happen to it. But thankfully, there are devices to protect the rest of your boat's wiring against short circuits.

Overload Protection Devices

If you have a boat that was built in the last two decades, it probably has magnetic circuit breakers controlling the circuits at the master panel. These neat little devices combine the functions of a switch and an overload-protection device in one package.

When a circuit is switched on, the current flows through the breaker. If the resistance of the circuit drops, the current flow increases. If it increases dramatically—beyond the circuit breaker's rating—the breaker trips and cuts off the supply of power to the circuit. If you look at the switch, you'll see that the handle has flipped toward the "off" position.

Older boats have conventional switches to turn the circuits on and off and small glass fuses mounted in fuse holders to provide overload protection. The function is the same: As the resistance drops down toward the short-circuit range, the current increases. When it reaches the rated value of the fuse that protects that circuit, the fusible link of metal in the fuse melts, opening the circuit and shutting off the current. (Unlike circuit breakers, fuses must be replaced when they "blow.")

These devices serve an invaluable purpose. If they weren't there, the current would increase to the capacity of the battery, which is a lot. At some point it would exceed the current-handling capability of the weakest link in the circuit—usually the wiring. The power would continue to flow until the wire melted through someplace between the battery and the device powered by the circuit. Not only would this be more of a pain than flipping a breaker back on or replacing a fuse, it also might start a wiring fire in some inaccessible part of your boat. Bummer.

Of course, if a breaker pops or a fuse blows, you shouldn't just switch the breaker back on or replace the fuse. First, you need to figure out what caused the overload condition. Don't ever be tempted to put in a larger fuse to eliminate this problem either. If breakers pop or fuses blow, there's something wrong with the wiring or the device supplied by that circuit. You must find the problem and fix it.

Ampacity

Electricity in a wire is a lot like water in a pipe. The larger the diameter of the pipe (or wire), the more water (or electrical current) can flow within. That's what is behind an important concept that you must understand to make and maintain boat wiring. The concept is called ampacity.

Have you ever tried to run an electric drill or other appliance at the end of a few long extension cords and have the appliance burst into flames when you put a load on it? It happened to me once. The problem was that the extension cords I was using didn't have enough ampacity for their length.

To understand this phenomenon, you should know that the diameter of the conductor in a piece of wire is expressed by a number called its gauge. These numbers work backwards from the way you might expect: the larger the wire the smaller the gauge.

The gauge numbers typically used in boat wiring run from a very light #22 wire, which might feed the tiny light bulb inside your boat's compass, all the way down to 0 (pronounced "aught") gauge, which is a typical size for a battery cable (the highest-current circuit on most boats). There are even heavier cables than 0. For example, there are 2/0, 3/0, and 4/0A, each succeedingly heavier than the last. Unless your boat is powered by a diesel engine, you won't find any conductors this heavy in your boat's engine room. (You might have noticed that after the cable gauges get bigger than 0, the numbers go up again. How else could they do it?)

The longer the wiring run, the heavier the conductors must be to deliver a satisfactory amount of current to the end of the line (the device being fed). To help you determine what size wire to use when adding an accessory circuit to your boat, an ampacity chart is reproduced opposite.

It's important to remember that when selecting a gauge of wire, you have to count the distance from the battery to the device being fed *and back to the source of the current*. So when you use the chart to pick the gauge of wire to use for an accessory mounted 10 feet from the source of power, you have to look in the 20-foot column.

For example, a piece of equipment that requires 10 amperes of current to operate and is installed 10 feet away from the battery requires 10-gauge wire. Now to prove my point about the need for a heavier wire: Check out what you'd need to feed that same device if it were installed twice as far from the battery. Moving from the 20-foot column to the 40-foot column, you'll see that the circuit now calls for 8-gauge wire, which is one size larger.

If you installed our hypothetical device at that longer distance and stayed with 10-gauge wire, too much of the voltage would be "dropped" inside the conductor. That wouldn't leave enough left at the end of the line to properly feed the accessory. When

CONDUCTOR SIZES FOR 3% DROP IN VOLTAGE

Length of Conductor from Source of Current to Device and Back to Source—Feet

12 Volts—3% Drop Wire Sizes (gauge) — Based on Minimum CM Area

Total Current on Circuit in Amps.	10	15	20	25	30	40	50	60	70	80	90	100	110	120	130	140	150	160	170
5	18	16	14	12	12	10	10	10	8	8	8	6	6	6	6	6	6	6	6
10	14	12	10	10	10	8	6	6	6	6	4	4	4	4	2	2	2	2	2
15	12	10	10	8	8	6	6	6	4	4	2	2	2	2	2	1	1	1	1
20	10	10	8	6	6	6	4	4	2	2	2	2	1	1	1	0	0	0	2/0
25	10	8	6	6	6	4	4	2	2	2	1	1	0	0	0	2/0	2/0	2/0	3/0
30	10	8	6	6	4	4	2	2	1	1	0	0	0	2/0	2/0	3/0	3/0	3/0	3/0
40	8	6	6	4	4	2	2	1	0	0	2/0	2/0	3/0	3/0	3/0	4/0	4/0	4/0	4/0
50	6	6	4	4	2	2	1	0	2/0	2/0	3/0	3/0	4/0	4/0	4/0				
60	6	4	4	2	2	1	0	2/0	3/0	3/0	4/0	4/0	4/0						
70	6	4	2	2	1	0	2/0	3/0	3/0	4/0	4/0								
80	6	4	2	2	1	0	3/0	3/0	4/0	4/0									
90	4	2	2	1	0	2/0	3/0	4/0	4/0										
100	4	2	2	1	0	2/0	3/0	4/0											

COURTESY OF THE AMERICAN BOAT AND YACHT COUNCIL (ABYC)

it was put under load, it would either burn dimly (in the case of a lamp) or burn out or catch on fire, like my drill motor did (in the case of a motorized device). Ampacity is important if you want to have happy electrical equipment.

Once you've got the right size wire running in all your boat's circuits, you've got to move on to the next potential trouble area—the quality of the connections.

CONNECTIONS

When a piece of electrical gear on your boat fails to work, the problem is often with the wiring, the switch, or the connections; not the device. To minimize these kinds of problems, first make sure that your wiring has as few connections as possible. When you add an accessory, don't patch together a bunch of short pieces of wire. Instead, work the wiring into your boat right off a full-length spool and don't cut it and install the terminals until you've securely routed and bundled it in place. (If you cut it to what seems to be the right length and then bundle it, you might find yourself a few feet short when you get to the end of the run.)

Solderless Connectors

These connectors are ubiquitous. If you're a do-it-yourselfer, you should make up a small electrical box with a good assortment of the various types and sizes that you'll need. Make sure the metal parts of the connectors you buy are tinned copper. There are some with plated steel inside; avoid them like the plague. You can use a magnet to test them if you're in doubt. It should not be attracted to your connectors. Buy good-quality connectors and expect to pay at least 50¢ apiece for them.

There are different connectors for different jobs. The most popular is the so-called butt connector. This is a small hollow cylinder designed to accept the ends of two wires (one in each side) and join them in an electrical connection when the ends are crimped.

There's a cylindrical copper sleeve inside the butt connector. That's the part you crimp with your electrical pliers to make the connection. A tough plastic shell surrounds the crimpable part to protect it from moisture (which it doesn't really do very effectively—more on that later).

There are also the so-called Scotchlok connectors from 3M. These are for tapping into an existing wire. They have a snap lid that pierces the conductor of your wire. In my experience, they stink. I wouldn't use them on a boat or anywhere else.

When you need to tap into a wire, it's far better to cut the wire you're tapping into and twist one of its ends together with the branch wire. Then you can use a butt connector and heat-shrink tubing to make a proper splice.

Wire: Buy the Best

You can't do good work with lousy materials. Wire is a critical component and it pays to buy the best you can. There are two types of conventional wire, solid and stranded, referring to the copper conductor inside the insulating jacket. Solid wire is made with a one-piece conductor. It doesn't abide flexing and *should not be used anywhere on a boat*. In stranded wire, as its name suggests, the conductor is made of a bundle of small strands of continuous copper. *Stranded wire is the only type you should use for boat wiring*.

There are a few variations on the stranded wire theme, called types one, two, and three. Type one is the least flexible. It has seven strands of copper inside and is used only on circuitry that is rigidly secured so the wire is not subjected to any flexing whatsoever.

Type two has anywhere from 16 to 127 strands of copper inside, depending on what gauge it is. It can withstand more flexing than type one, and is what you'll typically get if you ask for stranded wire at your boatyard or auto parts store.

Type three is the most flexible. Depending on the wire's gauge it has anywhere from 26 to 655 strands inside. The only place I've ever seen it used is in cars to wire harnesses that are flexed by opening and closing all the time (places like doors or tailgates). There's nothing I know of on a boat that requires this degree of flexibility, which is just as well because I've never seen it offered for sale to the marine market anyway.

Insulation Specifications

Insulation is the colored plastic that's around your wire's conductor. There are a few types and grades with letter designations like THWN, MTW, AWM, XHHW, and THW. THWN and XHHW are the best for our purposes, but according to the American Boat and Yacht Council, all are suitable for marine wiring.

Multiconductor Cable

When you run an accessory circuit in a car, it usually only takes one wire—the so-called hot lead. That's because the car's chassis and body are made of metal and serve as a ground path for the circuit. Boats, though, are made of nonconducting materials such as fiberglass and wood. Therefore, except for the engine wiring, we need to have a hot lead *and* a ground lead running to each accessory to have a complete circuit.

That's where two-conductor cable comes in handy. This is simply two discrete wires that are bundled together in a rugged vinyl plastic sheath. Run a length of cable wherever your wiring needs to travel and, when you get to the end of the line, strip off the jacket and make your connections with the individual wires.

Cables are available with various gauges of wire inside and are designated by the wire gauge and the number of conductors inside. For example, a two-conductor cable with 14-gauge wires inside is called 14-2; simple, eh?

Heat-Shrink Tubing

No connection will last long in a marine environment unless it's properly sealed. The best thing I've found for sealing things is heat-shrink tubing, a neat, flexible plastic sheath that shrinks down tightly over your connections with the application of heat. The only drawback is that you can't put it on after you've made the connection. That means you have to remember to cut an appropriate length of this tubing and slide it along one of the wire ends *before* you make your crimped connection. If I had a nickel for every time I've had to cut a connection apart and redo it because I forgot this step, I'd be pretty well off.

I'll tell you how to shrink this tubing after I give you some pointers on making successful connections. I just thought I'd mention it now, so you'd remember to do things in the proper order.

Making Solid Connections, Step by Step

Connectors are made in several sizes. Each can accommodate a range of wire sizes. Before you make a connection, you have to make sure that you've selected connectors that will fit the wire and allow it to be properly crimped. If you can fit the wire into the connector and get enough of a squeeze so it can't be pulled out after crimping, it's just right.

In addition to wire, heat-shrink tubing, and solderless connectors, you'll also need a couple of tools to make rock-solid connections. You should have a source of heat and high-quality crimping pliers in your bag of tricks.

I use a disposable cigarette lighter for heating heat-shrink tubing. It's quick, though you have to carefully play the flame over all portions of the tubing to avoid applying too much heat. If you're careless, you'll char the tubing and your connection. The other drawback with a cigarette lighter is that it has an open flame, which isn't safe in an engine room or other enclosed space unless you're absolutely sure there are no gasoline vapors. So be careful.

When it comes to crimping pliers, you get what you pay for. The cheap ones that come with an assortment of equally cheap solderless connectors are not worth messing around with. A good pair sells for around $22. If you can't justify spending that much, see if you can borrow them from a friend.

Better-quality crimping pliers have well-ground stripping dies for cleanly stripping the insulation off the wire, which is the first step in making a connection. The better-quality crimping pliers also have more leverage and cushion-grip handles, two features that make it easier to make a solid crimp that will retain the wire in the connector. There's nothing more frustrating than finishing a connection and tugging on it, only to have it come apart in your hands.

The very best pliers—which can cost as much as $60—have male and female crimping dies that punch a dimple into the crimp. This type also uses compound leverage to ensure solid crimps. If there's any way you can pony up the money for this type, you'll really be in fat city. But the midpriced ones will serve you just fine if you mind your P's and Q's.

Here are the promised step-by-step directions for making a proper butt connection.

1. Select the smallest diameter of heat-shrink tubing that will easily slide over the connector body. This stuff doesn't shrink that much. If you select a size that's too large, it won't effectively shrink down and seal over the wire (which is skinnier than the connector).
2. Cut a piece of heat-shrink tubing that's long enough to go well beyond both ends of the connector when you're done. I usually make it twice as long as the connector body, which always works out just about right.

   Slide your length of heat-shrink tubing onto one of the ends of the wires and push it up out of your way. (Secure it with a piece of masking tape if it keeps sliding back down and getting in your way.)
3. Strip the wire ends with the correct size stripping dies on your pliers. These sharpened holes are marked with the wire size they're designed to strip. If you use a too-small pair of stripping holes, you'll nick the conductor; too large and you won't be able to pull the insulation off.

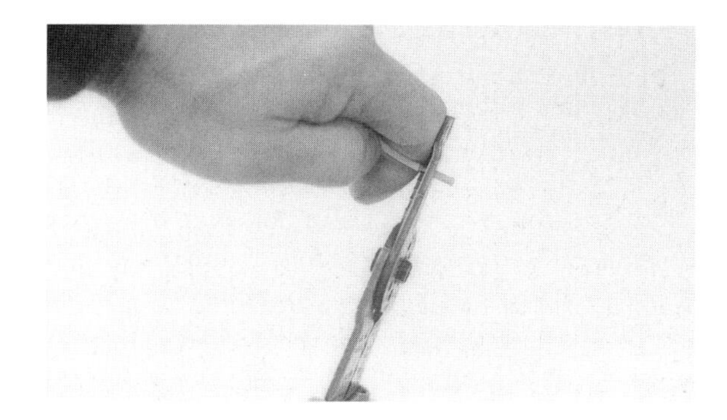

Stripping the wire end. Don't strip off too much at this step or you'll wind up with a weak joint.

You should strip off only enough insulation to let the bare wire reach in to the middle of the crimpable shell inside the connector, with the insulation butted up against the inner sleeve. This is a shorter strip length than you might think. It's better to strip off too little insulation than too much; you can always take another nip. If you strip off too much insulation, there will be a short length of exposed conductor that's not supported by the body of the connector. When this is flexed it can fatigue and break off, so make sure you get this right. Some connectors have a dimple inside that will stop the wire end from going more than halfway through.

When you've stripped off the right amount of insulation, the inner conductor will reach into its half of the connector body and the end of the insulation will butt up against the crimpable shell inside.

There are other types of connectors besides butt connectors. You will also use ring lugs and spade lugs in your boat wiring projects. For these you should strip off enough insulation to let the wire end peek through at the ring or spade end of the connector, but not to stick out and interfere with the function of the connector.

Finish off the stripped wire end by twisting the conductor's strands clockwise. This gives them more strength and stiffness and also makes it easier to insert the wire end into the connector.

4. Make sure you remembered to slide your length of heat-shrink tubing onto the end of the wire; then push the wire end home in the connector. Locate the correct crimping dies on your pliers and put the connector body in with the dies right in the middle of the half that you're crimping.

   While you're holding the wire securely in the connector so it won't slip out, give a mighty squeeze of the pliers to securely crimp the wire in place. If your hands aren't too strong or you're using cheap crimping pliers, you might want to put one handle on a solid surface and bear down on the other handle with your body weight.

   After you've made your crimp, put down the pliers and test the job by tugging on the connector body. Give it a couple of pounds of pull. If the wire doesn't pull out, your crimp is a good one. Repeat the above operations with the other wire end. Test this connection, too, before proceeding to the last step.

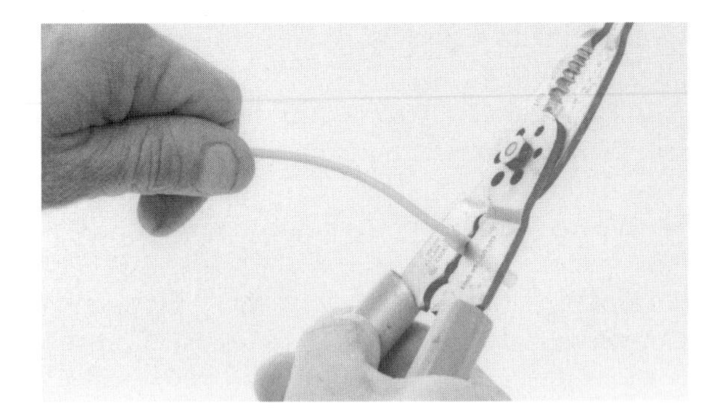

Crimping the terminal on the first wire end.

5. Slide the length of heat-shrink tubing down over the connector body and center it before beginning to apply the heat. Heat the tubing and twirl the wire around. Move the heat from end to end, too. If you follow these steps, the tubing will shrink all the way around and along its entire length.

Some connections don't lend themselves to heat-shrink tubing. For example, how are you going

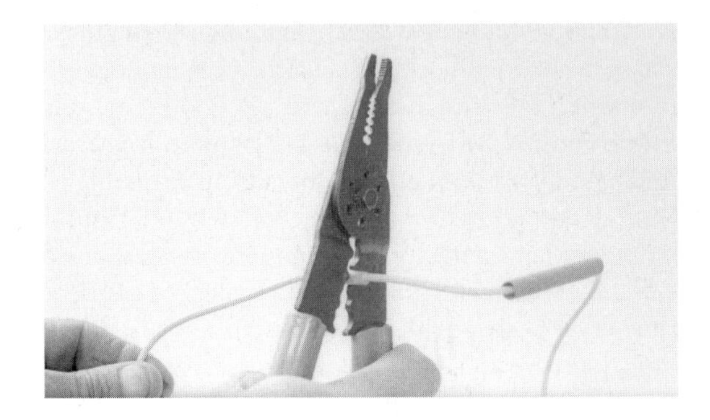

Crimping the terminal onto the second wire to be joined. Note that the heat-shrink tubing has already been slid onto the wire end. If you neglect this step you will have to cut the joint apart and redo it.

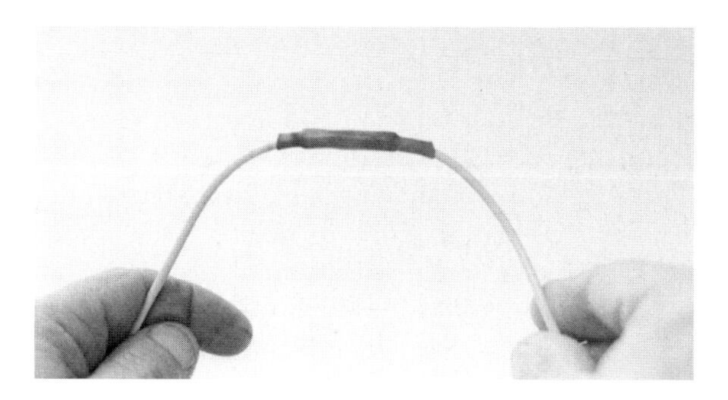

The completed butt joint with the heat-shrink tubing securely shrunk in place over the connector.

to make a moisture-proof seal where you attach a ring lug to the back of a magnetic breaker or slide a spade lug onto a bus bar?

Simple—use my secret weapon: Liquid Electric Tape, a liquid dielectric coating that comes in a can with a brush in the cap. It's sold by Star brite, which means you can find it in chandleries everywhere. It's even made in different colors, though I tend to stick with basic black. (It goes with everything, right?)

Brush this product on any exposed metal portions of your connection and on the body of the connector. When it dries, it polymerizes into a tough, flexible coating that excludes moisture and corrosion. Connections treated with this product can still be easily disassembled and, when they're reconnected, the sealing can be restored with a quick reapplication.

Congratulations! You've made a perfect connection. Now let's secure the wire and bundle it into the rest of your boat's wiring to complete the job.

Electrical Housekeeping

If you want a reliable electrical system on your boat, there's more to it than the connections—you need to practice good housekeeping. That is, you must snake wires through the nooks and crannies of your boat so they can follow a short, sensible path from source to accessory. You must also bundle them into organized harnesses and run them where they won't get wet, tugged, or stepped on. In this section, I'll provide tips on these important wiring issues.

Neatly bundled wiring on back of instrument panel. These wires are carefully routed and secured with ty-wraps.

Wiring Color Codes

If you've ever poked around in your boat's wiring you might have noticed that the boatbuilder and engine manufacturer used a lot of different wire colors. They didn't do this because they thought it would look nice. There's actually a standard color code, promulgated by the ABYC, for boat wiring. The beauty of this system is that when you're poking around under the helm panel looking for the fuel-gauge sender wire, it's easier to find if you know it's pink. That narrows things down considerably.

When you add accessories, you might not need to use color coding since most of the circuits that have predetermined wire colors are already in your boat. But it is nice to know the code. So I've provided a copy here.

Keeping It Neat: Harnesses

There are a lot of handy little hardware bits on the market that are designed to help you keep your boat's wiring in shipshape condition. A well-stocked chandlery should be able to furnish most of these products. You can also find some at RadioShack or at well-stocked hardware and auto parts stores.

One warning though: Provided they're stoutly constructed, nylon wiring clips and other plastic parts are fine no matter where you buy them. Metal hardware, however, should come from a chandler. You don't want to install any screws on your boat

ABYC COLOR CODE CHART

Wire Color	Usage	Runs where?
Yellow w/ Red Stripe	Starting Circuit	Starter Switch to Solenoid
Yellow	Alternator Field Bilge Blower	Alternator Field Terminal to Regulator Fuse or Switch to Blower
Dark Gray	Navigation Lights Tachometer	Fuse or Switch to Lights Tach Sender to Gauge
Brown	Generator Armature Alternator Charge Lt. Pumps	Gen. Armature to Regulator Generator Term./Alternator Aux. Term. to Light to Regulator Fuse or Switch to Pumps
Orange	Accessory Feed	Ammeter to Alternator Output and Acc. Fuses or Switches
	Accessory Common	Distribution Panel to Accessory Switch
Purple	Ignition	Ign. Switch to Coil and Electrical Instruments
	Instrument Feed	Distribution Panel to Electric Instruments
Dark Blue	Cabin & Inst. Lights	Fuse or Switch to Lights
Light Blue	Oil Pressure	Sender to Gauge
Tan	Water Temperature	Sender to Gauge
Pink	Fuel Level Gauge	Sender to Gauge

Courtesy of the American Boat and Yacht Council (ABYC)

unless you know they're made of high-quality, non-magnetic stainless steel.

Here are some thoughts on the most common types of harness-making accessories you'll probably use on your boat.

Ty-Wraps

What a great invention these things are. I don't know what we did before they came on the market. A ty-wrap is a tough, ribbed plastic strap with one pointed end and, at the other end, a notched opening. The wires are gathered up in the ty-wrap, then you feed the pointed end into the ratchet-equipped hole in the other end and cinch the wires up snugly. Then snip off the excess. These are indispensable for gathering up bundles of wires or for securing one new wire to a bundle that already exists.

It gets even better. Ty-wraps are also made with screw holes in the end. If you gather up the wires, cinch them up in the ty-wrap, snip off the excess, grab a panhead, self-tapping, stainless steel screw, and put it through the hole, you can secure that ty-wrapped wiring almost anywhere you want. If the mounting site is fiberglass, you should predrill the mounting hole so you don't crack the gelcoat. Wiring secured this way is not going anywhere.

Avoid like the plague self-adhesive wiring clips. They aren't worth messing with. They'll fall off after a week or two. I don't know where they're useful, but it certainly isn't on a boat.

Plastic Raceways

If your boat was built in the last fifteen years or so, you'll probably find some of these in the engine room. A raceway is a U-shaped track that screws on a surface (usually overhead). Most are about 1¼ inches square in cross section, which provides room for a whole bunch of wiring. The sides of the raceway are slotted so wires can be led out at any point along the line. The whole thing is capped off with a snap-on cover, which can be removed to add another wire or reroute the existing ones.

These act as "manifolds," if you will. Although they carry the bulk of the wire, they don't do the whole job. When you break a wire out of the raceway to route it to its final destination, you'll still need ty-wraps and the other little hardware bits mentioned in this chapter. The most popular raceways are made by Panduit (Panduit Corp., 17301 Ridgeland Ave., Tinley Park, IL 60477; 800-777-3300; www.panduit.com).

Nylon Wiring Clips

After your wiring leaves the harness or conduit that it follows on the way to its destination, it's on its own. It won't do to just string a wire from this point to the accessory that it powers. You need wiring clips.

Using them is simple. Just tuck the wire or cable in an appropriately sized clip and secure it with a short, self-tapping stainless steel screw. To keep things from snagging on the wire, it's best to support it with a clip every foot or so whenever possible.

Pigtailing

Wire often reaches a point where it has to take a leap to get to its destination. I've got a neat trick for dealing with this—it's called pigtailing. Wire leads that are pigtailed make a job look neat and professional and the wiring survives vibration and movement better. Here's how it's done.

1. If your wire has to take a 1-foot leap, for example, provide an extra 9 to 12 inches of wire before you cut it and install the terminal. In other words, make a 75 to 100 percent allowance for a perfect pigtail. (By the way, it's best to install the ring lug or whatever kind of electrical terminal is going to go on the end before you do the pigtailing.)
2. Wrap the wire around a cylindrical mandrel or form. I usually use a pencil for this. Wrap it tightly and evenly with the wraps right next to each other. Leave a couple of inches straight at each end of the section being pigtailed.
3. Slide the pencil out of the wire and stretch the pigtailed lead out just enough to reach its connection point. Attach it to the terminal and you're done. Now does that look professional or what? Pigtailing is almost mandatory for wire

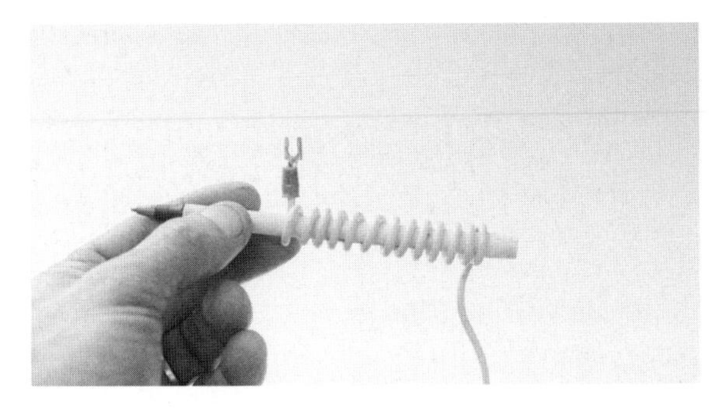

The first step in pigtailing a length of wire is to wrap it around a pen that serves as a mandrel. Wind it evenly and push the wraps against each other.

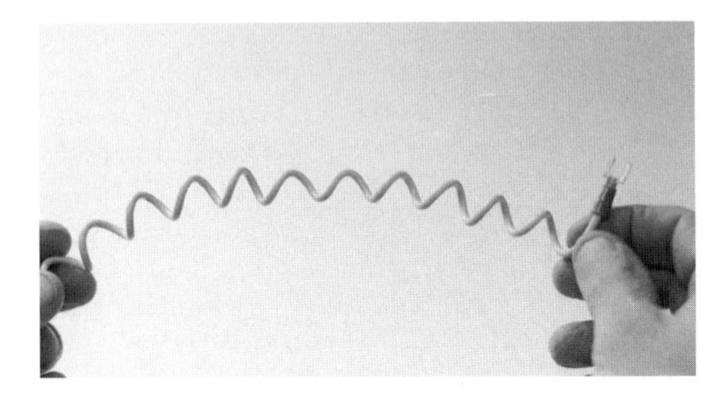

The completed pigtail job. This technique provides a good strain relief and a professional appearance. It's especially useful for wires that are subjected to vibration such as those that attach to the engine or other machinery.

leads that attach to the engine or any other machinery that's subject to vibration. It's also a nice treatment for fuel-gauge sending unit leads at the tank. But use your imagination—pigtailed wires look good just about anywhere. Happy pigtailing.

Snaking Wires

If you've ever tried to make a wiring run in your boat, you might have discovered that the task can be a real pain. But routing wires from a switch or source of current to the destination—that is, the device being fed—can be made easier with a procedure called snaking. Here are some tips and techniques to make it easier.

Start by looking for a conduit. Most boats have preinstalled lengths of plastic pipe to carry the wiring. If you're lucky, your boatbuilder will have installed one of these that's large enough to accommodate some extra wiring.

If you've found a length of plastic pipe or some other kind of conduit to carry your wiring, great. Now, how do you get the wiring from point A to point B? You need something to snake the wiring through the conduit. For a short wiring run, you can probably get by with a straightened-out wire coat hanger or a length of brazing rod.

But, if you have to snake a wire for a distance of more than a couple of feet, you're going to need a special tool. The best item I've found for this job is a wire snake, sometimes called a fishtape. It's a length of stiff, flat steel that unwinds from a reel. You can buy one at an electrical supply house or a serious hardware store. Using one is pretty simple.

1. Unreel enough of the fishtape to reach from one end of your conduit out to where the wire will emerge. Gently push the end of the fishtape into the conduit. Keep pushing it in gently. If it gets hung up, don't push hard; you might damage the existing wiring that's already occupying the conduit.

   Instead, back it up half a foot and twist the entire tape by rotating the reel. That action will usually make the tape flop over to the other side of the conduit, at which point you can start pushing again.
2. Continue in this fashion until the fishtape emerges from the end of the conduit. Now you can securely tape the end of the wire or cable that you're going to run to the protruding end of the fishtape.

   Make sure you tape it on tightly, so it won't detach when you've pulled it halfway back. I usually lay the fishtape and wire end butted up against each other on a strip of stiff, strong tape (like sailboat rigging tape). I don't wrap the tape around the connection here; instead, I run it the long way and press it tightly against the two pieces being joined. Then I fold over one edge at a time and press them down securely against

Fishtape (wire snake). Note that this is a professional tool. For short wiring runs you can use a length of brazing rod or even a straightened-out wire coat hanger.

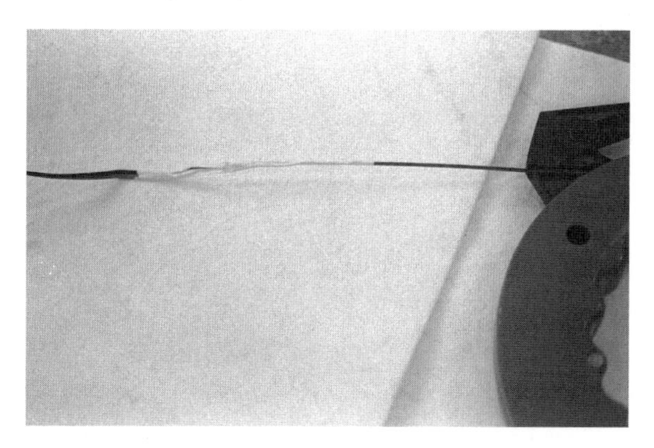

Attachment of wire end to fishtape (wire snake) in preparation for pulling through to make a wiring run.

the wire and the fishtape. This scheme lessens the likelihood of the tape pulling off when the wire is reeved through its passage.

3. Now, the wire is ready to be pulled back through the conduit. Make sure you have enough wire free of its spool and that it won't kink when you get to the other end and start pulling. (Sometimes it pays to station a helper at the wire end to make sure the wire feeds in properly with no resistance as you pull.)

   Smoothly and gently begin to pull the fishtape back out, bringing the wire along for the ride. If it gets hung up, push it in a bit and try pulling it out again. If it gets hopelessly hung up, you have nothing to lose by pulling hard or having your helper pull the wire back from the other end. There's a good chance that if you have to do either of these things, the joint will come apart—but not to worry. Just snake the fishtape through again, reattach the ends, and start over. It will probably work fine. (Now you know why it's important to get a strong connection between the wire and the fishtape.)

   If I have to snake a wire in a length of conduit that I expect to revisit with another wire at a later date, I often install a "messenger." That's a length of thin synthetic rope ($^1/_8$-inch diameter flag halyard line works great) that's snaked into the conduit. The next time I want to reeve a wire through this passage, I'll simply attach my new wire to the messenger and pull it through.

Twelve-Volt Troubleshooting

Troubleshooting your boat's 12-volt wiring system is not a black art. In fact, if you learn a few basic rules and techniques, you can be a troubleshooting whiz.

Remember: For your boat's electrical devices to work, there must be a complete path for current. It starts at the source of power—the battery—goes through a switch and fuse (or a magnetic breaker that combines both of these functions in one unit) along a wire to the device being powered, through the device to its other terminal, and then back through the ground side of the circuit to the negative terminal of the battery.

If the battery is capable of sourcing current, the path is complete, and the device is in good order, the circuit will work. If anything along the line is out of commission, things won't work. It's as simple as that.

When the entire path is complete, we have what's called continuity. If you look at the drawing on page 66, you can trace the path that the electrons follow when they light the lamp (or spin the motor in the bilge pump or what have you).

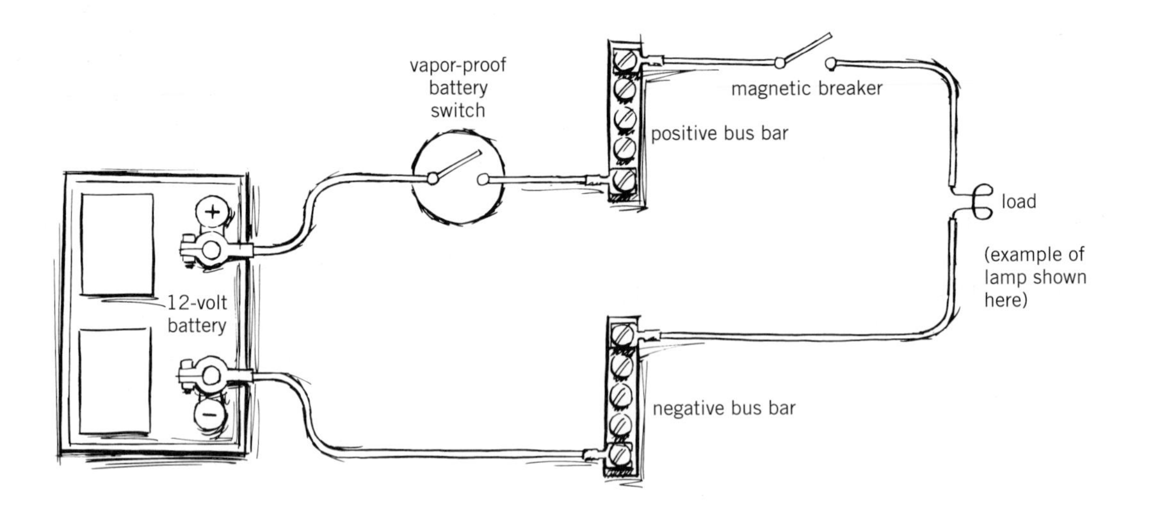

Basic DC electrical circuit, shown schematically. Note that some older boats may have a switch and fuse to serve the functions of the magnetic circuit breaker shown.

First Things First

I've seen people tear apart a carburetor because they knew they had a fuel system problem, only to find out that the fuel system problem was an empty fuel tank. Don't make the same mistake when troubleshooting your electrical system.

Start with the simple, obvious stuff. Does any of the electrical gear on the boat work? If not, you probably have a dead battery.

Similarly, if a running light isn't working, don't get out your meter and other troubleshooting tools and start tearing things apart. Instead, grab a screwdriver and take the fixture apart to check for a burned-out lamp or dirty contacts. Make sure the metal base (or ends in the case of cylindrical lamps) is solidly attached to the glass envelope. If you're in doubt, you can either test the lamp with a meter—more on that later—or replace it temporarily with a known good lamp from your spares box.

Similarly, if your boat is an older model that has glass fuses instead of magnetic breakers, take out the fuse that protects the faulty circuit. Is it burned out? Twist the metal ends here, too; fuses can fail without burning out. Make sure the ends are clean and shiny for good conductivity too.

Also remember that, even if your boat has magnetic breakers, some electrical devices, such as certain radios, GPS computers, lorans, etc., have their own built-in fuses. These are usually mounted in the back panel of the unit and are easy enough to check.

Second Steps

If none of the simple tests disclose the problem, you've got to move on to some circuit inspection work. There might be a fault in the wiring or you might have a bum switch or magnetic breaker. Here are some pointers for digging a little deeper.

Make a careful visual inspection of the wiring, concentrating on the connections—that's where troubles usually lie. If you find a connector that looks suspicious, it's time to get physical. Turn on the circuit and wiggle and tug on the connector. Does the circuit intermittently spring to life? If so, you've found the problem. Cut the flaky connection out of the circuit and renew it following the procedure outlined earlier in this chapter.

How about the switch? The same wiggling and jiggling technique works here as well. Exercise both the switch handle and the connection points on the back to see if things suddenly start working.

You probably noticed some parts marked bus bars on the drawing. These are distribution points for feeding power to a group of circuits, or for making a common ground path for a number of circuits. In some cases, these have screw terminals. The wires that attach to this type of bus bar are terminated with ring lugs and usually don't cause any trouble.

Then there's the other type of bus bar. It has a series of metal blades that are designed to receive wire ends that are terminated with female spring lugs. This type of connector is attached to the wire end with a crimp like all solderless connectors. Then the end of the connector pushes on to the blade to make the connection. By nature, these connections are somewhat open and can be subject to corrosion problems, especially if they're mounted in a damp area.

If there's a problem with a bus bar of this type, you should be able to uncover it by pulling the problem circuit's connector partway off its blade and pushing it back on. Try this with the circuit powered up. If the device works intermittently, take the connector all the way off and clean up the offending blade with an ink eraser. You can't really clean the contact surface of one of these connectors, so if that's the problem, just cut the connector off and crimp a new one on in its place.

If none of the above-mentioned tricks correct the problem, it's time to bring out the heavy artillery: your multimeter.

Meter Troubleshooting

You have two choices when it comes to buying a multimeter: analog or digital.

If you can see your way clear to buying a digital one, by all means do so. They cost $40 to $100 (and even more for really fancy ones with features you probably don't need). Alternatively, a cheap analog one will set you back around $15 at RadioShack or your local True Value. Either type will do the job; the digital one is just a bit more versatile, harder to burn out, much easier to use, and way more rugged.

Continuity Testing

This is the simplest type of electrical troubleshooting you can do with a meter. Remember, continuity refers to a complete path for current to flow in a circuit. If the switch is closed (turned on), the fuse is in good shape, the wiring is OK, and the device is in good order, we have continuity. If any one of these things is out of order, we don't. It's as simple as that.

To test for continuity, use the resistance-measuring (or ohms) function on the meter, which is sometimes marked with the Greek symbol omega (Ω).

When a multimeter is used as an ohmmeter, the battery inside it supplies the power that's used to test the circuit. Therefore, make sure that the circuit is powered down before hooking the meter probes up to anything. Shut off the battery switch. You can't measure continuity in a live circuit. Worse yet, if you try to do so with an analog meter, you'll wreck the meter movement.

To get the hang of continuity testing, let's start with the magnetic breaker, or the on-off switch that controls the circuit. Set the meter to ohms. If you're using an analog meter, zero the reading by touching the probes together and turning the adjuster knob to move the needle to the zero ohms mark on the dial. This step is necessary with an analog meter because, as the built-in battery gets weaker, the circuit has to be adjusted to yield accurate results. If you're using a digital meter, there's nothing to zero.

Now, with the circuit power shut off, attach the two meter probes to the terminals on the back of the switch. When the switch is closed (turned on),

Digital multimeter being used for continuity testing of a switch. The meter reads zero because the switch is closed (turned on).

Digital multimeter being used for continuity testing of a switch. In this photo, the meter reads overload (or infinity) because the switch is open (turned off).

the resistance should drop down very close to the zero ohms end of the scale. When it's opened (turned off), it should move to the opposite end of the dial. This is sometimes marked with the symbol for infinity (∞).

Digital meters are a bit different and they're easier to use. With the circuit power shut off, set the meter to the ohms function and hook up the probes to the wire or device you're checking for continuity. When there's continuity the display will show the resistance, which should be a low value (a few ohms perhaps). When there's no continuity the display will read "OL" (overload)—or something like that—depending on your particular meter.

If the resistance of the switch or magnetic breaker doesn't drop to near zero ohms when you turn it on, it's no good. This is the essence of continuity measurements. You can measure the continuity of a piece of wire, a fuse, or a lamp (the resistance of any of these should be just a few ohms).

Voltage Measurements

Unlike continuity measurements, voltage measurements are made with the circuit powered up. With an analog meter, first select the correct range of DC volts. For measurements in a 12-volt system, you have to pick the lowest range that exceeds twelve volts. For example, if your choices are 0 to 5 volts, 0 to 50 volts, and 0 to 500 volts DC, you should pick the 50-volt scale. On some meters the choices are 0 to 1.5 volts, 0 to 15 volts, 0 to 150 volts, etc. In that case, select the 15-volt scale. By picking the lowest range, you get the best accuracy. You could use a 150-volt (or 500-volt) scale, but the needle would just barely move when you measured 12 volts.

Most digital meters are "auto-ranging." You just select DC volts and the meter senses the voltage present in the circuit and automatically chooses the lowest range that will work. This ensures maximum accuracy.

There's no need to zero the meter or anything like that when measuring voltage. You might start to familiarize yourself with voltage measurements by putting the probes on the terminals of the battery. You should get a reading somewhere between 12.2 and 12.8 volts. The lower number indicates a battery that's nearly dead and the upper end of the scale indicates a full charge.

Open Circuits

The voltmeter function of your multimeter is handy for finding open circuits. Here's how to do it.

As you know, an open circuit is a break in the continuous path for current that makes a circuit work. With your meter set to an appropriate DC voltage range, connect its negative lead to the negative terminal of the battery or to a known good ground point (such as a clean ground attachment on the engine block). You can use a jumper lead if you're working in a part of the boat that's not handy to either of these.

Now, use the positive lead of your meter to check the battery side of the switch or magnetic breaker that controls that circuit. If you measure full battery voltage, the wiring between the battery and the switch is good.

Turn on the switch and put your probe on the other (downstream) terminal of the switch. If you don't measure battery voltage here, the switch is an open circuit (in other words, no good).

If you did get a reading of full battery voltage, the switch gets a clean bill of health. Leave it in the "on" position and continue to probe along the circuit path toward the load or device that's not working. Check each connection point. As long as you keep getting readings at or near full battery voltage, the part of the circuit between you and the battery is in good order.

If you get to a point in the supply side of the circuit when you don't measure battery voltage, the open circuit is between that point and the last point you tested that did give you a battery voltage reading.

This technique will tell you if there's an open circuit in the supply side of a circuit. But what about diagnosing a fault in the ground side? I usually use the ohmmeter function of my multimeter to sniff these out. Here's how.

As with all ohmmeter testing, start by shutting off power to the circuit; that is, turn the battery switch to the "off" position. (Don't ever do this with the engine running or you'll blow the diodes in your alternator's rectifier assembly—an expensive mistake.)

If you have an analog meter, touch the probes together and zero the ohms reading. Then attach one probe to the negative terminal of the battery or a known good grounding point, such as a clean spot on the engine block. Next, connect the other meter lead to the negative bus bar. The meter should read somewhere near zero ohms. If it doesn't, then the fault is between the negative terminal of the battery and the bus bar. If that's the case, none of the equipment that is connected to ground through that bus bar should be working.

Assuming you got a near-zero ohms reading at the bus bar, it's time to follow the negative side of the circuit toward the load. Each time you get to a connection point, take a reading (while keeping the first meter lead attached to the same ground). When you reach a point in the ground side of the circuit that doesn't give you a meter reading of near zero ohms, the open circuit is between that point and the last point that checked out OK.

In some cases, you might get a reading that's neither fish nor fowl. It isn't a low ohms reading that indicates a good ground path, but it isn't an open circuit either. Instead, it's somewhere in between. This almost always points to a poorly made connection in the circuit. There might be a ground lead connection with a corroded or loose attachment. When you get this reading—same as with an open circuit—it's time to find and correct the problem.

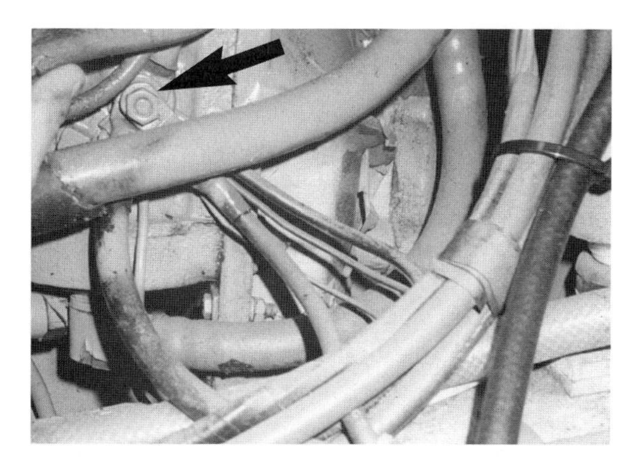

Ground wire attachment on an engine block. Periodically disassemble, clean, and seal these connections with Liquid Electric Tape.

Ground path connections that are made through the engine block can give troubles if the metal connection point is corroded, the bolt that secures the connection is loose, corroded, or missing its toothed washer, or the connector itself is "looking for better weather." Marginal ground problems provide a good opportunity to use the "wiggle test" I talked about earlier. If the circuit intermittently springs to life when you wiggle a connection in the ground circuit, that's where the problem lies.

Inspect for each of these potential problems in turn and, when you find the source of the flaky ground path, replace the connector or clean up the connection as needed to make things right. Finally, power things up and check the circuit for function. If things are still not right, shut off the power and continue with your continuity checking.

Short Circuits

If the problem with your boat's wiring is a short circuit, as evidenced by fuses blowing or circuit breakers popping, here's how to use the voltmeter function of your multimeter to find the short.

1. Disconnect the load from the circuit. For example, if you're looking for a short in a lamp circuit, remove the bulb.
2. Remove the fuse that protects the circuit under test or, if your boat has magnetic breakers, disconnect the two leads on the breaker.
3. Turn on the battery switch and, if your boat has conventional switches and fuses (as opposed to magnetic breakers), turn on the relevant switch for the circuit with the short circuit.
4. With the meter set to the appropriate DC-volts range, connect the probes to the two terminals to the wires leading to the switch or the fuse.

If you measure battery voltage when you do this, the wiring leading to the load has a short circuit. If you don't measure any voltage when you perform this test, restore the connections at the load and the fuse (or magnetic breaker). Turn on the power. If the fuse or breaker blows again, the short circuit is most likely in the load, not the wiring.

Troubleshooting by Substitution

There's another way to troubleshoot that doesn't require any testing whatsoever. It's called substitution. If you suspect a wiring device, replace it with a known good replacement. If the problem goes away, the old component was no good. If it remains, then the problem was not in the component you exchanged.

Substitution should be done with care, though. You can damage certain types of electrical devices by installing them in a circuit that has a problem. This is especially true of engine electrical and electronic components. But this technique does have its uses. For example, if your boat has two of anything, you can swap one article for the other to see if the problem goes away.

Current Measurements

There's one more way to use your multimeter—you can measure current with it. But to do so, all of the

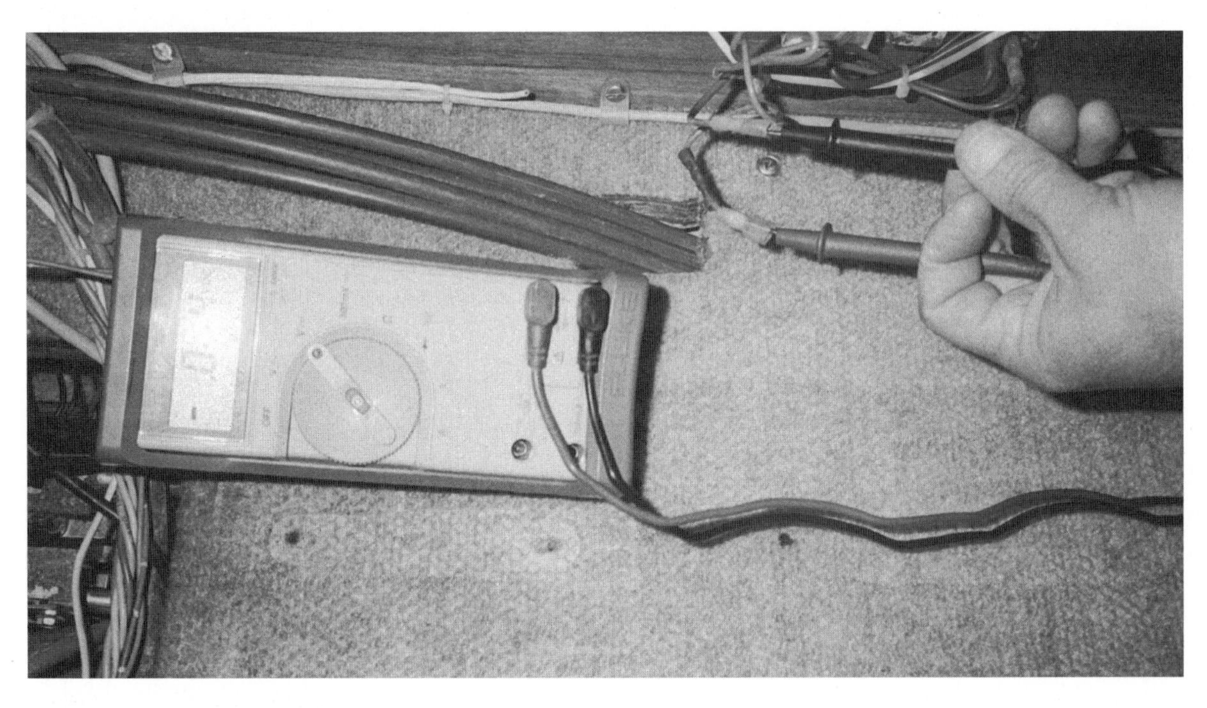

Digital multimeter testing for a short circuit.

electricity in a circuit has to flow directly through the meter. To do this you break the circuit and connect your meter's probes to both ends of the break.

The fact that the current has to flow through the meter introduces some limitations. Because a multimeter is a light-duty device, you can't measure the flow in a high-current circuit. For example, if you were to unhook the fat cable that supplies current to your engine's starter motor and connect it through your meter and turn the key, you'd immediately turn your meter into a crispy critter. (Actually, most better-quality meters have fuse-protected current measuring circuitry. As long as your meter was so equipped, all you would do is blow its fuse.)

But there's no point in trying to measure this type of current; it's way beyond the range of a multimeter's capabilities. Most inexpensive multimeters can measure 1 ampere or less of current. Better-quality meters have a current shunt built into their circuitry that lets them measure somewhat larger currents—something on the order of 10 amps or so. Considering that a typical starter motor draws at least 150 amps, that's still not very much.

If you do need to measure large current flows, accessories for high-quality meters make this possible. They usually take the form of an inductive pickup loop that surrounds the wire that carries current—the so-called amp-clamp. When these are used, the circuit isn't broken, so the large currents being measured don't actually flow through the meter.

There is one thing that the ammeter function on your multimeter is very handy for, though—measuring leakage current. In the section on electrolysis at the end of this chapter we'll cover this dreaded underwater-hardware eater and discuss how you can use your meter to sniff out the source of the problem.

AC Wiring Systems

Remember earlier when I said it would be hard to get a life-threatening shock from your boat's 12-volt electrical system? Well, as you know, most boats also have another electrical system: the shore-power system, which carries 110 volts of alternating current (AC). Unlike the 12-volt system, the power in this AC system will kill you in a jiffy.

Few boatowners have occasion to mess around with AC power, which is a good thing. If you're not a qualified electrician, you should leave additions and repairs to this system to qualified people.

There is, however, one bit of troubleshooting that you can (and should) do—get hold of an AC circuit checker and use it whenever you plug your boat into a shore-power circuit at a dock.

This is a small, solid-state electronic device that has three light-emitting diodes (LEDs) on its top. Its use is the essence of simplicity. Simply plug it into the receptacle on the dock, note which of the LEDs light up on top, and consult the legend printed on the tester to determine whether there are any faults in the wiring.

I think it's a good idea to plug it in whenever you're hooking up to a shore-power system in a marina other than your own. If the system you're connecting to has reversed wires, an open ground, or any of a host of other wiring faults, this circuit checker will tell you about it before you put the folks on board your boat at risk.

I don't trust any dock wiring. I've seen almost every kind of problem in the book. In fact, the first electrical box you should check out is the one at your boat's home slip. If the checker detects a wiring

AC circuit checker being used to check an AC outlet for proper wiring connections.

fault, don't plug in your shore-power cord. Instead, notify the dockmaster or yard manager and get the problem fixed or have your boat moved to another slip. (Then check that plug.)

A miswired electrical supply at a dock can be hazardous. It can also be destructive. Certain types of wiring faults can introduce stray current into your boat's wiring and hardware. This can cause rapid and very destructive galvanic corrosion of the sort that will consume a full complement of zinc anodes in short order, then set to work on the underwater hardware.

These checkers sell for around $30. Two popular brands are Hubbell and Marinco, which also happen to be the two biggest names in shore-power cords and receptacles for marine use.

ELECTROLYSIS

Electrolysis is widely misunderstood. It's always present to some degree, but it doesn't have to be destructive.

Electrolysis, which is more accurately termed galvanic corrosion, is a small electrical current that's generated whenever dissimilar metals are electrically connected and immersed in an electrolyte, such as salt water. Even fresh water has enough dissolved minerals in it to allow galvanic corrosion to occur.

Have you ever seen those kits that power a small digital clock with a potato battery? They work by connecting the digital clock (which will happily operate with very little current) to a pair of metal electrodes, such as copper and zinc. The electrodes are stuck in a fresh potato (the electrolyte) and, bingo! The clock works. The current flow that powers the clock is caused by galvanic corrosion.

Nobility

Metals can be arranged on a table called a galvanic series.

Whenever a metal is immersed in water, it has an electrical potential. When two different metals are immersed in the same bath of water and electrically connected, the less noble metal becomes an anode;

GALVANIC SERIES OF METALS IN SEA WATER
Metals and Alloys
(Anodic or Least Noble—Active)
Magnesium and Magnesium Alloys
Zinc
Galvanized Steel or Galvanized Wrought Iron
Aluminum Alloys
Cadmium
Mild Steel
Wrought Iron
Cast Iron
13% Chromium Stainless Steel, Type 410 (active in still water)
18-8 Stainless Steel, Type 304 (active in still water)
Ni-Resist
18-8, 3% Mo Stainless Steel, Type 316 (active in still water)
78% Ni—14.5% Cr—6% Fe (Inconel) (active in still water)
Aluminum Bronze (92% Cu—8% Al)
Naval Brass (60% Cu—39% Zn)
Yellow Brass (65% Cu—35 Zn)
Red Brass (85% Cu—15% Zn)
Muntz Metal (60% Cu—40% Zn)
Tin
Copper
50-50 Lead—Tin Solder
Admiralty Brass (71% Cu 28% Zn 1% Sn)
Aluminum Brass (76% Cu 22% Zn 2% Al)
Manganese Bronze (58.5% Cu 39% Zn 1% Sn 1% Fe 0.3 MN)
Silicon Bronze (96% Cu Max. 0.80 Fe, 1.50 Zn, 2.00 Si, 0.75 MN, 1.60 Sn)
Bronze-Composition G (88% Cu—2% Zn—10% Zn)
Bronze-Comp. M (88% Cu—3% Zn—6.5% Sn—1.5% Pb)
13% Chromium Stainless Steel, Type 401 (passive)
90% Cu—10% Ni
75% Cu—20% Ni—5% Zn
Lead
70% Cu—30% Ni
78% Ni—13.5% Cr—6% Fe (Inconel) (passive)
Nickel 200
18-8, Stainless Steel, Type 304 (passive)
70% Ni—30% Cu Monel 400, K-500
18-8, 3% Mo Stainless Steel, Type 316 (passive)
Titanium C
Hastelloy
Platinum
Graphite
(Cathodic or Most Noble—Passive)

CHART COURTESY OF THE AMERICAN BOAT AND YACHT COUNCIL (ABYC) the nobler one becomes a cathode. Even if no stray current is introduced into the equation, the anodic metal will be eaten away.

We use this phenomenon to our benefit by clamping sacrificial zinc anodes to our boat's underwater hardware (zinc is extremely low on the galvanic series). If the only current flow is caused by the various metals immersed in the water, the zinc will slowly erode over time. As it does, it is sacrificing itself to the galvanic corrosion to protect the more noble, or cathodic, metals immersed in the vicinity.

As soon as the boat is launched and the dissimilar metals are immersed, a small current begins to flow. The key here is that this current, which is called stray current, is small, hence manageable. Therefore, the zinc anode can provide adequate protection for the hardware because it erodes at a very slow rate. It might even last for years. If, at the end of the season, your boat's zinc anodes look almost as good as new, bully for you; your boat hasn't got a leakage current problem.

All of this gets real interesting (and destructive) on boats that introduce a lot of stray current into the surrounding water through their underwater hardware. Even a full complement of zincs won't provide much protection when the electrical leakage is quite pronounced. In that case, brand-new zinc can disappear like a tablet of Alka-Seltzer dropped into a glass of water. (Well, not quite that quickly, but certainly in a few hours.)

Once the zinc has been exhausted, the next metal up on the galvanic series that is electrically connected will start to be sacrificed. If that metal happens to be your boat's bronze propeller or through-hull fittings, look out.

Since you don't inspect the condition of your boat's zincs during the season, you might not know you have a problem until quite a bit of damage has been done. (In fact, if a through-hull fitting is attacked, you might not find out about the problem until your boat sinks.)

Most boats have current leakage to some degree between these two extremes. You don't have to be a passive party to these goings on. You can take an active role by inspecting your boat's wiring and keeping it clean, well connected, dry, and out of the bilges. And, there is a way to find out how much current is leaking into the water surrounding your boat.

You'll need a sensitive ammeter for this job. A digital multimeter really comes in handy here, although even a cheap analog one will have some value. Remember that, when we use an ammeter, we set it up so that the current being measured flows through the meter.

As an example, let's consider measuring the stray current flowing through a bronze through-hull fitting, since it's easy to isolate it from the boat's wiring.

Your boat probably has a network of bonding wires running to each of the pieces of immersed hardware to keep them at the same electrical potential. You have to disconnect this wire to measure leakage current. To do so, remove the bonding wire from the through-hull fitting. Then, with your meter set to its most sensitive amps scale, connect one probe to the wire end (clean it first) and the other one to the through-hull fitting (scratch this clean also to ensure a good electrical connection). Chances are you will measure little or no current flow.

On an inboard-powered boat, you can perform this same test with the running gear (propeller and shaft). Again, you've got to break the circuit to insert your meter and measure the current. Do so by unbolting the two halves of the propshaft coupling and pushing them apart so the electrical connection between them is broken. If your boat has a shaft wiper in its bonding system, you'll also have to lift it away from the shaft so it doesn't provide an alternate path for stray current.

Now your meter can be connected across the open part of the circuit—the coupling—to allow you to detect any stray current. Put one probe on each half of the coupling and make sure they're on clean spots.

When you make the measurements here and at the through-hull fitting, you can expect some current flow, though it will be negligible—something on the order of a few milliamps. (A milliamp is a thousandth of an ampere.) If, on the other hand, you get a reading of more than 20 or 30 milliamps, you'd better look further in your boat's wiring and systems for a fault.

Probable Causes

This is where things get a little snaky. There are a lot of potential causes for stray current leakage on a boat.

- Most often, poor wiring connections are part of the problem. The connections might be in good enough shape to keep the equipment working, but if they're just a bit dirty, corroded, or damp, they're likely to give you trouble. If you practice good housekeeping in your boat's wiring system, and all the connections are clean, shiny, bright, and well sealed against moisture, you've gone a long way toward preventing stray current problems.
- Ground circuits must have heavy enough conductors to provide a solid return path to the battery. Remember our discussion of the ampacity chart at the beginning of this chapter? If you add additional loads to your boat's wiring system and don't upgrade the ground path with a larger conductor (or additional ones), you will be setting the stage for stray current problems.
- Electricity, like water, takes the path of least resistance. If the electricity in your boat's accessory wiring can find an easier path back to the negative terminal of the battery, it will take that path, believe me. That's stray current.

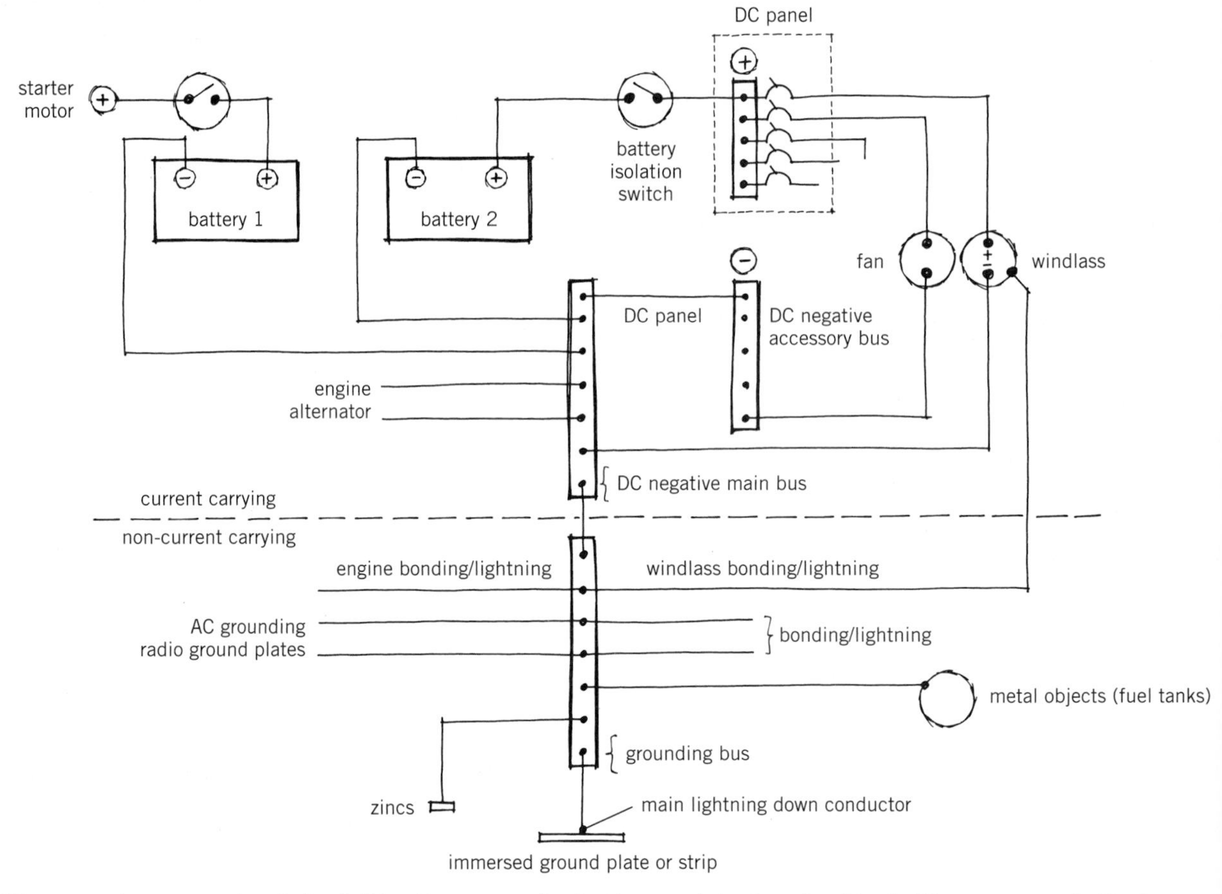

Diagrammatic representation of a boat's DC wiring system, showing the ground circuits and positive feed lines to some typical loads.

• Using electrical equipment that isn't specifically made for use on a boat is another big source of stray current. The best example of this is bringing a shoreside battery charger or sump pump onto your boat to charge the batteries or pump the bilges. (If you have to use this kind of battery charger, disconnect the battery before you charge it and then get the charger off the boat as soon as the battery has been brought up to a full charge.) Marine battery chargers contain isolation transformers to keep the boat's electrical system separated from the shore-power supply.

• Dock wiring or defective shore-power wiring in your boat is another frequent cause of stray current problems. In fact, you can even have problems if the boat in the next slip is improperly wired (or has an automotive battery charger humming away in its bilge).

• The neutral leg of your boat's shore-power system should not be connected to the DC ground in your boat's wiring. If it is and you hook up to a shore-power outlet with reversed polarity, your boat's AC equipment will work fine, but you will have stray current in spades. Instead, hook it up to the shore-side electrical network, which provides its own path to ground.

As you can see, poor electrical housekeeping isn't just messy. It can cause electrolysis and damaged hardware. If the connections and wiring don't look so good down in the bilges of your boat, get after them now, before your boat starts to suffer the ravages of electrolysis.

Also, keep tabs on your boat's zincs. If you can't haul your boat out for a midseason check, at least hop in the water with a mask and flippers periodically and make sure the sacrificial anodes are still intact and doing their important job.

Wiring needn't be a mystery. Like most boat systems, when it comes to wiring, an ounce of prevention is worth a pound of cure. The basic goal is to keep moisture away from the easily corroded metal conductors. The only way to stay on top of this before corrosion overwhelms your boat's wiring system is with inspections, heat-shrink tubing, Liquid Electric Tape, and Teflon grease on the O-ring seals of the running lights. In short, your boat's wiring system needs regular attention.

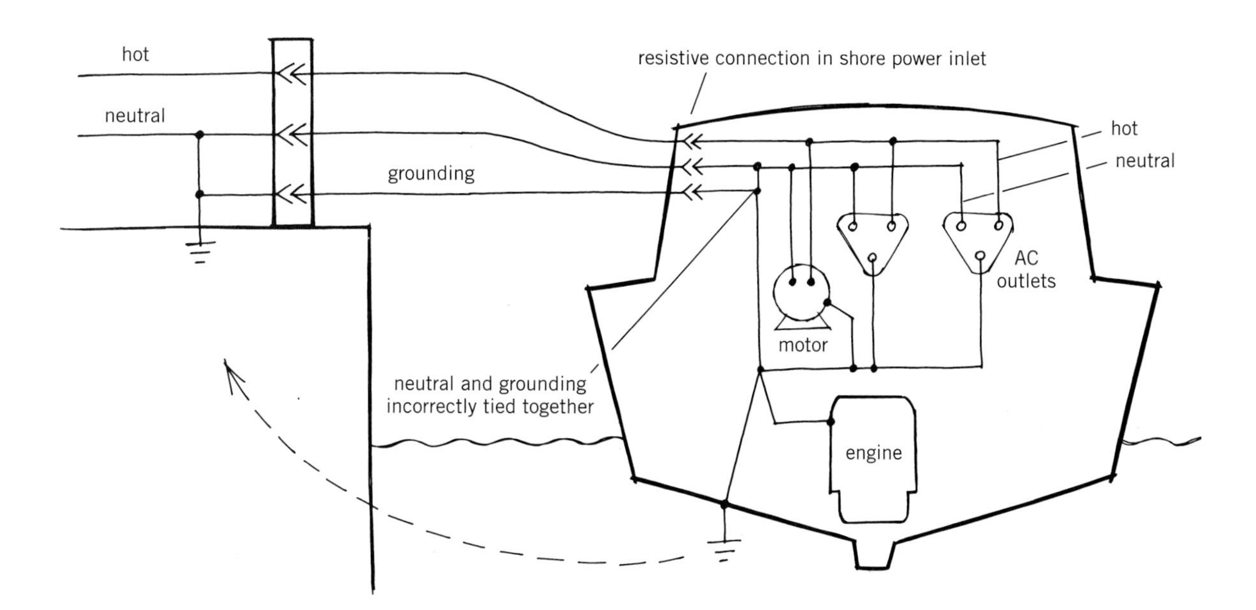

Boat wiring diagram, showing an improper common ground connection between the AC and DC wiring systems.

Questions and Answers

Question: I have a 25-foot cruiser. Recently, I was washing the boat, using a wood brush with bristles. The hose was attached to a faucet on the dock and my shore-power cord was plugged in and operating properly. I temporarily put the hose nozzle on a cleat and, while the hose was hanging, it touched the shore-power cord (which was not in the water). I knelt down, put my right hand against the boat, and scrubbed the waterline with my left hand and the brush. I was touching neither the cord nor the hose, but when the brush dipped into the water I got a shock. This happened twice.

I tried to duplicate this while the yard mechanic watched, but it didn't happen again. The mechanic suggested changing my shore-power cord. Do you think I should, or could the problem be the boat or the dock? Also, if I had been using my stainless steel brush, would the shock have been stronger?

Answer: If your boat's AC wiring system has not been modified or tampered with, and the shore-power cord and plug ends have not been crushed or damaged, I'd usually suspect the dock wiring first. But your boat's problem sounds more offbeat and I'm sure you wouldn't have written if the shore-power cord were cut or damaged.

Was your boat in her home slip, or did this happen while cruising away from home? If the latter, your boat might have been in a slip with improper wiring.

If you were docked at your home slip, you could eliminate any question about the wiring by using a Hubbell 5200 circuit checker. These are most useful when cruising for pretesting outlets before plugging in.

Have you or any of your guests ever gotten shocks before? I gather yours was just a "tingle" since you were willing to do it again for the mechanic. (Either that or you didn't turn out quite as clever as your mom had hoped you would.)

I ask this because your problem seems more like a ground fault between the boat's inlet receptacle and the distribution panel. With this scenario you might have had a long-term leak of current to ground—and all sorts of strange and potentially dangerous things can happen.

Here's how I think you got your shock: When the hose was draped over the cleat, it might have provided the leaking current with a much less restrictive way to drain to ground. (Like water, electricity follows the path of least resistance.) You grabbed the hose, which was carrying current, and got a shock. If this is correct, the fact that the hose touched the cord is irrelevant. If I've guessed right, you've got a serious problem that calls for the services of a professional who is conversant in AC wiring on boats.

If I'm wrong and your dock is improperly wired, you'll need that Hubbell outlet checker. (Marinco also makes a similar device.) The crew at your marina probably has one and should be willing to lend it to you or use it themselves to test your dock's outlet.

Start by checking the outlet that your shore-power cord draws its power from. If you need an adaptor, use a known good one. If the tester indicates a fault, tell your marina manager what the problem is; it's theirs to fix, not yours.

If the outlet checks out OK, plug the cord in and turn on your boat's shore-power system. Test the outlets in the boat with the checker and see if a wiring fault is indicated. (Troubleshooting is usually done by isolating the problem step by step until it's been narrowed down to a specific link in the chain or part of the circuit.)

If you have any doubt about what the problem is and whether or not you've corrected it, you'd be well advised to unplug your boat from shore power whenever you wash it. This is not really the hot setup; wiring difficulties don't heal themselves and your boat is less than safe with suspect wiring. Therefore, I wouldn't use the shore-power system until I was sure that I'd found and corrected the problem.

Question: I own a 1977 Carver 2896 Mariner with twin Ford 302 engines. When the steering wheel is turned back and forth from the 12 o'clock position to about 3 o'clock, the VHF radio, depth-finder, and instrument lights blink. They all seem to short out. The radio reverts back to channel 16 and the depth-finder restarts. The boat doesn't have power steering and the steering cable is sheathed in plastic. Any ideas?

Answer: Your boat has one very weird problem. You don't mention whether you've got sterndrive or inboard engines; Carver built that model both ways. If it has inboard power, I'd look for a problem near the rudders. It could be that one of the rudder quadrants is rubbing or tugging on a battery cable, which could explain why the problem occurs between the 12 o'clock and 3 o'clock positions.

Whether sterndrive or inboard-powered, another possibility is that the steering cable is moving under the helm panel and perhaps tugging on the wiring.

But I suspect a different scenario. Since the three faltering devices are probably not all fed through one circuit, it's more likely that you have an intermittent open circuit rather than an intermittent short circuit. You might have a problem with the ground wiring. It's easy to check it out—simply add a substitute ground wire. Run it from the common ground section of the helm panel wiring to the negative terminal of the battery. Then try the wheel turning operation again.

If the problem is solved by this additional wire, look for a loose connection someplace in the original ground wiring; most likely behind the instrument panel or the master electrical panel. You can, if you wish, simply install the new ground lead permanently by securing it to the existing wiring harness, though the battery end should not go all the way to the battery. Instead, connect it to the negative bus bar at your boat's main panel.

Question: Everyone seems to know about cranking batteries and deep-cycle batteries, but I wonder if you know anything about "combination cranking/deep-cycle batteries." That's how the battery that came with my 19-foot sterndrive runabout is labeled. Can you comment on these "dual-purpose" batteries and their suitability for a typically equipped runabout (with a stereo, depth-finder, etc.)?

Answer: A combination battery is occasionally used in small boats to save the cost of having two batteries (one starting battery and one deep cycle). Its rating allows it to pass muster as a starting battery with a CCA (cold cranking amperage) designation, yet its chemistry and construction lets it function in a deep-cycle application as well.

This is somewhat of a compromise, as one battery can't be as good as the best of each individual type. The only practical effect that you will probably notice is that this battery will lose more water than a starting battery would in the same application. No big deal as long as you regularly check the electrolyte (acid) level and top it off, as you should anyway.

Question: I bought a used 23-foot Sea Ox with a 200 hp Mercury outboard last summer. Recently, I installed a cockpit light. After I had run the hot wire to the switch on the dash, I realized there was no ground wire. The light gets grounded to whatever you mounted it to. The easy way to get around this was to ground my boat's hardtop. Does this cause any problems?

Answer: Most likely your boat's hardtop is already grounded. But this is no way to provide a return path for current in an electrical circuit on a boat. The one-wire system works with cars because they're made of tightly fastened together pieces of conductive metal. But on boats, ground paths aren't so easy to make and maintain.

Except for engine electrical equipment, the wiring for marine circuits must have two wires: a "hot," or feed wire and a ground lead running back to the negative terminal block or bus bar (which is electrically the same as the negative terminal of the battery). Two-conductor cables make this requirement easy to comply with.

Question: I would like to dedicate a battery to my boat's 12-volt cabin system. However, I can only fit one alternator to the engine. Is it possible to charge a bank of batteries for the engine separate from a bank for the cabin electrics with one alternator?

Answer: Sure it is. In fact, you've got two options—

stick shift and automatic, if you will—to accomplish what you want.

The stick shift approach is to install a battery switch and take charge of the system yourself. In your mind you will dedicate one of the batteries as a starting battery. Let's call that battery #1. After shutting down the engine at the end of a day's cruising, you will change the battery switch to battery #2 (the house battery). No matter how much you draw down the 12-volt system by running cabin lights and stereo, battery #1 will remain unaffected.

Before starting the engine for the next day's cruise, switch back to the "both" position. When you do, your single alternator will charge both batteries, as you wished.

Remember that "both" position well—it's your emergency parallel switch. If the starting battery is ever wanting for current, when you move the battery switch to "both" and put the batteries in a parallel circuit, you combine their amperage potentials.

For the automatic transmission equivalent, just install an automatic battery isolator such as Guest's 2401A. The isolator will automatically ensure that whichever battery needs a charge the most will get it first.

6 PLUMBING AND PUMPS

Plumbing Overview

Flare fittings, inverted flares, pipe connections, hose barbs—there's no doubt about it, plumbing can be confusing. But when it comes to boats, it's important. If you have plumbing problems you don't merely wind up with water in the basement (well, actually, you do). But the consequences on a boat can be much more serious than they are at home. Sinking comes to mind.

Your boat's plumbing doesn't have to be a confusing forest of hoses and fittings—the systems are really pretty simple. This chapter will demystify the subject, give you a handle on how all the pieces work, and let you know what you can do and what you can't.

Types of Plumbing Connections

The first step in understanding your boat's plumbing is learning to recognize the various types of fittings and connections that are used in its systems. There are four main types of plumbing connections—hose barb, pipe fittings, flare fittings, and inverted flares—and you need to know why a particular type of connection is used for each application. It's also important to note that there are hybrid fittings that adapt from one type of connection to another. As an example, the end of your boat's flexible fuel line leading from the tank most likely terminates in an adaptor fitting with a hose barb at one end and a pipe-thread or flare fitting at the other to allow it to connect to the primary fuel filter.

Hose-Barb Fittings

These are probably the most popular style of fittings you'll find in boat plumbing. They're used in low-pressure applications such as sink drains and the connections in heads and holding tank systems. Hose-barb fittings are also the easiest type of connection to make. Ordinarily, there's no sealing compound needed. Simply slide an all stainless steel hose clamp onto the hose, push the hose onto the male portion of the fitting that's sized to mate with it,

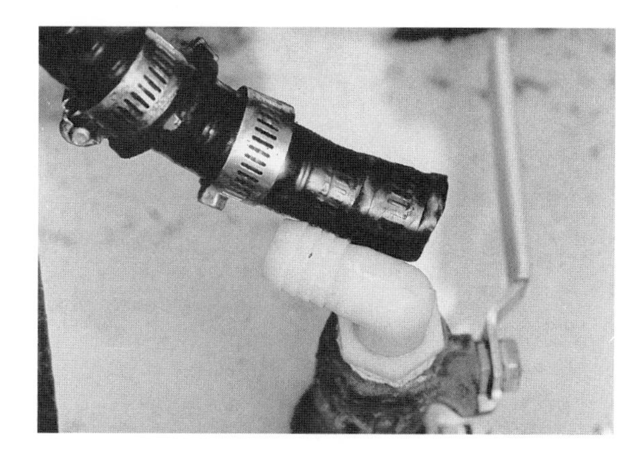

Raw-water inlet showing barb-type hose connection. The shut-off valve here is a ball valve; note that, since this hose is below the boat's waterline, the hose clamps are doubled.

place the hose clamp over the right part of the end of the hose, and tighten it securely.

For hoses that run below the waterline anywhere along their length, it's necessary to use two hose clamps when making the connection. Here are some specific pointers to remember for making these connections.

- It's important to cut the end of the hose squarely because there isn't much room for the hose to clamp on to the fitting. If you make a sloping or jagged cut you'll compromise the integrity of your finished connection.
- When you have to use two hose clamps, stagger their worm drives opposite one another. You'll even up the clamping action and improve the reliability of the finished connection.
- You don't need to use any pipe dope or sealing compound on these fittings. The tight seal is furnished by the tightening action of the hose clamp, which causes the hose to conform to the male fitting inserted into it. If the joints leak after tightening, don't try to correct them with some kind of goo. The problem is that the hose and fitting don't fit each other properly. The only way to correct this is to get the right size hose for the fitting it must mate to. You will know it's right if the hose is a little difficult to push on to the fitting.
- Use the right type of hose for the application. There are several different types. These include fuel hose, which has a two-minute fire rating; wire-reinforced hose, which is rugged and won't collapse when subjected to suction; sanitation hose, which blocks sewage odors from escaping; and water hose, which works, doesn't impart a bad taste, and is inexpensive.
- If the male fitting that goes into the end of the hose is barbed (has annular ridges), make sure the hose clamp is placed so it tightens over the barbs. Some fittings have a single ridge, near the end. To get a proper connection with one of these, the hose clamp must tighten on to the fitting inboard of this ridge—not directly on top of it. (By "inboard," I mean toward the fitting body from the ridge.)
- Use worm-drive hose clamps for most of these connections. The only exceptions are certain engine applications, especially on outboard motors, where other types might be specified to prevent loosening caused by engine vibration. In those cases you will often find spring clamps or special ratcheting ones made of tough plastic. When those kinds of clamps need to be replaced, make sure you replace them with identical clamps. (You can get these from your outboard motor dealer's parts department.)
- Choose the right size hose clamp for the end of the hose. Using one that's too big leaves a long tail that can gash your leg or hand when you're working in the vicinity. Larger clamps are also wider than small ones; if you use an oversized one, the band of the clamp might be too wide to allow proper seating of the hose on the fitting's barbs.

Pipe Fittings

Pipe fittings are threaded connections. The distinguishing characteristic of a pipe-thread connection is that the thread is tapered. That is, on a male pipe-thread fitting the diameter gets smaller out toward the end. The female pipe-thread fitting has a matching taper. When you tighten one of these connections it gets progressively tighter as you go.

Pipe sizes don't make much sense because they're based on the inside diameter of the smallest fitting. For example, a fitting that's described as ¼-inch pipe doesn't measure a quarter of an inch. The male fitting has an outside diameter that's considerably larger than ¼ inch. If you're going to the store to buy fittings, take the part that you're connecting to if you're not sure how to describe it.

There are a host of different kinds of pipe-thread fittings and they have names that you're probably not familiar with. For example, a short length of pipe with male pipe threads on both ends is called a *nipple*. If it's the shortest length available, it's called a *close nipple*. A fitting with female pipe threads at both ends is known as a *coupling*. A fitting that goes around a 90° bend is called an *elbow* if both ends are of the same gender. If one end is male and the other end is female, it's called a *street ell*. Weird, eh? The best bet is to bring what you need to connect to the parts counter with you and let the experts tell you what you need.

The hallmark of good plumbing is to use as few fittings as possible. For a complicated connection, there are often a few different sets of fittings that will do the job. If you use as few fittings as you can, you cut down on the likelihood of leaks and you won't wind up with a pound and a half of fittings weighing down your boat's plumbing. (It's cheaper, too.)

Materials are important. For boat plumbing, use brass fittings. If you are at a plumbing supply counter and they tell you they've got what you need but only in steel, go to another supply house. Your best bet for buying fittings is to buy them from the mechanic's shop at a well-stocked, busy boatyard. They are inclined to have the types of fittings you need and to stock them in the only suitable material—brass.

Here are some tips for making pipe-threaded connections.

Before you make up a connection, put a smear of pipe dope or thread-sealing compound on the threads of the male component. Several kinds of dope or compound are available. The old reliable is Permatex No. 2, but it's not suitable for connections in your boat's drinking water system (that system has few pipe-threaded connections anyway). Because Permatex is a pain to get off your hands, I like to use Teflon thread paste for all pipe-thread connections. It's easy to clean up and easy to use. Since it contains Teflon, it actually lubricates the connection, which makes it easier to tighten it securely. Some people like to use Teflon tape for sealing pipe-thread connections. I'm not one of them. It's a pain to work with and if a small piece of it gets into the plumbing it can mess things up, especially in engine fuel-system plumbing.

Securely tighten pipe-thread connections. The tapered threads in these fittings don't make an effective seal unless the fittings are really tight. After you've applied the pipe dope, start by winding the fittings together by hand to make sure they're not cross-threaded. When they're hand-tight, put wrenches on the connection and make it as tight as you can. Use a little judgment here; if you're tightening a tiny pair of fittings with a big wrench, you will have enough torque to overdo things and ruin the fittings. But remember—they do have to be tight to make an effective seal.

Flare Fittings

Like pipe fittings, flare fittings are also threaded. However, the thread on a flare fitting isn't tapered—it's straight, like the thread on a machine screw. As a consequence, tightening these together is different from tightening pipe-threaded fittings together. When you make up a connection with flare fittings, spin them together hand-tight and then just snug them up a bit with your wrenches. Don't wind them together. Why? Because flare fittings have a pair of precisely machined surfaces that make the gas-tight seal when they're joined. If you have a gas grill at your house, you're already familiar with flare fittings—they're used at the end of the hose where it connects to the valve on top of the propane tank. Perhaps you've noticed the male flare at the end of the hose and the matching female seat in the valve.

The strength of the flare fitting—that precisely machined surface—is also its Achilles heel. If the flare gets nicked or scratched, or has a piece of sand or dirt on it when you assemble the fittings, it will leak. No matter how much you tighten it, you won't stop the leak. Only a *new pair of fittings* will correct this problem. Here are some flare fitting pointers.

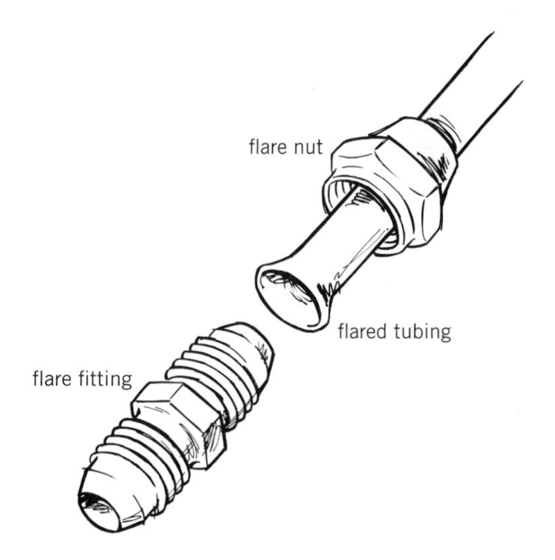

Exploded view of a conventional flare connection. Any debris or damage to the male or female portions of the mating flare surface will cause a leak.

• Don't use any pipe dope or thread-sealing compound on the threads of a flare fitting. Since the threaded parts don't make the seal it won't do any good.
• Don't overtighten these fittings. Spin them together by hand so you know they're not cross-threaded, then snug them up a little bit with your wrenches so the connection won't vibrate loose. If you overtighten them, you can stretch the threads or damage the flares, which ruins the fittings.
• When you buy fittings, make sure you get ones with the correct angle on the flares. They're available in 45- and 37-degree (on hydraulic fittings) flares. These *can't* be mixed and matched. Most fittings on boats have the 45-degree flare angle, but certain hydraulic components might have the other type. If you have any question about which ones you're dealing with, bring the device you're connecting with you when you buy the fittings.

Inverted Flare Fittings

As the name suggests, these are flare fittings with a twist. Think of them as the gender-bending cousins of flare fittings. The male fitting has the female flare seat inside and the female fitting that mates with it has a male flare inside. The only place you're likely to come across inverted flare fittings in your boat is in the fuel system—specifically, the hard steel line that connects the fuel pump and the carburetor.

I don't know why they even invented these things (maybe just to confuse us). Since they're not widely used, you're not likely to ever need to buy them and, unless you take that hard line off the carburetor, you'll probably never even see the inside of one.

All the rules and tips for the flare fittings apply equally to inverted flares.

Pumps, Pumps, Pumps

Modern powerboats are loaded with pumps. If you count the ones inside your boat's engine, it's likely that you'll find at least ten. There are diaphragm pumps in the freshwater system, centrifugal bilge pumps, flexible impeller pumps for the deck washdown, and—if your engine is freshwater-cooled—the engine's coolant circulating system.

Most of these pumps can't be serviced. When they wear out they're designed to be thrown away and replaced with new ones. The main exception to this rule are the flexible impeller pumps. They can be serviced and overhauled when they're damaged or worn.

Servicing Flexible Impeller Pumps

Most boats have one or more flexible impeller pumps. These give pretty good service but they do need to be checked from time to time. Typical applications include the raw-water coolant pump on freshwater-cooled engines, deck washdown pumps, and some types of macerator–transfer pumps in the head and holding tank system.

You should know where these pumps are and how to disassemble and service them. To work properly, flexible impeller pumps depend on a tight seal between the thin feathered edges of the rubber impeller blades and the inside of the pump housing.

When these pumps gobble up some seawater that's laden with sand or silt, the impeller, cover plate, cam, and pump body can be scored and damaged. Even in the absence of outright abuse—sand or mud—the impeller is a rubber part that is subject to wear and aging.

It's this aging that can cause headaches. If the pump goes more than a few seasons without being overhauled, the impeller can start shedding blades. If it's being used as a deck washdown pump, that's no big deal. But if it's your engine's circulating pump, the broken impeller blades have a habit of drifting along in the plumbing, lodging in inconvenient spots, and causing overheating. (Of course, an impeller with a blade or two missing will contribute to overheating as well.)

When you replace a damaged impeller, you must track down all the missing parts. In freshwater-cooled engines, the happy hunting grounds for these bits is usually the raw-water circuit of the heat exchanger. To avoid that unpleasant situation, it's best to simply overhaul and inspect all of your flexible impeller pumps each year at spring commissioning.

Modern impellers are made from pretty impressive rubber compounds but, just the same, over the winter lay-up season even the best of them can take a "set." When that happens they remain somewhat bent and the pump works with reduced efficiency.

The replacement parts don't cost much and overhauling one of these pumps is a piece of cake.

1. Remove the screws that secure the brass cover plate. Put them aside where you won't lose them and, for heaven's sake, don't drop any of them in the bilge. (Since they're made of brass, you won't be able to retrieve them with a magnet.) The cover plate might fall off in your hands or it might need a light sideways tap with a rubber mallet to dislodge it from its gasket. Whatever you do, don't pry the cover plate off with a screwdriver—you will damage the cover plate and the pump body. When the plate is off, remove the gasket and inspect the underside of the cover plate for scoring. If there is any, replace the plate because, even with a new impeller, the pump will never perform up to snuff.
2. With the cover plate off, the impeller is right there in front of you. Impellers are secured in several ways to the shafts that drive them. The simplest arrangement is no arrangement at all. The impeller is secured by virtue of the cover plate holding it in place. Happily, this is the system that's employed most often. Once the plate has been removed you simply grasp the impeller's hub with a pair of pliers and yank it out.
3. Inside the housing of these pumps is a cam. It has the important job of bending the impeller blades, which is what makes the pump work. If it has any scoring—even superficial—in its surface, replace it. The pump housing itself must also be smooth with no scoring. Don't cheat on this inspection. A new impeller will not work effectively if other parts of the pump are worn out or scored.

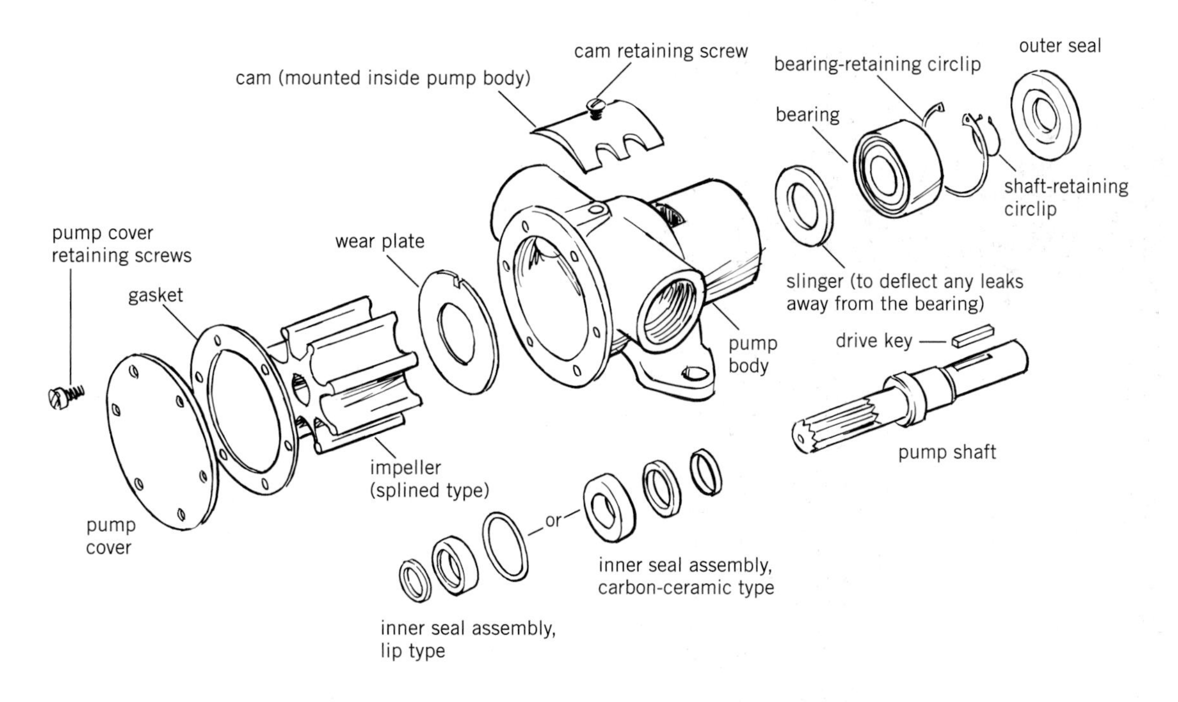

Exploded view of a typical flexible impeller pump. With seasonal maintenance these pumps usually serve reliably year after year.

4. When you reassemble the pump, don't forget to install the thin gasket or O-ring that goes under the cover plate. If your pump uses a gasket, retighten the cover plate screws again after an hour's operation.

Centrifugal Pumps

The typical modern bilge pump is an example of a centrifugal pump. This pump's strengths are its low cost, high capacity, and tolerance for running dry without harm. It works by rapidly spinning a vaned impeller inside a housing. The water is thrown to the outside of the inner housing by centrifugal force, hence the name. The outside case of the pump has a slotted grate to keep trash that's big enough to clog the pump outside in the bilge so it won't harm the pump.

Since they work by centrifugal force, not direct displacement, this type of pump can't create much pressure, nor can it lift the outlet flow of water very high. But none of this matters for bilge or shower pumping duty, which is why these pumps are usually used for these purposes.

Centrifugal pumps are simple. The only moving parts are the motor and the vaned impeller that are directly attached to one another by a shaft. There are no check valves to wear out or break. Since these pumps can't be overhauled, your best bet is to carry a spare for immediate replacement in case one fails.

Centrifugal bilge pump and float switch.

There's also a vane-type centrifugal pump. These can't be run dry without burning out. They're often used for pressure water systems. Shurflo is the most popular brand. They really aren't worth servicing. If one of these craps out, your best bet is to replace it.

Diaphragm Pumps

This is another type of pump that is often used in pressure water systems on board boats. They're more expensive than the centrifugal vane type so they are typically found in costlier boats

In a diaphragm pump, an electric motor imparts a pulsating motion to a flexible rubber wall on the side of a compartment for water, changing the volume of the compartment by alternately pulling and pushing. A pair of one-way check valves take turns admitting supply water and allowing discharge water to be pushed out of the chamber as the diaphragm moves in and out. When the diaphragm is pulled, the inlet check valve opens and allows water to flow into the pump. When the motor pushes on the diaphragm, the inlet check valve closes and the water is pushed out the outlet one, which opens because of the pressure of the outgoing water.

When a diaphragm pump fails, the problem is often with the check valves. The better-quality diaphragm pumps, such as the ones made by Jabsco, can be serviced. If you own a diaphragm pump and don't have a copy of its exploded view and parts list in your boat's service information binder, contact the manufacturer to have them mail you one.

A diaphragm pump typically has a pressure switch built into the pump body that automatically senses the pressure drop when a faucet is opened and a supply of water is demanded. When this happens, the switch turns the pump on. Conversely, when the faucet is closed, the pump builds up pressure in the system and the switch signals it to shut off. These pressure switches occasionally fail. Here are some troubleshooting suggestions for freshwater system diaphragm pumps.

• If the pump does not come on when the system is switched on and a faucet is opened, use your voltmeter to make sure that a supply of 12 volts is making it to the pump. If voltage is present, the next suspect component is the pressure switch. It works by closing a set of contacts when the pressure in the system falls. The pressure drop indicates that someone has opened a faucet. When the faucet is shut back off, the pump will build up pressure inside, which causes the switch contacts to open and shut off the pump. Thus, the system works automatically on demand.

• If you shut off the power to the system you can check the pressure switch with an ohmmeter to make sure that it's functioning properly. With a faucet open and low pressure in the system, the

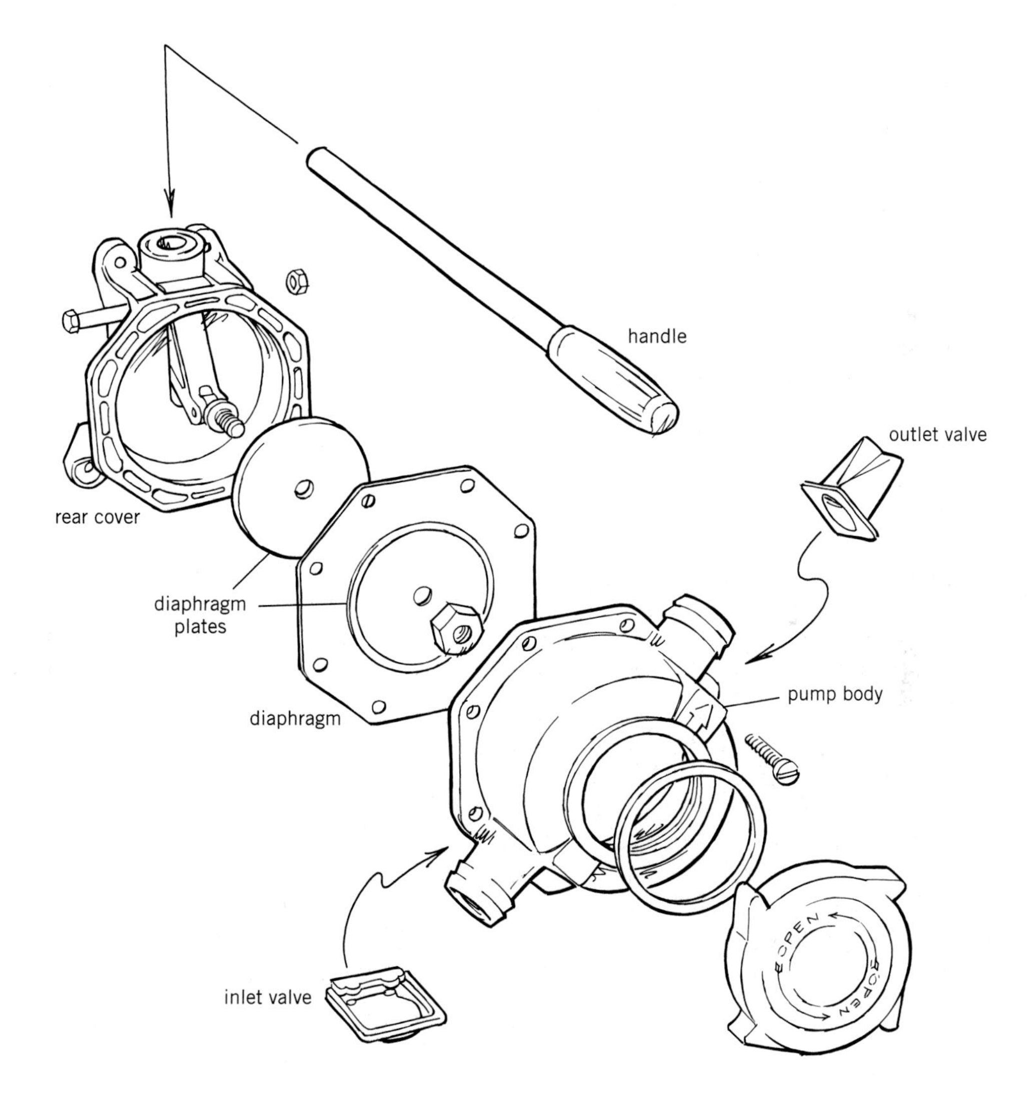

Diaphragm-type hand bilge pump. All diaphragm pumps work by alternately opening inlet and outlet check valves as the diaphragm travels in and out. Each cycle moves a slug of water in and out of the pump.

switch should close, giving it a resistance of near zero ohms. If its resistance (as measured with your ohmmeter) never drops, the switch is defective.

- Most of today's pressure switches are sealed modules that can't be opened, serviced, or adjusted. If the one in your pump is acting up, simply remove it and replace it with a new one. Use Teflon paste on its threads and protect the electrical connections with Liquid Electric Tape (see page 61 for directions).
- If your boat's pressure water pump periodically cycles on and off when no one is using the system, chances are there's a leak somewhere in the plumbing. It could be something as simple as a dripping faucet.

Float Switches

In most bilge or shower sump applications, the pump is controlled by a device known as a float switch, which is a small mercury switch mounted in a hinged, floating arm. When the water level gets high enough to call for the pump to operate, the switch arm floats up on its pivot, closes the circuit, and turns on the pump. As the pump reduces the water level in the sump or bilge to the lower limit level, the switch floats back down and breaks the circuit, shutting off the pump.

Float switches cause more problems (usually mechanical, not electrical) than the centrifugal pumps they control. What typically happens is that gunk and goo in the bilge or shower sump clogs the hinges that the switch arm pivots on. Another possible troublemaker is the mounting of the switch bracket. It must be positively secured to the boat. If the switch assembly is free to float around in the bilge, it might force the pump to operate when it's not needed or never to turn on at all.

When troubleshooting a float switch, first make sure that it's securely mounted and that the arm is pivoting freely. Use the tip of a pocketknife to clean the pivots if they're gummed up. If you can't resurrect the switch by cleaning it, you'll have to bite the bullet and buy a new one.

Sometimes a float no longer floats. The float arm is typically a sealed plastic assembly that floats by virtue of the air trapped inside. If it cracks and fills with water, it will never float (and never signal the pump to turn on). You'll need to install a replacement switch.

Float switches occasionally suffer from an electrical failure. If you suspect that's the cause, shut off the power to the circuit and exercise the float switch with your ohmmeter attached. When you lift the arm, the switch resistance should drop to near zero ohms. When it's in the "down" position, it should have a resistance reading of infinity.

The pumps and plumbing on modern boats are pretty reliable. If you are like most boaters, chances are you will never have to do any maintenance or repair work beyond periodically replacing the flexible impellers.

Make sure you don't overdo the tightening when you make up fittings in your boat's plumbing. If you have to make plumbing repairs and you're uncertain of the size or type of fittings you need, bring the components you're trying to mate to the plumbing counter with you. Most important, get fittings that are suitable for use on board a boat. Pass over the steel ones. They cost less than brass—and that's exactly what they're worth.

Questions and Answers

Question: We bought our boat two years ago and I don't think anyone ever serviced the holding tank system. Last summer I overhauled the macerator pump. Since then, we've been plagued with an odor in the boat.

I've been able to trace the problem to a bad cuff on a hose and a leak on the elbow on the macerator pump. I have removed the holding tank and all the hoses to make repairs. My questions are as follows:

1. Should I use a sealer when installing new cuffs on the hoses?
2. What type of sealer would you recommend for the elbow on the macerator pump? The existing sealer has a gritty appearance.
3. The holding tank still has some solid matter on the bottom. What would you recommend to dissolve it?

4. The hose to the macerator pump connects to a T fitting and the other side of the T connects to the pump-out outlet. The hose to the macerator is routed up over the tank in what I would assume to be some form of a trap. Could I lower this hose to allow the macerator to completely pump out the tank or would this cause some other problems?

Answer: The cuff-style fittings in your system are prone to causing odors. You can seal the ends with 3M's 5200 adhesive-sealant, but you'd be better off replacing the hoses and ends with the proper type.

Many types of hoses are permeable to odors; they are the most common causes of foul odors in marine sanitation systems. Try wiping the outside of any suspect hose with a clean piece of cloth and then sniff it. If there's any odor on the cloth, replace the hose with a nonpermeable type.

I like Raritan's sanitary hose (Type SH), which is smooth inside and out and impermeable to odor. Instead of relying on a threaded cuff, this hose mates with barb-type male fittings that are secured with stainless steel hose clamps. No sealer is used on these connections. (Remember, below the waterline you must use two hose clamps.)

You can seal the threaded fittings on the macerator with Teflon thread sealing paste. That is probably the gritty material you found when you disassembled the system. Teflon tape is not suitable for this application. It's designed for use on threaded fittings only.

I'm not sure about the trap you describe. Most marine sanitation systems have a vented loop in the discharge line from the head, which has a siphon breaker installed at its high point. This is designed to accomplish two objectives. First, it prevents backsiphoning from the through-hull fitting, which could sink your boat. Second, for heads with an antibackflow device in their discharge pump (all Raritan, ITT, and Groco models, to my knowledge), it keeps a slug of water in the discharge line and allows the head to retain some water in its bowl.

As for dissolving the sludge in your holding tank, here's my advice: Empty the tank as much as possible and add a dose of holding tank chemical. Then add just a gallon or two of water (perhaps three times that for a large tank). Let this concentrated mixture stand for a day or two. If you can get access to the tank, so much the better. Let the concentrated chemical stand for a few hours, then, with a sprayer-equipped garden hose, loosen the sludge. Try either of these techniques as many times as necessary to clean things up.

If, on the other hand, your holding tank has mineral deposits, you might try using a 50 percent solution of white vinegar in water.

Question: I have a problem getting the vented loop to work on one of my Raritan Crown heads. It's supposed to let the water stand in the bowl after flushing, but I can't get it to work as it should. I have replaced the vented loop and the air vent two times.

The vented loop worked fine until about a year ago. The air vent on top of the loop unscrews and air escapes, and when this is done, water stands in the bowl each time. When water is otherwise pumped into the bowl, it drains out.

I have replaced the flapper valve on this head twice but it hasn't helped. The instructions that came with the head don't help either.

The head works fine in all other respects. The other head on the boat works fine with no problems—its vented loop is OK.

Answer: The vented loop fitting installed in the discharge line from your boat's head functions as a siphon breaker. First, it keeps some quantity of water in the toilet bowl between uses. If it weren't there to admit a slug of air into the high point in the discharge hose, the head would completely drain out the through-hull fitting—because of gravity and the siphon effect, of course.

Its second—and arguably more important—function is to break the discharge siphon to prevent water from coming back through the discharge line. Depending on how low the toilet is installed, this could overtop the bowl and sink your boat.

Even though you've replaced the vented loop twice, I suspect that it's still causing the bowl to drain empty after flushing. You might want to try installing another one. Perhaps you should pick a different brand this time.

The other possible cause of this problem might be some kind of restriction—like a plastic bag—on the inlet side. A tired pump is another possibility. If the pump's mechanism is worn, your head might discharge more water than it draws in from outside, which would leave you with the dry bowl you describe. (If this is the problem, however, the bowl will be dry immediately, not after a while.)

A Raritan Crown head does indeed have a flapper valve, but I doubt that it's the cause of your problem.

Question: I own a Sea Ray SRV 240 and have recently rebuilt the macerator pump. After reinstalling the pump and the plumbing hoses, the pump doesn't self-prime. In fact, even after priming it manually, it will not take hold. Can you suggest a repair that will get this thing going?
Answer: I'm sure you're talking about an ITT Jabsco 18590 macerator pump. They make about 25,000 of them each year.

A few things might have gone wrong. Because you removed and reinstalled the macerator pump, I'd start by checking the hose connections. They must all be airtight for the pump to prime. In fact, depending on how the system is plumbed, even a bad O-ring in the deck-mounted pumpout fitting can prevent the pump from priming. The hoses must not be kinked and they must be the reinforced (wire wound) type so they don't collapse under suction.

If the hoses are OK, check to make sure that you assembled the pump correctly. The recesses in the pump body and the macerator pump have to line up, and so do the holes and cutouts in the two gaskets and the wearplate that's sandwiched between them. It's easy to mess up here; each part can go together four different ways—but only one of them is right. There are raised bosses on each layer of this five-part "sandwich." If they all line up, you've assembled it correctly.

The pump body in the 18590 is plastic (the most recent ones have stainless steel wearing surfaces installed). If the all plastic version (like yours) is run dry—even briefly—the housing can become distorted from heat. The pump will never prime again. This is rarely evident from outside; you'll have to disassemble the pump to inspect it.

Jabsco makes a service repair kit (part number 18598-1000) that includes a seal, an impeller, the pump body, and a handful of other small hardware bits. It does not include a wearplate, so check the condition of that before you buy the kit.

Sometimes, when one of these units lays idle for awhile, the flexible impeller gets stuck in the pump housing. Are you sure the motor is turning? In the newer models, there's an easy way to check. The back end of the motor's shaft has a slot in it. Insert the biggest screwdriver that will fit and try giving it a turn. Unfortunately, the earlier versions of this pump don't have that feature. You'll have to disassemble it to see if it's stuck. But I'll bet you a nickel that one of the gaskets or other parts I mentioned in that five-part sandwich is out of place. I would check there first.

Question: I'm considering reworking the freshwater plumbing on my boat. Some people tell me to get rid of all the copper pipes and replace them with synthetic hose; others say that copper can't be beat. Who's right and who's wrong?
Answer: Copper is pretty good stuff. Its main drawback is that it doesn't abide vibration. When it's inadequately supported and then subjected to vibration, it fatigues and ultimately fails. The metal actually crystallizes.

Few boats have copper plumbing. It's more difficult to make connections with it and it's certainly not as easy to route as flexible plastic tubing. (It's also way more costly.)

If the soldered joints are not made with lead-free solder, the water that travels through the joints can pick up unhealthy doses of lead and other heavy metals, particularly when it stands in the plumbing for some length of time. Maybe that's why people are suggesting you get rid of the copper plumbing.

If you're going to redo the plumbing, your easiest course of action would be to install flexible plastic lines. Of course, water that stands in this kind of plumbing gets an off taste. But it's a simple matter to run the water a few seconds to flush out the lines before you fill a pan or draw a drink of water.

In my experience, boat water is not usually very tasty no matter what the plumbing is made of. On most boats the potable water is stored in polyethylene tanks. Yuck. Once it's been in there for a while, it doesn't really matter what kind of plumbing it runs through. Most folks I know use the boat water for washing dishes and their bodies and stick with bottled water for cooking and drinking.

7 WINTERIZING

Which do you suppose is rougher duty for your boat's engine—working hard all summer long or being laid up for the winter? It all depends on you. If you practice a regimen of proper winterization and springtime commissioning, the winter lay-up season will provide a well-deserved rest for your boat's engine and other equipment. If you don't, it will be six months of torture.

Consider the lowly oil change. If you make sure this is done in the fall, your engine will hibernate with a coating of clean, fresh oil on its bearings and other moving parts. If you neglect to change the lube oil the engine will spend six months with a belly full of dirty oil, water, acids, and combustion byproducts.

Yuck! I know which way I'd rather treat my boat's expensive machinery. If you follow the maintenance advice in this book, your boat's engine and equipment will hardly notice the off-season. All of this machinery will enjoy a longer life as a result of your diligence; best of all, you'll get skinnier bills from the boatyard.

Speaking of boatyards, if you're not prepared to do a thorough job, pay the professionals to do it for you. It will be money well spent. The cost of replacing one piece of freeze-damaged machinery could equal five years of professional winterizing.

Laying up a boat for the winter is not particularly complicated; if you mind the details and take care of everything without being tempted by shortcuts, that is.

The key to winterizing is simple: lists, lists, lists. You'll find a suggested checklist beginning on page 92. This chapter describes in detail how to do all of the necessary tasks that comprise winterizing. The lists are coded to clue you in to what steps are required for sterndrives, as well as inboard- and outboard-powered boats. This chapter also provides a list of the tools required for each chore, and warns you about potential trouble spots and how to avoid them.

A Four-Part Program

There are four main groups of chores to accomplish when you tuck your boat in for the winter. They are servicing, inspecting, freezeproofing, and mothballing. In some cases, they must be done in a particular order. For example, some winterizing operations need to be completed before the boat is hauled out of the water, while others can't be done until afterward.

Servicing

Routine service is mostly concerned with the vital fluids in your boat's machinery. Most boaters only change their boat's engine oil once each season, in the fall. As mentioned, leaving old lube oil in an engine over the lay-up season is a bad policy.

Changing the oil in the spring is unnecessary. However, if you put a lot of hours on your boat's engine, you should consider an additional change of lube oil and filter in the middle of the season.

Freshwater-cooled engines should have their closed-cooling systems drained, flushed with fresh water, and refilled with a fresh batch of 50/50 antifreeze-water mixture. Unless you use really low-quality antifreeze, it's not necessary to do this flushing operation at the end of every season. Just the same, don't neglect it for too long. If you do, the heat exchanger waterways will start to become clogged and, as the coolant breaks down, scaly deposits can be precipitated out of solution in all the nooks and crannies in this important system.

If you don't drain, flush, and refill the closed-cooling system, at the very least use an antifreeze checker to test the coolant for its level of freeze protection. Finally, avoid using antifreeze that contains silicates.

Sterndrives and outboards require a change of gear oil in the lower unit. Similarly, the transmission fluid in inboard engines (and some sterndrives as well) must be drained and replaced.

And of course, no matter what kind of power your boat has, some important linkages need to be greased. When you do this, it's best to clean the old grease off with a rag before renewing the lubrication with a fresh smear of the factory-recommended grease. These grease points are spelled out in your owner's manual, or you can refer to the service checklist that follows for a generic guide.

Other servicing and lubrication items that need attention in the fall include the deck-fill caps for the water, fuel, and holding tanks. These have O-ring seals, which need to be periodically cleaned and lightly greased with white Teflon grease, such as WGL.

Inspecting

The inspection portion of your winterizing program can pay big dividends and is easy enough to do. In the course of winterizing, you're going to be poking around in all these nooks and crannies anyway. It doesn't take much longer to inspect V-belts, hoses, clamps, and the like while you're down there.

For many boaters, this is the only time that they check things over thoroughly. So be philosophical about it. Get yourself in the right frame of mind for playing Sherlock Holmes and don't cut any corners.

There's another nice feature of doing this inspection before you lay the boat up for the winter. If you find anything that needs attention, you can assemble the necessary tools and parts at your leisure. If the weather remains warm enough for working on the boat, you can tackle these projects before the cold weather sets in. If not, you'll have the parts on hand and be ready to get a jump on things before the next season gets a jump on you.

If you don't have the time and tools and capabilities to tackle the necessary work, you can still take advantage of the forward thinking that this inspection tour allows. If you know what you're going to need the boatyard crew to do for you next spring, you can put the work orders in now. This approach makes more sense and prevents launching delays. If you wait until the last minute at commissioning time, this can cause headaches for you and the boatyard.

There's one other subtle benefit to doing the inspection: You'll get a better understanding of how your boat's machinery is serviced and you might learn of some tools and spare parts you should be carrying but aren't.

Freezeproofing

If you store your boat in a part of the country where the temperature goes below freezing, you've got to make sure that there's no opportunity for water to stand anywhere within its machinery or spaces—you've got to freezeproof your boat. Although the other components of winterizing a boat are important, freezeproofing is arguably the most important. This is the one that, if neglected, can cost you the most money.

There are five main areas that require your attention. First, the supply and drain sides of the freshwater system, including the storage tanks, faucets, sinks and shower stall drains, and through-hull drains. Second, the head(s) and holding tank system. Third, the cockpit and deck scuppers and drains. Fourth, the engine's cooling and exhaust systems. And finally, the storage bins, lockers, and bilges.

i = inboard-powered boats
s = sterndrive-powered boats
o = outboard-powered boats
* = some engines—see your owner's manual for details

f = if your boat has this equipment
_ = all hoses that run below the waterline anywhere along their length must have double hose clamps at both ends
** = see battery storage tips on page 117

Winterizing Checklist

Before Hauling Out

Task	Application
inspect fuel filter for water	**i, s, o**
change engine oil and filter and genset oil and filter	**i, s, f**
check coolant in freshwater-cooled engines	**f**
change transmission fluid and/or gear oil	**i, s***
pump out holding tank	**f**
fill fuel tank and stabilize fuel	**i, s, o**
apply Teflon grease to fill caps and O-rings	**i, s, o**

After Hauling Out

Task	Application
wash the boat's bottom	**i, s, o**
remove barnacles from running gear and through-hull fittings	**i, s, o**
check running gear and through-hulls for electrolysis, corrosion, and damage	**i, s, o**
change gear oil in lower unit	**s, o**
disassemble, clean, inspect, and overhaul raw-water strainer(s)	**i*, s***
disassemble, grease, and reassemble seacocks	**f**
inspect hoses and hose clamps (especially below the waterline)	**f, _**
drain water tanks and winterize freshwater supply system	**f**
winterize water heater system	**f**
winterize shower drain system	**f**
winterize sink drains and icebox drain	**f**
check deck drains (scuppers) for water traps	**f**
winterize if necessary	**f**
winterize head and holding tank system	**f**
winterize engine	**i, s**

After Hauling Out *(cont.)*

Task	Application
fog out engine with fogging oil	**i, s, o**
winterize genset	**f**
fog out generator with fogging oil	**f**
shut off fuel supply at tank	**i, s, o**
remove, wash, charge, check, and store batteries in warm place**	**i, s, o**
seal engine inlet and exhaust with rags, plastic, and duct tape	**i, s**
clean engine with spray cleaner and rags or paper towels	**i, s, o**
spray light film of WD-40 over engine and machinery	**i, s, o**
establish a program for maintaining batteries over the lay-up season	**i, s, o**

Inspection Checklist

Task	Application
note engine water leaks	**i, s, o**
correct these by retorquing or replacing gaskets or hoses	**i, s, o**
grease all control linkages	**i, s, o**

Tucking In and Covering

- remove compass and electronics (store them at home)
- remove bilge drain plug and place in galley sink
- drain, pump, and sponge bilges dry
- add a little antifreeze to freeze-vulnerable nooks
- sprinkle rock salt in bottom of bilge near drain plug
- remove cushions to dry stowage place
- remove all food from cabinets and refrigerator
- open all lockers and compartments

(continued)

Inspection Checklist *(cont.)*

Required Tools

- oil changing pump (hand or drill motor-powered)
- container for drained engine oil (empty milk or bleach jugs)
- plastic funnel for draining oil filter
- disposable aluminum meatloaf pan
- oil filter wrench
- oil filler spout (only needed for oil in old-fashioned cans)
- pocketknife
- antifreeze checker
- 5-gallon plastic jerry jug
- plastic dishpan
- lever-action pump-type oil can
- multimeter (analog or digital)
- battery terminal cleaner
- ruler
- needlenose pliers
- combination wrenches
- screwdrivers
- bucket and sponge
- flush adapter and garden hose
- lever-action grease gun
- needle-tip adapter (for grease gun)

Necessary Supplies

- motor oil
- oil filters (engine and genset)
- gear oil
- nylon washers for gearcase screws (sterndrive and outboards only)
- fuel stabilizer
- factory-recommended marine grease
- white Teflon grease
- fogging oil
- WD-40 penetrating lubricant
- permanent antifreeze (ethylene glycol)
- nontoxic antifreeze (propylene glycol)
- rock salt
- Teflon thread paste
- wiping rags and spray cleaner (such as Fantastik or Formula 409)
- paper towels
- dish soap
- distilled water (for batteries)
- sheet plastic and duct tape
- fine-grade emery cloth

Some systems can simply be drained, provided you can be absolutely sure there is no trapped water waiting for freezing conditions to destroy things. Other systems must be flushed out with antifreeze.

There are two main types of antifreeze and they're not interchangeable. The antifreeze you will use for winterizing is propylene glycol. It's nontoxic and you will use it full strength. It's sold as RV antifreeze and you can find it at most chandleries and RV dealers. Whatever you do, don't mess up and use the toxic (ethylene glycol) antifreeze for winterizing. You certainly don't want to poison your boat's potable water system.

It's difficult to estimate how many gallons of antifreeze you will need to winterize your boat because that depends on what equipment your boat has and how effectively you use the stuff. Here's a useful pointer: You will get by with less antifreeze if you remove as much water as possible before winterizing. More details on this follow when I give you the specific directions for winterizing the various systems.

Mothballing

The main mothballing task is covering the boat to protect it against the elements for winter. But this is also the time to take care of a handful of other items that will help your boat lead a long life. At the same time, you will be ensuring yourself a snag-free commissioning experience next spring. I give you step-by-step instructions for mothballing your boat beginning on page 118.

Before Hauling the Boat from the Water

Inspecting the Fuel Filter

Some of the tasks you need to accomplish *before* you haul your boat for the winter concern the fuel system. You'll want to stabilize the fuel to keep it fresh and top off the tanks for reasons that I'll go into presently.

First, though, you must make sure that no water has settled in the sediment bowl of the fuel filter. Complete fuel filter servicing instructions are found in chapter 8. You may, of course, service the fuel filter now, but most of us do it in the spring at tune-up time. Remember that this task means opening the fuel system; therefore, all sources of sparks or ignition must be eliminated. Make sure the battery switch is shut off. Kick everyone else off the boat or make sure they know that you're working with flammable stuff. Needless to say, the smoking lamp is not lit.

Whether you're going to service the filter now or merely inspect it for water, you should jump to the next chapter now for particulars on accomplishing those operations. At a minimum, drain the sediment bowl and make sure there's no water sitting in the fuel system all winter.

If you detect any water in the filter, use the information in the following section to help you purge it from the system. Once all the water is gone, you'll replace the filter element. Also, make sure you remove the water from the filter housing and the fuel tank. Leaving a load of water in the bottom of the fuel tank over the winter will cause corrosion and subsequent fuel system troubles.

Since water is heavier than gasoline, any water in your boat's fuel tank will have handily settled to the bottom. As a rule, boat fuel systems have the pickup tube for the fuel line located a bit off the bottom of the tank to leave room for a little water down there, before the engine starts to ingest it. That means if you found some water in the filter, there's almost certainly a good-sized slug of it in the tank. Here's how to eliminate the water before it starts to cause fuel system troubles.

Getting Water out of a Tank

If your boat has an access port in the top of its fuel tank, you're in luck. Most likely, however, it does not. Don't despair—there's still a way for you to get into the tank to remove the water.

Remove the fuel-gauge sending unit. This is usually secured with five or six screws. Carefully lift the float mechanism out of the tank and set it on a clean rag on top of the tank. Using an *explosion-proof flashlight* (make sure it's so labeled), peer down into the tank through the small sending unit opening.

Water in gas is usually pretty easy to spot. The two do not mix, so the water forms small round balls that roll around in the bottom of the tank as the boat rocks. Of course, if there's a huge load of water in the fuel, the water doesn't form balls—it makes a homogenous boundary layer of water beneath the gas.

If you're not sure that you're seeing any water, get some Kolor Kut water-finder paste. It's a chemical indicator that you smear on the end of a probe. When you push the probe down to the bottom of a tank where you suspect there's water, the paste turns bright red if water is present. You can order it from Quality Yacht Service (10701 5th Ave., P.O. Box 500567, Marathon, FL 33050; 305-743-2898; www.wecleanfuel.com).

You can remove the water with a small, explosion-proof hand pump, such as the ones made by Jabsco and Beckson. They come in a kit with a couple of rigid plastic inlet and outlet tubes. Feed the pump's pickup tube all the way to the bottom of the tank where the water should be and start pumping the suspect gasoline into a small disposable aluminum loaf pan. Once you've pumped a bit of fuel out, look at the contents of the pan. Do you see any balls of water? Good. Keep pumping until you don't.

You might have to pump quite a bit of fuel out to ensure that you've removed all the water from the bottom of the tank. When you think you're done, smear a new application of water-finder paste on the end of your probe stick and insert it to the bottom of the tank again. Do not button up the tank by replacing the fuel-gauge sender unit until you're sure you've removed all traces of water.

Now hook up to the fuel line at the filter inlet and draw the contents of the fuel line into your pan so you can inspect it for the presence of water.

Ask the crew in the boatyard office how to safely dispose of the gasoline and water mixture in your pan. Do *not* throw it into the water or onto the ground. This stuff is highly toxic.

My sister runs a boatyard in Connecticut, and in order to be able to properly dispose of contaminated gasoline, she had to invest tens of thousands of dollars in a facility to handle the stuff. Connecticut law requires a roof over the facility, ventilation, secondary containment, a secure lockup, and, because the boatyard is in a flood plain (aren't all boatyards?) the containment had to be proofed against floating away in a hurricane storm surge.

I think the only thing tougher for her would have been to build a nuclear power plant. She pays an environmental company $6 per gallon for gasoline disposal and, to help defray costs, charges customers $10 per gallon. (At that rate, given the volume of contaminated gasoline she disposes of, her facility should pay for itself in about three hundred years.)

Now refer to chapter 8 again for details on installing a new fuel filter element.

Once you've installed the new fuel filter element and disposed of the contaminated gasoline and gasoline-soaked rags, you can start venting the engine room and the bilges where the fuel tank and the fuel filter are.

Then run the blowers for at least five minutes and check for gasoline fumes by performing a sniff test. If things are clean you can proceed to start the engine. Run it for a while with the new filter element and then check the sediment bowl again for the presence of water. Don't be shocked if you find some; it's possible that some nook or cranny in the fuel system had some in it, or perhaps you didn't get it all out of the tank at the first go-round. Water in a fuel system can be perverse that way.

Continue to probe, pump, and replace filter elements until you're absolutely sure there's no water in the fuel system. If you think this operation is a pain, trust me—it pales in comparison to the kind of work you'll have to do next season if you don't fix the problem now.

Checking the Coolant on Freshwater-Cooled Engines

It's best to use your antifreeze checker to check the freeze protection of the coolant in a freshwater-cooled engine's expansion tank. You'll want to do this with a cold engine.

Sometimes it's impossible to draw enough of a sample from the tank to float the needle (or balls) in an antifreeze checker. If that's the case with your engine, pull off one of the hoses and allow some coolant to drain into a tall, relatively narrow container, such as a clean olives or capers jar.

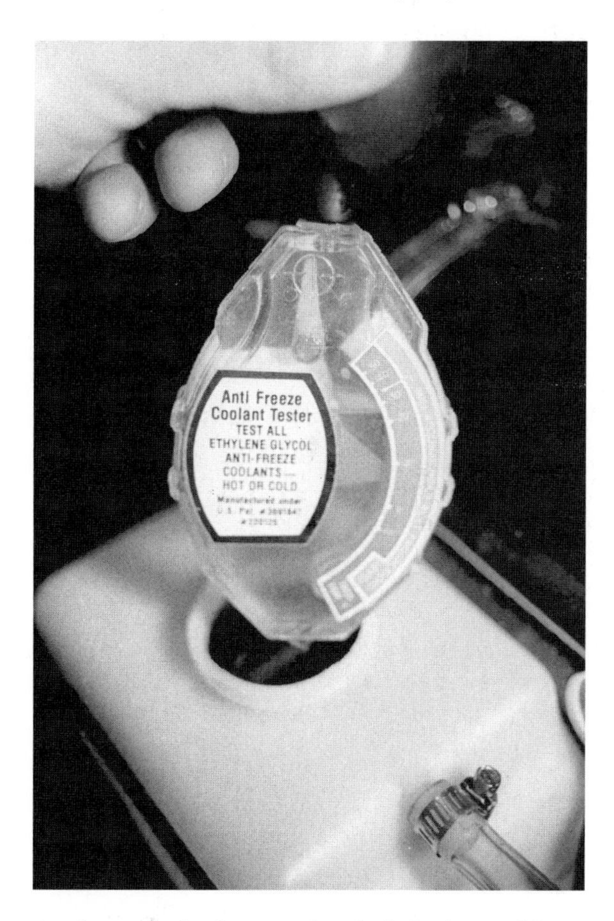

Antifreeze checker being used to check the degree of freeze protection in the coolant in an expansion tank.

Changing the Engine Oil

If you've ever changed the oil in a car, you'll find that, as a rule, marine engines are a bit more difficult. Chances are there isn't a drain plug in the bottom of the oil pan. Therefore, in most cases, you have to extract the old oil with a pump.

But first, a few words on buying new oil. Make sure, of course, that the oil you choose is the correct grade and specification.

"Grade" refers to the oil's viscosity, commonly known as the oil's "weight." Your engine owner's manual will specify the correct grade for use in your engine. Choose the oil that's recommended for summer operating conditions, not the winter weight oil specified in the chart, since you won't be running the engine over the winter.

The oil's specification is noted by a series of letters such as CD, SG, or SE. They indicate that the oil conforms to a set of standards promulgated by the American Petroleum Institute; hence this is also called the API designation. Again, your owner's manual will clue you in about which oil specification is required by your engine.

Now, back to pumping out the old oil. The secret to success here is to first get the old oil good and hot; doing so makes it less viscous—a fancy way to say runnier. And runnier, warm oil is a lot easier to pump out than cold, which means you're more likely to get almost all of it out. So, run the engine for ten or fifteen minutes before beginning this task. To warm up the engine most effectively, you need to put a load on the engine. There are two ways to accomplish this. You can either take the boat out for a little cruise around the bay or run it in gear at idle speed with the boat securely tied to the dock.

Warning: If you decide to warm up the engine with this latter method, make sure the boat is really securely tied off to the dock and be sure the cleats or rings that you are tied off to can stand the strain. You definitely don't want the boat to rip loose and slam into the dock during this operation.

There are electric oil changing pumps on the market, but one of the hand pumps sold for this purpose works just fine for the weekend mechanic. Jabsco and Beckson make suitable models that sell for $25 to $35. If your engine has a threaded dipstick tube, you should use Beckson's model 12PGA. It threads right onto the top of the dipstick tube, which means you don't have to snake the pickup tube down into the dipstick tube.

Before you get started, assemble disposable plastic gloves, oil, oil filter, an oil filter wrench, rags, milk jugs, a bucket, cleaning supplies (paper towels and a spray bottle of Formula 409), and a funnel. I also use a special tool that I make from a plastic laundry detergent jug to catch the drips and dribbles from the oil filter.

If you want to make one of these, here's how. Cut the top of the jug into the shape of a scoop. Use a utility knife for this operation. The photo shows this special tool to give you an idea of the final shape you want to get.

Once your engine's oil is hot and you've got all your tools and supplies at the ready, shut off the engine. It's time to start pumping out the old lube oil.

If you can't use the thread-on type of hand pump, you'll need to snake your pump's pickup tube down inside the dipstick tube. Push it in until it bottoms out in the oil pan and then stop. If you push any more tubing in, it might actually bend back up away from the bottom of the sump. If it's in too far or not

If you cut down a laundry detergent jug, you can make this handy dandy oil drip catcher. To use it, get the filter loose, then put this scoop in place underneath before you spin off the filter. You can drop the filter right in, then use the tool to drain the mess into one of your collection jugs. Saves a lot of messiness.

far enough, you will leave some of the old oil behind, and you don't want to do that.

Have a couple of 1-gallon plastic milk jugs on hand for the waste oil. Screw-top ones are the most secure. Brace the jug securely so it won't tip over and make a mess. Insert the pump's outlet tube into the jug, then start pumping. When the first jug is three-quarters full, cap it securely and shift over to filling the second one. If you have a typical V-8 marine engine (most sterndrives and inboards), two jugs will be more than enough for one oil change.

When you think you've gotten all the oil out, move the tube around and pump some more. Keep moving the pickup tube around and pumping it until you think you've truly scavenged all of the old lube oil out of the engine's crankcase. (The fact of the matter is you'll never really get every bit but you should make sure you get as much as you possibly can.) Set the first jug aside but keep the second jug handy; it will receive the oil from the filter in the next step. (Cap it securely for now, though; you don't want any unnecessary spills.)

The next step in the oil change procedure is to remove the old oil filter. Before you start this step, make sure you're wearing gloves, because things are about to get messy. Get your special tool (the one you made from a laundry detergent jug) ready.

Now you can use your oil filter wrench to loosen the filter. There are several types of oil filter wrenches. The ones with a metal band are the most effective. If you're using the kind with a plastic strap, it may just slip around on the filter. If that's the case, you may be able to improve the traction by wrapping a rag around the filter before you put the strap wrench on.

Don't loosen the filter too far with the wrench. The trick is to get it loose enough so that you no longer need the wrench but not so loose that oil starts to leak out and make a mess. Once you've reached this point, get the wrench out of the way and put your cut down jug underneath the filter. Push its lower lip in as far under the filter as you can. With any luck there won't be any stray oil that runs out underneath.

Now you can finish spinning the filter off its mounting boss by hand. Let the filter drop into the cut down jug when it comes off. Now stand the whole ensemble up in a secure place so it won't tip over and make a mess. Leave the filter in here with its open end down so that the oil within can drain.

Once the filter has drained, you can throw it in a Ziploc bag and dispose of it in the garbage. Then tip your special tool over and drain the captured oil it contains into your second drain oil jug.

Wipe up the mess with rags, taking particular care around the mounting boss where the filter screws onto the engine block. Don't let any lint from your rag get on this area, though. You don't want it getting sucked into the engine's lube oil system. Make sure the neoprene gasket from the bottom of the old filter isn't stuck on the engine block.

While the filter is draining into the funnel, use your squirt-type oilcan to drizzle a coating of clean motor oil onto the gasket on the base of the new filter, then smear it around with your finger.

Different engines have their oil filters installed in various orientations. If you're lucky enough to have one that's installed open end up, it's a good idea to fill the filter with new oil. This will allow the oil pressure to come up faster when you start the engine.

Spin the filter on by hand until it seats against its mounting boss on the engine block. Then tighten it as tight as you can by hand. Do not use the oil filter wrench for this step. Resist any temptation to overtighten the filter. If you do, the gasket will

Applying a film of motor oil to the neoprene gasket on the bottom of an oil filter before installation.

squirm out of place and the new filter will leak when you start the engine. Once the filter is in place, you are ready to add fresh oil to complete the oil change.

Add the oil to the oil fill cap, which is typically located in one of the valve covers. It's best to add about a quart less than the engine manufacturer specifies. That way if you didn't scavenge all the old oil out with your pump, you won't wind up with an overfilled crankcase.

Once you've added the new oil, you should make sure the oil fill cap and the dipstick are reinstalled securely, and then prepare to start the engine.

Run the blowers for at least five minutes, sniff the engine room to make sure there are no gasoline fumes, and then, if all is well, start the engine and run it for thirty seconds or so. Unless you prefilled the filter, for the first few seconds the oil pressure gauge will give a reading that appears dangerously low. If your engine has a low oil pressure alarm, it will probably be sounding too. Don't race the engine at all during this run. Once the oil pump has filled the filter, the pressure should jump up to the normal operating range.

Shut down the engine and check for leaks at the base of the filter. Wait five minutes or so for the oil to drain into the oil pan then remove the dipstick, wipe it clean, and check the oil level. Add oil as necessary to bring the level up to the full mark.

If there were no leaks, great. Now you can restart the engine and bring it up to a fast idle—1,200 to 1,500 rpm—for two or three minutes to allow the fresh oil to circulate throughout the engine. This will bathe the bearings and all the other moving parts with fresh clean oil for the winter lay-up season ahead.

Shut the engine off and wait ten minutes or so for the oil to drain down into the pan; finally, check the oil level again. If necessary top it off to bring the level right up to the full mark on the dipstick. *Warning:* Don't overfill the crankcase. Too much oil is worse for an engine than too little. If you somehow finished up with an overfilled crankcase, you will have to use your oil-scavenging pump to bring it down to the full mark on the dipstick.

Move your tools and gear out of the way and dispose of the used oil in an environmentally responsible way. Sometimes, you can return the oil to the outlet where you bought the new oil. Failing that, your boatyard might have a drain oil tank that you can dump it into, though they may have to charge you for this service.

Your best alternative is to check with your town. Many municipalities have drain oil collection tanks at their dumps. This is almost always a free service; the town picks up the cost of proper disposal. If you call your local Department of Public Works, they should be able to guide you to a safe disposal site.

Checking and Changing Transmission Oil

All inboards and some sterndrives have a transmission mounted abaft the engine. In most cases it's not necessary to warm up the engine before draining and refilling this gearbox.

Depending on the brand of transmission and its mounting configuration, you will have to either remove one of the hoses connecting the transmission to the oil cooler or pump the oil out through the fill hole. If you drain yours by removing a hose, you might find a small spring and a filter screen under the bushing in the hose end. If you do, wipe these parts clean and lay them out in their proper orientation. When you reassemble these parts, it's imperative that they go together the same way.

Consult your owner's manual for the quantity and specification of fluid to refill the gearbox. Do not use any other type of gear oil than the exact one specified in the manual; doing so might damage the transmission or make it operate erratically (if at all).

As with the engine lube oil, it's critical that you dispose of the used transmission fluid in an environmentally responsible fashion.

You're in the homestretch for the in-the-water portion of your boat's winterizing. You only have a few more chores to attend to before hauling the boat out for the winter. You will take care of these last few operations at the gas dock.

Here you can add stabilizer to the fuel, top off the fuel tanks, and pump out the holding tank. Since the batteries are strong, this is also a good time to run all the drinking water out of your boat's tanks.

Winterizing the Fuel System

There are a few simple steps you need to take at lay-up time to make sure your boat's fuel system and the gasoline it contains are ready to go next year. Although you might be tempted to drain your boat's fuel tanks for the lay-up season, there are two good reasons you shouldn't.

The first reason is condensation. As the air in your boat's fuel tanks is warmed and cooled during the warm days and cool nights of autumn, water vapor is condensed from the air. This condensed moisture collects on the inside walls and the top of the tanks. Then it dribbles down the sides of the tank, mixes with the gasoline, and begins to cause trouble.

The water, which is heavier than fuel, settles in the bottom of the tank and starts causing corrosion. Worse, when you try to start your boat's engine, the first thing it does is gulp a load of water into the fuel system. Then the trouble really begins. If you allow your engine to ingest water, you might never really be able to fix the resulting problems.

The good news is that condensation only occurs when there is unoccupied airspace in a tank. So you can easily minimize this potential problem by keeping fuel tanks filled all the time—especially when the boat is laid up for the winter.

The second reason for keeping the tanks topped off is an important matter of safety. Which do you think is more of an explosion hazard: a nearly empty tank of gasoline or one that's filled to the tip-top? If you guessed the full one, you're wrong.

Liquid gasoline is not nearly as much of an explosion hazard as gasoline vapors are. The vapor form of gasoline is much more volatile. In a fire, a boat with a nearly empty tank of gasoline is much more likely to explode than a boat with a tank that's chock-full.

Stable Gas Saves Grief

Gasoline degrades when it is stored. Thankfully, this deterioration can be slowed down if you add a dose of fuel stabilizer to the gas in your boat's tanks. Several reputable companies make fuel stabilizers, but Stor-N-Start, made by MDR (Marine Development and Research Corp.), seems to be the most widely distributed. It keeps the fuel in the tanks from forming varnish and gum deposits during the lay-up season. (Marine Development and Research Corp., 2116 Merrick Ave., Merrick, NY 11566; 516-546-1162; www.mdramazon.com.)

Whatever product you decide to use, start by determining the capacity of the first tank to be treated. (*Hint:* If your boat's owner's manual doesn't specify the tank capacity, you can often find this information on the builder's plate attached to the tank.) Then consult the chart printed on the bottle of stabilizer and add the recommended amount to protect the entire tank of gasoline. Lastly, fill the tank with fresh fuel. It's best to do things in this order so the stabilizer will be well mixed with the gasoline in the tank.

After you've added the stabilizer and topped up the tanks with fresh fuel, run the engine for ten or fifteen minutes to distribute the stabilized gasoline throughout the fuel system. This leaves stabilized fuel in the carburetor. This last step is particularly important because the varnish and gum deposits that form in unstabilized fuel cause the most problems in the small passageways in the carburetors. If the treated fuel doesn't make it that far, neither does the protection.

Fuel Cap Care

Before tucking in the fuel system for the winter you should take a few minutes to treat the fuel caps on your boat. Most boats have deck-fill caps that are sealed with O-rings. Their maintenance is minimal. Simply open them up, inspect the O-rings to make sure they're not cut or squashed, and give them a light smear of white Teflon grease. The threads of the caps should be lightly greased as well. The two most popular brands of Teflon grease are WGL and Star brite.

These O-rings are there to keep water out of your boat's fuel system. If the O-rings are looking for better weather, replace them now. They are inexpensive and provide a cheap insurance policy against water in the fuel. Remember to inspect and grease the deck caps on the holding tank and the freshwater tank while you're at it.

Pumping out the Holding Tank

Now that the fuel system has been taken care of, you've got one more task to attend to before you leave the gas dock: pumping out the holding tank. I like to rinse the tank out by adding 10 gallons of water and pumping again. For best results, repeat the pump and rinse procedure at least two times.

Once the holding tank is empty you can run the boat back to her slip and tell the yard crew that she's ready to be hauled out for the winter.

After the boat is out of the water, one of your chores will be to winterize the MSD system or head and holding tank. To do this properly, you must start with an empty holding tank. Once you've done the pumpout routine, put a sign on the head saying that it's out of commission for the season, and get ready to haul your boat.

WINTERIZING CHORES AFTER HAULOUT

Cleaning and Inspecting the Bottom and Running Gear

If possible, clean your boat's bottom immediately after hauling. While the bottom is still wet, the slime and sea life will be fresh, which makes them a lot easier to remove. If you have your boat hauled out by a boatyard, chances are the yard crew will pressure-wash the bottom as soon as the boat comes out of the water. As a rule, they do a good job, but there's always a bit more cleaning to be done.

If you haul out the boat yourself, you probably don't have a pressure washer. No matter; if you tackle it immediately, a hose and scrub brush will work fine. It's important to do a good job, though. If you don't, next season's bottom painting job will not be as smooth as it can be, which will cost your boat some speed and efficiency.

Regardless of who cleans the bottom, the barnacles will still be attached—pressure washers and scrub brushes won't usually budge them. You'll get the best results by scraping barnacles off with a stiff, thick-bladed putty knife, although you'll probably only be able to remove their shells. Each former barnacle attachment site will have a stony ring of barnacle glue. Don't bother trying to remove these while they're wet. Wait until they're dry and then gently sand these spots with some fairly coarse—say, 80-grit—sandpaper.

Barnacles will also probably be on the drive unit (if you have a sterndrive), or on the running gear of an inboard-powered boat. Look even further while you're on barnacle patrol. These little critters like to establish themselves inside through-hull fittings and on the transducers for your boat's knotmeter and depth-sounder as well. These can be carefully removed with a paring knife or lock-blade pocketknife. Get 'em while they're fresh.

Below-the-Waterline Inspection Tour

While you're looking for barnacles, it's also a good time to give your boat's underwater hardware a thorough going over. Using a "beater" pocketknife, pick some bottom paint off any bronze through-hull fittings to give them a critical examination.

If you find a pinkish tinge on any metal, you've found evidence of galvanic corrosion or electrolysis. The bonding wires inside the boat might have come unattached or your boat might have had stray currents circulating in the water. Or, the problem might be in the wiring of a boat that's in a slip near yours.

Bronze is a metal alloy comprised of 86.3 percent copper, 9.7 percent tin, and 4 percent zinc. The pinkish tinge is caused by dezincification. If you look at the galvanic series chart on page 72, you'll see that zinc is at the active end of the list of metals; copper and tin are quite a bit toward the passive end. (That's why we use zinc anodes to provide sacrificial protection for underwater hardware.)

When dezincification occurs, the zinc molecules are actually leached out of the bronze alloy. If this process is left unchecked, the metal hardware becomes spongy, brittle, and weak. A through-hull fitting in this condition can fail with catastrophic consequences (like sinking the boat). See chapter 5 for more information on this topic.

How's Your Stern Bearing?

If your boat has inboard power, wiggle the propeller end of the shaft and check for excessive play in the stern bearing. If you find more than the allowable amount of axial play here, it's time to replace the stern bearing.

Here are the allowable play dimensions in thousandths of an inch. For example, 0.005 is 5/1000 of an inch.

AXIAL PLAY OF STERN BEARINGS

Shaft Size (in.)	Allowable Play (in.)
3/4–1 3/8	0.005–0.008
1 7/16–1 7/8	0.004–0.010
2–2 3/8	0.005–0.012

If there's any fishing line or other junk tangled in the stern bearing, now is the time to clear it away. If debris of this sort gets lodged between the propshaft and the stern bearing, it can quickly ruin the bearing. Worse, it can score the shaft, necessitating replacement.

Check the nuts and cotter pin that secure the prop at the end of the shaft. If they are eroded or otherwise in poor shape, put them on your list for replacement before launch time next spring. If you want to get a jump on your springtime chores, remove the spent zinc anodes on your boat's running gear and hardware.

Prop Talk

I would conservatively estimate that at least half the boats on the water have propellers that are at least subtly damaged. That's a shame because almost nothing—save a fouled or barnacle-encrusted bottom—erodes performance and efficiency more than a damaged propeller. To check yours, you'll need nothing more complicated than a ruler.

Start by making sure your engine is in neutral

Using the ruler technique for measuring propeller damage.

and, for safety's sake, pocket the ignition key. Hold the ruler against your boat's bottom (or the gearcase, if your boat is sterndrive-powered). Rotate the propeller until one of the blades just contacts the ruler with its tip. Now adjust the ruler so it clears the prop by a small fraction of an inch—about 1/16 inch is fine.

Hold the ruler firmly in place and continue to rotate the propeller by hand to make sure each blade clears the ruler by the same dimension and in just the same place. If any of the blades don't clear by the same dimension or are swinging in a different arc from any of the others, your prop requires reconditioning. Pull it off and send it out now so it will be ready next spring.

If you had to remove the propeller for reconditioning, you should repeat this test on the bare propshaft to make sure that it's not bent as well. If your boat is inboard-powered, have a helper rotate the shaft from ahead of the stern bearing so you can be sure you're measuring shaft runout and not the axial play of the stern bearing.

The end of the shaft should not have more than 0.003 or 0.004 inch of runout. The dimension is less than the thickness of a typical business card. If the shaft is bent, remove it for straightening or replacement during the lay-up season.

Changing the Oil in the Lower Unit

If you have a sterndrive or an outboard, you're not quite done with oil changing yet. Now that the boat is hauled out, you also have to drain and refill the lower unit of your drive.

These call for the correct, factory-specified gear oil. See your owner's manual for the gearcase capacity specifications; the amount will be listed in fluid ounces. I find it easiest to simply buy the branded gear oil furnished by the engine manufacturer. It usually costs a bit more, but you'll be sure of getting the right stuff. This product is usually a multiweight oil, but much more viscous (thicker) than lubricating oil. For example, a typical lube oil might be 10W-30; gear oil is often something on the order of 85W-140 weight.

Assemble the following tools and supplies: enough gear oil to fill the gearcase, a wide-blade screwdriver, clean rags, a drain pan to catch the used oil, a funnel, and a 1-gallon screw-cap milk jug to carry the spent oil to the disposal center.

Prepare the drive unit or outboard motor by lowering it until it's vertical. This is important to ensure that the old oil drains out properly and you get the right amount of fresh oil in the drive when you refill it.

Place the drain pan underneath the gearcase and remove the lower screw carefully. Put the screw in a safe spot, where it won't get lost. I usually wipe it off with a clean rag and stick it in my pocket. Not much oil will dribble out at this point because the vacuum in the gearcase tends to hold it in.

Next, remove the upper screw. At this point you can expect gear oil to start running out of the lower hole in earnest. Allow it to drain out completely—it might take five to ten minutes.

When it's empty, use a clean rag to wipe any residual oil from the fill and vent holes. Each of these holes is sealed with a plastic washer or neoprene O-ring that is captured under the screw head. In most cases, these sealing washers come out with the screws, but in some cases they remain stuck in the hole. Replace the washers—they cost about $1 each.

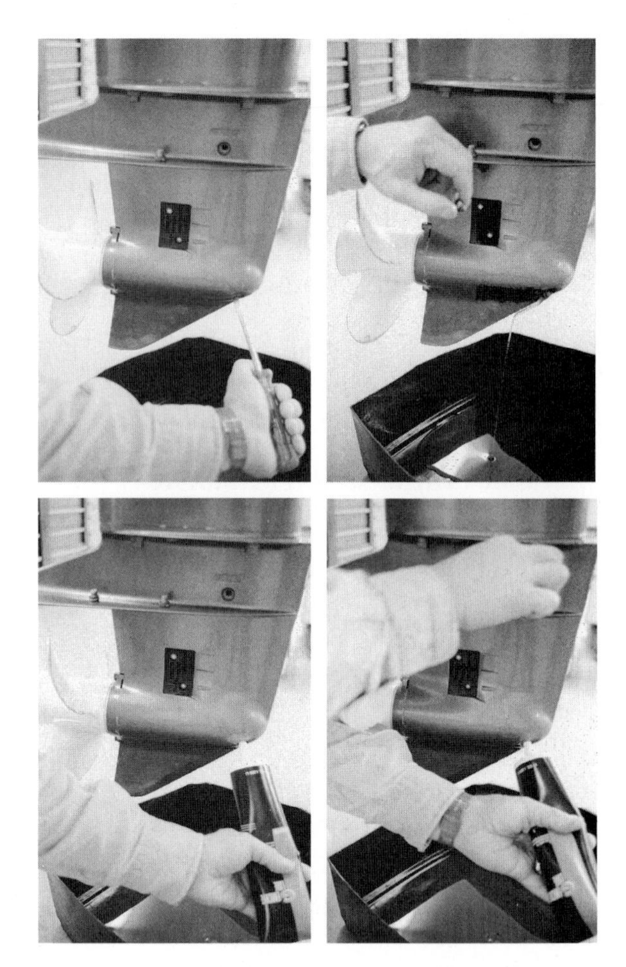

(TOP LEFT) *Loosening the (lower) gear oil drain screw in an outboard motor gearcase. The upper screw has already been removed in this photo.*

(TOP RIGHT) *Allowing the old gear oil to drain out of the outboard motor's gearcase.*

(BOTTOM LEFT) *Inserting the tube of fresh gear oil into the lower hole in preparation to refill the gearcase.*

(BOTTOM RIGHT) *Oil has dribbled out of the upper hole. Now it's time to reinstall the upper screw. Once this screw is tightened, the tube of gear oil can be withdrawn in preparation for installing the lower screw. The vacuum in the gearcase will hold the oil in place while you start the screw.*

If for some reason you can't replace the washers and must recycle the old ones, make sure that each screw and hole gets one washer. In other words, if one washer is stuck under the screw head, make sure you put that screw back in the same hole when you refill the gearcase. If you wind up with two washers under one screw and none under the other, water will infiltrate into the gearcase as soon as you launch the boat next season.

Speaking of water in the gear oil, now that you have the old oil out of the gearcase, inspect it. Does it have a slug of water in it? Is it milky looking? If the answer is yes to either of these questions, the gearcase has a leaking seal which should be replaced before you refill it with fresh oil. Gearcase seal testing and replacement is a job for a professional mechanic.

Does the oil appear burned or smell that way? If so, you might be running the wrong gear oil or you might be subjecting your engine to extra hard usage. If the latter is the case, you should drain and refill the gearcase more often; perhaps one additional time in the middle of the boating season.

Fill 'Er Up

If the gearcase passed muster with no evidence of leaks, you're ready to refill it with fresh gear oil. Strangely enough, it gets filled from the lower hole, not the top one. This ensures that there are no voids or air bubbles in the gearcase and that it's solidly filled with oil.

Remove the cap from your first tube of gear oil. These tubes are usually factory-sealed with an end that has to be cut off to dispense the oil. To make things easier, go ahead and cut the tips off all the tubes before you begin the operation.

Insert the tip of the first tube into the lower hole and squeeze it so the contents flow into the gearcase. It's best to fill the gearcase slowly. That way the oil is less likely to squirt out around the tube.

If the gearcase holds more than the contents of the first tube, squeeze the oil out of the tube until it's emptied. (If you are filling the gearcase of a small engine that holds less than a tube's worth of oil, look for gear oil to dribble out of the top hole.)

If you need to continue filling with a second tube, insert the upper screw in its hole and tighten snugly before starting to fill from the second tube. When you've got the second tube ready, stick it in the lower hole, remove the upper screw again, and continue your filling operation.

Once gear oil has started to dribble out of the upper hole, the gearcase is full. Hold the tube in place and tighten the upper screw firmly.

Now that it's completely tightened, you can remove the gear oil tube from the lower hole and replace that screw, tightening it securely as well. You can usually take your time with this step because when you remove the tube from the lower hole, very little gear oil should dribble out. (The vacuum in the gearcase holds it inside.)

Once both screws are tightened securely, finish the job by wiping any stray oil off the outside of the gearcase, emptying the drain pan into the jug with your funnel, and disposing of the used gear oil in an environmentally responsible way.

Servicing Raw-Water Strainers

Your boat should have a raw-water strainer on each water inlet: engine, genset, water-cooled air conditioner/reverse cycle heat, deck washdown pump, head, and whatever else you have. They come in handy for filtering out eelgrass, trash, and small fish from your machinery's innards, but they must be cleaned out periodically.

If you don't know where they are and how to clean them, here are some guidelines.

Strainers are made from bronze or tough plastic. Periodic maintenance consists of loosening the bail or large hand nut and removing the stainless steel mesh strainer and cleaning off any trash that has collected there.

At the end of the season, take this a step further by completely disassembling the strainer's body to carefully inspect its component parts. Pay particular attention to the clear plastic outer body and the O-ring seals that keep things tight. The plastic body or sight glass is made of a tough, clear plastic, but it can become crazed (riddled with fine cracks), which will ultimately weaken it, causing it to fail.

The O-rings can become flattened from the pressure of their confines. If they don't spring back to a nice round shape (in cross section) after the strainer is disassembled, replace them. Whether you recycle the old O-rings or replace them with new, give them a thin coating of white Teflon grease before reassembly.

Examine the strainer basket to make sure it hasn't become mashed. If it has, it will allow the trash it's supposed to filter out to pass into the machinery. This is definitely not a good thing. In most cases, you can bend a distorted strainer back into perfect order with your fingers. Test it by fitting it into the recess that receives it. If you can't make it right, you'll have to replace this part.

Over time, these strainer baskets become brittle. If that's the case, order a new one and install it before launching the boat next spring.

Maintaining Seacocks

Every raw-water inlet on your boat should be fitted with some sort of a shutoff, either a conventional bronze seacock or the more modern substitute—a ball valve.

If you have ball valves, good news—they don't require any maintenance or lubrication. If they begin to operate poorly, the soft Teflon parts inside (lip seals) can be replaced with an overhaul kit or—more likely—the entire valve can be replaced with a new one.

Conventional seacocks, on the other hand, do require maintenance. The good news is that you'd be hard put to find a simpler, more forgiving piece of equipment to work on. The typical seacock has two moving parts.

Remove the bolts from the side of the seacock

Raw-water strainer. The one pictured here is a bronze unit manufactured by Groco.

Raw-water inlet with ball valve shutoff. Note doubled hose clamps on this below-the-waterline hose connection.

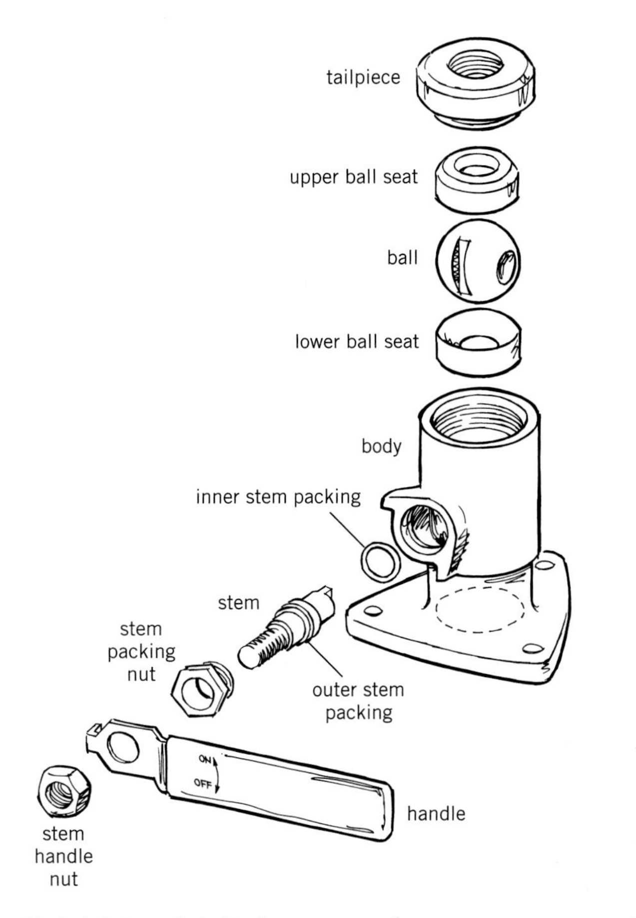

Exploded view of a ball valve on a seacock.

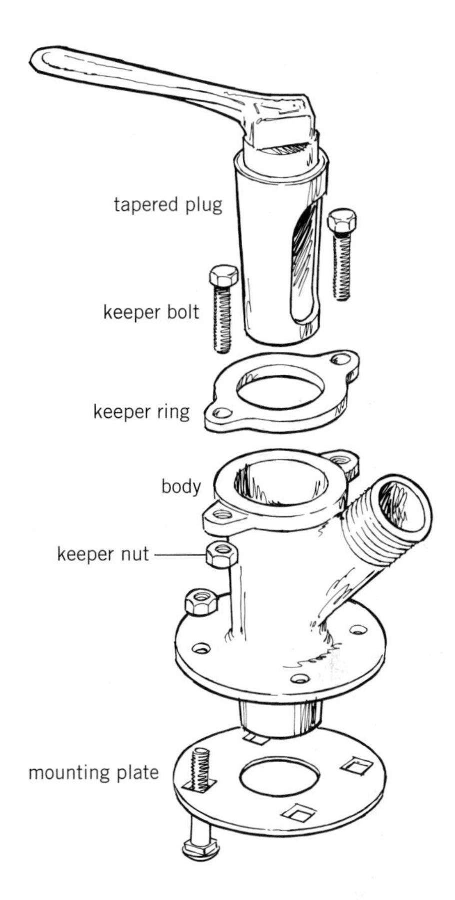

Exploded view of a typical seacock.

and slide the cock (the portion with the actuating handle) out of the body. Wipe the body of this part and the precisely machined receptacle in the seacock body off with a clean rag.

Inspect the surfaces of these two parts for cracks and pitting. Minor ones can be machined out, as I'll describe presently. While you're doing this inspection, pay attention also to the coloration of the parts. If you find the usual greenish corrosion, that's no problem. It will be cleaned up when you do the routine maintenance detailed below. What you don't want to see is any pinkish coloration, which is a sign of electrolysis. If you see any evidence of it, you need to find out why it has happened.

You might have to do some sleuthing to find the problem, but find it you must. Often it's something as simple as a broken bonding wire that is supposed to be attached to the through-hull fitting or seacock, but isn't. The culprit could be dirty battery terminals, damp, poorly made wiring connections, the use of a nonmarine battery charger on board, or even a problem with the wiring in your boat's dock. You'll find more information on electrolysis in chapter 5.

Clean and Greasy

Using a piece of fine-grade emery cloth, lightly polish or dress the mating surfaces of the seacock until they're shiny and bright. Do not oversand these parts or you will ruin the fit of the seacock parts.

Once the parts are cleaned, they should be reassembled. First, give the working surfaces a generous smear of a heavy-bodied, saltwater-proof grease. I like to use the Quicksilver Heavy-Duty Anti-Corrosion Grease, which is available from Mercury outboard and MerCruiser sterndrive dealers. Don't use this type of grease if your boat's seacocks have rubber parts as described in the next paragraph. Then put them back together and snug up the fasteners. Don't go crazy tightening these machine screws; they're made of bronze and, if you overdo the tightening, you'll snap off their heads.

Warning: If your boat's seacocks are made by Groco, the cock has a bonded rubber surface over a bronze core. This shouldn't be sanded with emery cloth; merely wipe it clean and grease it, making sure you use a nonpetroleum grease. Silicone or Teflon-based grease is fine. In my experience, the Teflon stuff is more heavy-bodied and tenacious and holds up longer. The interior of the seacock body is a bronze casting that can be lightly dressed with your emery cloth before reassembling the seacock.

Once that's done, tighten up the locking screw enough so the cock can't be actuated accidentally. Don't overtighten this part either; doing so might distort the seacock body and invite leaks and trouble. When I'm finished with this job, I leave all seacocks in the closed position for two reasons.

First, this prevents any surprises on launching day if I've done something stupid, like left a hose off. Second, it holds antifreeze in the system when I winterize. That's better for engines, heads, pumps, etc.

During the season, you should make it a point to exercise your boat's seacocks from time to time. The handles can get stuck if they're never moved—and the last thing you want if water is pouring into your boat is a balky seacock that can't be shut off.

Inspecting Hoses and Clamps

Boaters are inclined to forget the multitude of hoses down in the bilge, which is fine until one of them lets go. Therefore, take a little time to check them over now, while the boat is out of the water.

Hoses degrade from the influence of ozone in the atmosphere and the overheated conditions that often prevail in bilges, engine rooms, and other machinery spaces. That's on the outside. On the inside of a hose, even worse things can go on. The only way to properly inspect a length of hose is to remove it from its fittings and check it carefully for delamination and/or deterioration.

Below-the-waterline hoses need to be especially reliable for obvious reasons (how long can you tread water?). They must be made of the wire wound-type; that is, reinforced with stainless steel wire.

Shields is the most popular brand. They make two types of hose for wet exhaust applications. The first is designated 250 series and is used in applications where flexibility and tight bends are not important. The second type is designated 252 series. It's a newer product with a ribbed construction that allows it to make relatively tight radius bends. (They also make a hose designated 200 series, which is suitable for dry exhaust systems, but that's not likely to apply to any of your boats.)

The stainless steel should not be piercing the inside or outside of the hose at the ends and the hose clamps must be in good shape.

By the way, all hose clamps on a boat should be constructed entirely of stainless steel. Be forewarned: Some of the clamps on the market that are marketed as being all stainless are not—the band portion of the clamp is stainless but the worm screw is not.

Here's a tip for making sure yours pass muster. A magnet will not stick to high-quality stainless steel. If a magnet sticks to any part of a hose clamp on your boat, replace the clamp with a known good one.

There's another important thing to remember about hose clamps below the waterline. Any hose that runs below the waterline anywhere along its length must have double hose clamps at both ends. Don't forget the shower sump, bilge pump, and sink drains. If these exit the hull near the waterline, they should have double clamps.

Although they're not quite as critical, you should also inspect your boat's other hoses (the ones that run above the waterline). Any hose that is starting to look a bit suspect should be replaced now—not later—before it can cause any trouble. They don't get any better with age.

Emptying and Winterizing Freshwater Tanks

The basic premise behind freezeproofing your boat's freshwater system is that you must remove any standing water and replace it with antifreeze.

Let me remind you again that you must only use antifreeze that is suitable for potable water systems—that is, propylene glycol: the so-called RV antifreeze. If you inadvertently put ethylene glycol—conventional antifreeze—in your boat's freshwater system, you will poison your family and guests next season when they begin to use that water. Make sure you get this right.

Propylene glycol is sold in 1-gallon jugs at chandleries and recreational vehicle dealers. It comes prediluted to a 35 percent solution, which is how you'll use it. Expect to use 4 or 5 gallons to winterize a typical freshwater system on a boat that has a couple of sinks and a shower. (If your boat has two water tanks, add at least 3 or 4 gallons to that figure.)

If there's a handy access port in the top of the tank, open it and take a peek inside. If you see any water left inside, pump or sponge it out before you proceed. If much standing water remains, you will have to winterize the system twice to make sure that the antifreeze protection is adequate. (The standing water will dilute the antifreeze, thereby reducing its effectiveness.)

If you followed my advice, you opened the faucets, and let the pressure pump evacuate the water for you when the boat was still in the water.

Winterizing Your Water Heater and the Freshwater System

The next step is to bypass the water heater by disconnecting it from the rest of the water system. Otherwise you'll have to use a lot more antifreeze to do the job.

If your boat's engine is freshwater-cooled the water heater will probably have four hoses attached to it. Two of them are connected to the closed-cooling system (the so-called freshwater side, which as you know is actually filled with operating antifreeze).

You can ignore the two hoses that lead to the engine; leave them hooked up to the engine—they're already winterized.

The two hoses you need to concern yourself with are the ones marked "inlet" and "outlet" or "cold water in" and "hot water out." Disconnect these two hoses where they attach to the water heater and allow the water heater to begin draining. Expect a lot of water to drain from the lower hole. (If your water heater's capacity is 6 gallons, that's how much water will be draining out.)

Note: If the water heater is not mounted where the water will drain into the bilge, connect a length of hose to keep the water from puddling up on a shelf. Standing fresh water on plywood can cause mildew at best, dry rot at worst.

You can speed up the draining process by opening the pressure-relief valve. Do this by swinging its lever straight out and away from the water heater. Once the draining has begun you can move on with the procedure.

Since you're bypassing the water heater, you're going to have to find the necessary fittings to connect the two hoses to each other. If the system is plumbed with hoses, you'll just need a short piece of the right size of pipe, which is properly called a nipple. You'll also need a couple of hose clamps to secure the hose ends to the nipple. If the water heater plumbing uses some other kind of connections, you'll have to collect whatever fittings you need to connect the inlet and outlet lines.

If you're really lucky, your boatbuilder has already plumbed a bypass into the system to make winterizing easy. In my experience that's only about one in fifty boats, but you never know. If your boat is so equipped, set the valves to bypass the hot water heater and forget having to mess around with fittings.

As the heater is draining, connect the inlet and outlet hoses together with two hose clamps and a short length of copper tubing or a nipple. Once it has drained, close the pressure-relief valve (if you opened it). To bypass the water heater altogether, once the heater has drained completely, winterize it by pouring pure propylene glycol antifreeze (remember, please—the nontoxic type) into the upper hole.

You will probably need a short length of hose with a funnel attached to accomplish this. Again, if the drain doesn't lead into the bilge, attach a hose to the lower fitting to keep the antifreeze from puddling where you don't want it.

At first, pure water will drain out of the lower hole. But as you add a bit more antifreeze, it will begin to take on a stronger color as the antifreeze replaces the water in the tank. Once the color of the liquid that's draining has become as dark as the antifreeze you're pouring in, you can stop. The water heater is now winterized. Allow the unit to drain and you're done.

Hint: Once you've gotten the necessary parts together to do this bypass, and you've done your winterizing, you should mark the parts and set them aside for future years.

Now you can move on to winterizing the system. (You'll get back to the water heater when you've finished.) Start by adding 3 or 4 gallons of RV antifreeze to the water tank. Simply open the deck-fill fitting and pour it in. If your boat has more than one tank, add antifreeze to each tank.

The next step is to circulate antifreeze through all the water lines, faucets, and drains. Make sure you remember all of your boat's faucets. For example if there's a swim shower at the transom, don't forget about winterizing it. The same goes for any freshwater washdown pumps.

Now switch the pressure water system circuit breaker on. Go to the farthest cold-water faucet from the tank, open it up, and let it run until the color of the liquid running out of the tap matches the antifreeze you added to the tank.

This color change is subtle, so here are a couple of other cues that will help you be sure that antifreeze has made it to the faucet: RV antifreeze feels slimy, gets just a bit foamy when it splashes in a sink, and tastes sweet. (Don't try this last trick when you're winterizing the head and holding tank system.)

Run a little extra antifreeze from the faucet to protect the drain in case there are any low spots that hold water. Now you can shut this tap off and move to the next farthest cold-water tap from the tank.

Repeat this procedure at each cold-water tap, moving toward the tank(s) until they're all done. Don't forget the shower and the galley sink faucets. Then repeat this same procedure with the hot-water taps in the system starting with the one farthest from the tank.

If your boat has two freshwater tanks, now is the time to switch the valves to select the other tank, and run through the procedure again. If you were never able to get the antifreeze that spouted from the faucets as dark as the stuff you added, run the system dry, add another few gallons of antifreeze to each tank, and repeat the procedure. Don't give up until the color intensifies, indicating good protection against freeze damage.

If your boat has a dockside water hookup, be sure to add antifreeze from the outside hookup through the regulator with a faucet open—it might require a pump to force the antifreeze through.

All this work is a bit of a pain, but it's trivial compared to spending the beginning of next season chasing down water system leaks caused by freeze-damaged plumbing over the winter.

Drains Freeze, Too

As I mentioned, make sure to run enough pure antifreeze down the sink drains to protect them as well. Get down under the sinks and check for water-trapping low spots. If you find any, pull the hoses off from the bottom of the sink or the through-hull fitting, swing the hose down to let it drain, and then reconnect it. Then, just to be sure, pour a little more propylene glycol through.

Speaking of drains, if your boat is plumbed like most, the shower probably drains into a sump that's equipped with a small bilge pump. Sponge the water out of this sump before winterizing and pour antifreeze into the shower drain until the sump is half full or so. Flip on the switch that powers the pump and allow it to drain the sump out.

Most powerboats have refrigerators, but if yours is equipped with an icebox instead, you'll have to winterize the icebox drain. These are either plumbed to drain into the bilges, or there will be a hand pump to pump the meltwater into the galley sink.

In any case, the object is to pour RV antifreeze in

the icebox and make sure that you displace any water. If yours has a pump, before you add the antifreeze, operate the pump until it's sucked the line dry. Then add your antifreeze and pump again until the discharge is pure antifreeze. That way you don't have to worry about any trapped water freezing in the low spots in the line.

Back to the Water Heater

You're almost done with the freshwater system. Finish up by reconnecting the inlet and outlet hoses to the water heater. That's it; you're done winterizing your boat's freshwater system.

Bilge Pumps

Your boat's bilge pumps and their discharge hoses need winterizing too. The procedure is pretty much the same as described for the shower sump pump. Pump the bilges dry, sponge up any water that remains, then dump enough RV antifreeze in to cover the pump inlet.

Now you can turn on the pump and let it pump antifreeze through the discharge hose. If there wasn't enough antifreeze to make the pump run for at least ten seconds, do it again. If your boat has more than one bilge pump, make sure you perform this operation for each of them in turn.

Will the Scuppers Be OK?

It's seldom a problem, but if your boat's deck drains or scuppers have any water-trapping low spots in them, they need attention, too.

Have a look and, if you find any low spots, you can either remove the hose end to drain it or even tip it up to make sure that it drains. Then, pour a little RV antifreeze through until the standing water has been displaced. Make sure you replace any hoses that you removed and tighten the clamps securely.

The Head and Holding Tank

First, make sure that the holding tank is empty. I trust you took care of this when you made that last trip to the gas dock.

If your boat has a dual discharge system, start by moving the Y-valve to the overboard discharge position. Find the inlet through-hull fitting and remove the hose from the fitting or the seacock. Open the seacock to drain it, then close it. Stick the end of this hose into a jug of RV antifreeze, then start pumping the head with the control valve in the "flush" position.

At first, the water swirling around in the head will be pale. As the antifreeze begins to displace the water in the system, the color will intensify. Keep pumping until the discharge is the same color as the antifreeze from your jug, then switch the valve on the head over to the "dry bowl" position.

Do this a couple of times so you can be sure that any standing water in the system has been replaced by antifreeze. Once you know the head and its associated inlet and outlet hoses are full of antifreeze, switch the Y-valve selector over to send the head's discharge into the holding tank and pump a couple of gallons of 50/50 antifreeze solution in there. Now you can replace the hose on the through-hull or seacock. Finish up by closing all the valves in the system. That's it; you're done with the head, the holding tank, and the associated plumbing.

Winterizing and Fogging Out the Engine

Now that you've winterized the freshwater system and heads, you're ready to tackle something a bit more complicated—the engine. Winterizing an engine involves not only freezeproofing it, but also, at the same time, fogging it out with a special preparation known as fogging oil.

Fogging is mandatory with outboards. Not everyone bothers with this procedure for inboard and sterndrive power plants, but I strongly advocate that you do. The beauty of fogging is that it coats all the interior surfaces of an engine with rust-inhibiting oil. Since condensation in an engine is a fact of life, an engine that doesn't get the fogging treatment will rust in all sorts of curious locations. A fogged engine won't.

What Flavor Engine Do You Have?

For inboard and sterndrive engines, the first step is to determine what kind of cooling system your engine has. There are two possibilities: freshwater-cooled or raw-water cooled. If you don't already know, here's an easy way to figure it out. Look at the top of the engine. If you find an expansion tank with a pressure cap (like the radiator cap on a car) or a coolant-overflow bottle, you have a freshwater-cooled engine. (It's also called a closed-cooling system.) If there's no pressure cap, your engine is raw-water cooled. It's as simple as that.

Winterizing a Freshwater-Cooled Engine

Freshwater-cooled marine engines are cooled much like automotive engines. A closed-cooling system circulates a mixture of operating antifreeze through the engine block and cylinder heads. In almost all cases, this operating antifreeze is ethylene glycol antifreeze and water (usually in a 50/50 ratio). This operating antifreeze is what draws off the heat generated by the friction and the combustion of fuel in the engine.

In an automotive engine, the heat that is absorbed by the coolant is dissipated by running the hot coolant through a radiator. The radiator has relatively cool air flowing over the exterior of its myriad small tubes. After passing through this air-cooled radiator, the coolant is cooled down and ready to be circulated back through the engine to remove more waste heat. Round and round it goes, drawing off heat and getting rid of it into the air.

A freshwater-cooled marine engine has essentially the same system except that, instead of a radiator, it has a heat exchanger. In this case the tubes aren't exposed to cool air. Instead, they run through a bath of cold seawater in a closed tank called the heat exchanger.

This cold seawater is circulated and constantly replaced with new cold water by the engine's raw-water pump. The used seawater and the waste heat it contains are dumped out of the boat's wet exhaust. (The wet exhaust keeps things cool enough to allow rubber hose to be used for the exhaust system.)

When winterizing a freshwater-cooled engine, you have to winterize both systems: the freshwater side (filled with antifreeze and water) and the raw-water side.

The Freshwater Side

If you followed my earlier advice, you checked the degree of protection afforded by the coolant in your freshwater-cooled engine when your boat was still in the water. I urged you to check it then because, if you have to drain the system down a bit to add some straight ethylene glycol antifreeze to increase the freeze protection, you'll have to run the engine to mix up the coolant then allow it to cool before you recheck it with your antifreeze checker. If you need to run the engine on land, it can be done. See The Sea in a Bucket section opposite for details.

Flushing a Freshwater-Cooled Engine

This system should be drained occasionally, flushed out with fresh water, and refilled with 50/50 antifreeze-water mixture. Here's how.

You begin by draining the system down. Before you proceed, it's wise to start by checking over the system and gaining an understanding of what the various hoses and components do.

There are usually a couple of petcocks in the engine block that will allow the coolant in the block to be drained. Check your engine owner's manual for particulars on where these are located. Open them with a wrench or a pair of pliers and allow the coolant to drain. Be careful, especially if they're made of plastic.

The stuff you're draining is ethylene glycol. It's toxic so you must rig up some means of catching it for safe disposal. Some petcocks are made to slip a hose over them. In other cases you'll need to rig a funnel, hose, and a catch jug. (In some cases there's not much room, in which case you may need to use a Coke bottle or the like to catch the spent coolant.)

Hint: You may find it helpful to poke a short length of coat-hanger wire or something similar in the petcock to dislodge any trapped crud that would impede the draining process.

Once the system has drained down, close the

petcocks and fill the engine with straight fresh water. Stick a garden hose in the expansion tank and fill it up very slowly. Don't try filling it up from the coolant overflow tank.

Filling it slowly is a must because otherwise air can be trapped, which will cause overheating when you start the engine up later. After it begins to balk at having more water added, you're almost ready to start the engine and keep topping up the fresh water in the expansion tank with your garden hose. But hold on; since the boat isn't in the water, you've got to do some rigging to provide a flow of fresh water to the raw-water side of the engine. (That's to substitute for the raw water that isn't being supplied.)

The Sea in a Bucket

1. Pull the raw-water inlet hose off the through-hull, seacock, or raw-water strainer. Make sure to drain the strainer of any standing water. Fill a bucket with water from your garden hose and immerse the engine's raw-water inlet hose that you removed from the strainer into the bottom of the water-filled bucket.
2. Station a helper with the garden hose at the bucket with instructions to regulate the flow from the garden hose to keep the water level in the bucket up near the top. Although it's easiest to do this with a nozzle, your helper can kink the hose to regulate the flow. When you start the engine, the raw-water pump is immediately going to start drinking water from the bucket, so *don't let it run dry*. If for any reason you can't keep the inlet hose immersed in water, shut off the engine immediately.
3. Now you're ready to start the engine. Allow it to run at a fast idle (1,500 to 1,800 rpm) for a few minutes with the heat exchanger cap off. Keep an eye on the coolant level in the expansion tank. Top it off as needed. When the thermostat opens, the engine will gulp some water and the tank will need topping off. This is sort of like burping a baby. Have your helper hand you the garden hose for a moment so you can top off the tank, then hand it back right away so the raw-water supply in the bucket isn't depleted.
4. When the engine has stabilized and run for three or four minutes, shut if off, let it cool down for an hour or so, and open the petcocks again. Let the engine drain completely, and observe the water that's draining out. *Note:* You may have to repeat the coat-hanger trick to ensure that the petcock doesn't get clogged with crud.

   If the water that's draining out isn't clean and clear, close the petcocks and repeat the filling and flushing procedure. Do this as many times as necessary until the water that's drained from the system runs clean and clear. Don't ever drain the engine and refill it with cold water when it's hot; you can crack the block.
5. When the flushing is complete, leave the engine drained and make sure the petcocks are tightly closed. Then fill the system with the recommended coolant; usually ethylene glycol and water in a 50/50 ratio. If your boat is liable to be subjected to temperatures below –34°F, you'll need to use a stronger mixture.

   Run the engine again, wait until the thermostat opens, and top off the coolant in the expansion tank as needed.

   (Keep the bucket, garden hose, and inlet hose arrangement rigged up; you'll be using it again in a few minutes when you winterize the raw-water circuit of the cooling system.)
6. Test the coolant in the expansion tank with an antifreeze tester to make sure that it provides enough protection for the lowest temperatures that are likely to prevail during the lay-up season.
7. If the coolant in the block is not a strong enough mixture for the temperatures expected, yet the tank is full, you will have to open a petcock and drain some out and add pure antifreeze in its place. Start the engine again and wait for the thermostat to open so the coolant mixes thoroughly. But please don't forget that your boat is out of the water. Any time you run the engine, you'll need your helper with the bucket and garden hose. After the engine has warmed up and the coolant has begun to circulate, check the

protection level of the coolant again with your antifreeze checker.

Remember, too, that it's the true outside temperature that you want to protect the engine against—not the wind chill. You don't need to take into account the wind chill factor because a body with no heat in it—like your boat's engine in the middle of the winter—isn't affected by it.

Finally, remember that a 50/50 coolant mixture doesn't suddenly freeze solid when it hits –34°F. Instead, it begins to get slushy. If this occurs, your engine will not be damaged as long as you don't try to start it before the ambient temperature comes back up.

Pressure Cap Maintenance

The pressure cap on a freshwater-cooled engine should be checked to make sure that the gasket is clean and the tabs that secure it are not bent. Scrape off any deposits on the gasket with a dull knife blade. I think it's prudent to replace this component every few seasons.

The Raw-Water Side

If you have a freshwater-cooled engine, you also have to freezeproof the raw-water circuit of the system. On the other hand, if your boat's engine is raw-water cooled, this is the *only* system you have to winterize in the engine. In that case, refer to The Sea in a Bucket section above for instructions.

The only difference in the procedure is that, instead of keeping the bucket topped off with water from a garden hose, your helper is going to refill it as necessary from a jug of nontoxic RV antifreeze (propylene glycol).

Now, before starting your engine to winterize the raw-water circuit, read the section below on fogging out the engine and assemble all of the necessary supplies and tools for that job. (You are going to fog out your engine, aren't you? If it's a gas engine, you should.)

Fogging supplies at the ready? Have you got your helper stationed with a bucket of RV antifreeze with a couple of extra jugs handy? Great; you're all set to winterize the raw-water circuit of your engine.

Winterizing a Raw-Water-Cooled Engine

If you have a raw-water-cooled engine (or a freshwater-cooled engine with the freshwater circuit previously taken care of), you can introduce RV antifreeze into the raw-water inlet and get set to fog out the engine at the same time. It gets complicated, so pay careful attention.

If your boat's engine has a raw-water strainer, it's a good idea to drain it first. That will save on antifreeze. The two most popular strainers are made by Perko and Groco. Here are details on draining both types.

The Perko is an all bronze unit with a pipe plug threaded into the bottom of the lower casting. If this is what you have, use a box end wrench to loosen the plug. Since this plug has a pipe thread, it may take a bit of oomph to loosen it. The unit will drain down faster if you vent it by loosening the upper (clean out) access port at the top. If you do this, make sure you tighten it back up before you reinstall the pipe plug and proceed with your winterizing operation.

Also before you reinstall the pipe plug, you should wire brush its threads and put some pipe dope, Teflon thread paste, or Teflon tape on them. That way this part won't get seized in place and will be easier to thread back in and remove. Tighten this plug securely.

Start it by hand then, once you're sure it's not cross-threaded, finish winding it in with your wrench. Remember, this fitting has a pipe thread, so you'll have to wind it in pretty tightly.

If your raw-water strainer is a Groco, the drain fitting is a plastic screw with a wing-type handle, and it's mounted in the side body of the strainer, not the bottom. Other than that the procedure is basically the same as with the Perko.

Once you've drained the strainer and reinstalled the drain plug, you're ready to proceed. Start the engine with the raw-water inlet hose immersed in the bucket of nontoxic antifreeze, and run it at a fast idle. The exhaust will start to deepen in color.

This will take a minute or two. As time goes by, the color of the exhaust water will intensify. (Also the exhaust discharge on the ground will start to get foamy as it changes over from water to antifreeze.) Remind your helper to top off the supply bucket so the hose doesn't start to pull in air.

When the exhaust water gets to the same intense color as the antifreeze being pulled in, the whole system is full of antifreeze mixture. Now there's no longer any trapped water to freeze; the engine is completely freezeproofed. Shut it off and leave the hose and bucket rigged up. Top it off one more time with RV antifreeze before you continue with the last step—fogging.

Flame arrester and crankcase ventilation hoses on carburetor. The carburetor's rainhat was removed to take this picture.

Fog It Out

The necessary tools and supplies for fogging out an engine are pretty simple. For sterndrives and inboards, you'll need a 7/16-inch wrench and a spray can of fogging oil. I find it easier to use a ready-made product (such as OMC Fogging Oil) than mix up my own home-brewed fogging oil preparation with Marvel Mystery Oil and LPS-66 as some mechanics do. The homemade stuff has to be squirted in with an oilcan whereas a ready-made product comes in a handy spray can.

Technique is everything in fogging. The object is to inject the oil into the engine's carburetor slowly enough so the engine continues to run long enough to be completely fogged out. Once it stalls, as it surely will, the plugs will be fouled. Then, you won't be able to restart it unless you replace them.

1. Use your wrench to remove the nut that secures the flame arrester on top of the carburetor. If your engine has a "rainhat," lift it off now. For safety's sake, leave the crankcase ventilation hoses and the flame arrester on for now.

   Warning: This procedure requires that you work around the engine when it's running. Make sure you stay clear of moving parts, drive belts, and engine accessories such as the alternator.
2. Check for gasoline fumes, run the blower for five minutes, and make sure your helper is ready with the RV antifreeze-filled bucket for the raw water. The helper should also have a backup supply of antifreeze in a jug to make sure the bucket doesn't run dry.
3. When all systems are go, start the engine and bring the rpm up to about 1,800—a very fast idle. Once it's running smoothly, pull off the crankcase vent hoses and remove the flame arrester. Begin the fogging by giving the engine a one- or two-second blast of fogging oil right down the throat of the carburetor (see photo next page). It will start to stumble, so don't overdo this first blast. Give the engine five or ten seconds to recover, then give it another shot.
4. By now, there should be some pretty rich smoke coming out of the exhaust. It's reasonable to assume that you've coated the engine's insides with oil pretty thoroughly. Now you're ready for the last blast. This final shot of fogging oil will be a few seconds long and will undoubtedly kill the engine with a serious case of fouled spark plugs. Have your helper bring the engine speed up to about 2,500 rpm or so. Then immediately give it the last blast of the fogging oil.
5. When the engine dies, you've completed the bulk of your engine winterizing chores. Replace the inlet hose on the through-hull, seacock, ball valve, or raw-water strainer. Leave the shutoff closed for the winter. Next spring, after the boat

Spraying fogging oil into an inboard engine's carburetor.

is launched and you're doing your commissioning, you'll reopen it. Reinstall the flame arrester, crankcase vent hoses, and the rainhat (if your engine has one). Tighten the nut that secures all this down snugly, then shut off the fuel valve on top of the tank if your boat has one.

Dotting "I's" and Crossing "T's"

After your freezeproofing and fogging chores are done, clean the engine with some spray cleaner (Formula 409 works well) and a roll of paper towels. Go outside the boat and stuff a rag in each exhaust. This will keep condensation from infiltrating into the engine through the exhaust system.

While you're outside the boat, wash the areas where the antifreeze has dribbled down from the engine exhausts, the sink drain outlets, shower drains, deck drains, etc. Don't be satisfied with just getting the topsides clean; do the bottom, too. (Antifreeze that has soaked into old paint makes it tougher for new paint to stick when you recoat the boat's bottom next spring.)

Once more back into the engine room. Grab a can of WD-40 or your favorite brand of penetrating oil and spray the engine with a light but even coat. This step helps keep corrosion at bay. When you do this, be careful not to spray any of the rubber or plastic parts such as the wiring harness, hoses, drive belts, ignition wires, distributor cap, etc.

Special Instructions for Sterndrives

When winterizing, sterndrive engines differ from their inboard brethren in just a few ways. All concern the raw-water inlet plumbing.

Sterndrives can be freshwater-cooled (closed cooling) or raw-water cooled, the same as inboards. On some of them, the raw-water inlet is a through-hull fitting; on others, there's a lift pump mounted in the gearcase.

The types with through-hull inlets are winterized exactly the same as inboards, and you're ready to do that now. (See the preceding pages for instructions.) The ones that draw cooling water in through a pump in the sterndrive have to be handled a bit differently. Here's how (and why).

You will need to attach a flush adapter with a supply of fresh water from a garden hose to the sterndrive when you run the engine. This water is not going to go in the engine. It's needed, however, to lubricate the flexible impeller pump in the gearcase. If you don't supply water and instead allow the pump to run dry as you winterize, you'll damage the impeller. In fact, you might even melt it and the pump housing.

You will have to run the engine in neutral to get it up to the necessary rpm for fogging. If your engine's controls won't let you advance the throttle in neutral, you'll have to run it with the engine in gear. If that's the case, remove the propeller before you start; a spinning propeller is very hazardous.

If you have this type of sterndrive, you'll find a water inlet hose leading to the engine from inside the gimbal housing inside your boat's transom. Find the engine end of this hose and disconnect it. Let it lie in the bilge where the water coming in from your flush adapter won't damage anything.

Then find a short length of hose, say 4 or 5 feet, and attach it to the engine where you removed the inlet hose. This hose will be immersed in your bucket of nontoxic RV antifreeze when you start the engine and winterize it.

Warning: Before you start the engine to do the winterizing and fogging procedure, turn on the water supply to your garden hose. Let it flow at a moderate rate while you run the engine and, for heaven's sake, don't forget to shut it off when you have finished these jobs. (If you leave it running you will fill your boat with water—a definite no-no.)

OK, we're just about ready. Run the blower for five minutes, do a sniff test to check the engine room for gasoline fumes, and make sure your helper is ready with the antifreeze-filled bucket and a handy supply of extra antifreeze to keep it topped off. Now you can jump back to page 112 and do your winterizing.

Special Instructions for Winterizing Outboards

An outboard-powered boat is the simplest of all when it comes to winterizing, but there are a few points that differ from the inboard process.

- Don't use antifreeze when you winterize an outboard. Theoretically, all the water that circulates through an outboard motor drains out, provided the engine is stored vertically. That vertical storage is key. If you lay an engine down, water can be trapped in the exhaust housing or gearcase. If it is, and the temperature in your storage area goes below freezing, these castings will most likely be destroyed. Therefore, if you possibly can, store your engine where it won't be subjected to freezing temperatures.
- You will have to connect a flush adapter and a garden hose to the gearcase during the fogging procedure. For safety's sake, you must remove the propeller, since you will have to put the engine in gear to run it up to the necessary rpm for fogging.

Note: If your outboard's control lets you advance the throttle in neutral, you can leave the prop installed and fog out the engine in neutral.

- Most outboard motors have a molded plastic air silencer cover shrouding the carburetors. As a rule, these covers don't have to be removed to inject the fogging oil into the carbs. If you look carefully, you will find removable plastic plugs near the air inlet for each carburetor. Pop these out with a screwdriver to gain access to the carburetor throats.
- When you fog out an outboard, follow a procedure similar to the one outlined earlier in this chapter. The main difference is that you have to give each carburetor air inlet a spritz of fogging oil at each step.
- As with all engine fogging, you should avoid dosing the engine so heavily that it strangles and stalls early in the fogging procedure. Start by dosing the engine with a little fogging oil, then let it recover somewhat, then squirt in a little more oil. That way the engine will run long enough to thoroughly coat all the internal parts and surfaces with a protective coat of oil.
- Once it recovers again, you can begin spraying in the heavy dose of fogging oil that will strangle the engine. This will foul the spark plugs and the engine will die. Then, if you're removing the engine, you can unhook the fuel line, steering cable, battery cables, control cables, and the wiring harness.

Warning: Disconnect the terminals at the battery before you unhook them at the engine. That way you won't have to worry about short circuits, sparks, or exploding batteries.

Now finish up the job by removing the cowl from the engine and greasing the linkages with a good-quality, saltwater-proof grease. That's it; your outboard motor is ready to be moved inside for storage.

- After the engine has stood vertically and drained for a day or two, wrap the gearcase with a plastic garbage bag taped on securely. This serves two purposes. First, it helps prevent water and condensation from infiltrating inside the exhaust housing and the engine. Second, it catches the inevitable drips of nasty exhaust housing residues and keeps them from staining the floor where you store the engine.

Remember: if possible, store the engine where it won't be subjected to freezing temperatures.

The Care and Feeding of Batteries

It's time to give your boat's batteries the winter off. But don't just haul them out of the boat, stick them in the basement, and forget about them. Here are a few points to keep in mind in order to ensure long and faithful service. Ignore these at your peril (and your wallet's).

Warning: Batteries contain a lot of stored electrical energy. If you short-circuit one with a wrench when you're unhooking it, it will probably explode in your face. Always use a wrench that's too short to touch both terminals at once and always disconnect the negative terminal first. If you have to haul the batteries out of the boat through a hatch, make sure that the terminals can't come in contact with the aluminum frame around the hatch. If they do . . . kaboom!

If, after loosening the terminal bolt, you can't wiggle the terminal clamp and slide it off the battery post, don't lever it off with a screwdriver—you might break the seal where the post enters the battery case. Instead, use a large screwdriver or small wrench to spread the jaws of the clamp open. Then it should be a simple matter to wiggle it back and forth a bit and pull it straight up off the post without causing any damage.

Cleaning Batteries for Storage

Use the female part of a wire brush battery post and terminal cleaning tool to remove any oxidation from the battery posts before you haul the battery off for storage. You should also treat your batteries to an end-of-season washdown. The bath will remove any powdery deposits from the top and slow down the rate of self-discharge while the battery is in storage. I mix up some strong detergent and scrub the top of the battery with a throwaway paint brush then rinse the top off generously with a bucketful of fresh water.

Battery servicing tools, left to right: Bucket of sudsy water with throwaway brush, digital multimeter, battery terminal-post cleaning tool, bucket of clear water for rinsing off battery after cleaning.

Use the female portion of the battery terminal-post cleaning tool to clean the battery posts for a good electrical connection.

Battery Storage Tips

If a battery is kept fully charged, it can survive being stored at temperatures below freezing (even below 0°F, in a pinch). However, if you can manage it, it's better to find a place that doesn't get so cold. The basement or an attached garage is perfect.

No matter where you store your boat's batteries over the winter, they're going to require periodic recharging. A fully charged battery in good condition loses about 2 percent of its charge every day that it's laid up. If you're tempted to think, "What the heck, as long as I charge the battery every couple of months it will be OK," think again. If it's stored in a warm storage space, it might be OK, but that's no way to treat an expensive battery.

Worse, if your battery is in cold storage and it gets below three-quarters charge or so, it will freeze. If a battery freezes, it has to be replaced. That's kind of expensive compared with putting a battery charger on it for a few hours every couple of weeks.

So check them regularly and charge as needed. You can check their condition with a voltmeter, which is much safer than using an old-fashioned hydrometer. You should get an open circuit reading of about 12.7 volts. If the reading is less, put a charger on them for a few hours and then check them again.

Testing the condition of the battery with a digital multimeter.

You might have heard that batteries shouldn't be placed on a concrete floor. That was true of the old ones with hard rubber cases. With modern polypropylene-cased batteries, you can safely ignore this dictum. Old habits die hard though. I still always hunt up a piece of plywood to rest my batteries on when I lay them up for the winter. It can't hurt, right?

Charging and Topping off Batteries

If you want your batteries to last as long as possible, top off the water in the cells each time you apply a charge. (Of course, if you have gel-cell batteries you can skip this section.)

Don't be tempted to think that the tops of maintenance-free batteries can't be opened—they can. If you have the so-called maintenance-free batteries that don't have conventional screw caps or pop-off caps on each cell, here's how to open them up to add water.

Usually, there are a couple of large rectangular covers on the battery tops. If you look carefully, you'll find that each of these covers has a small screwdriver slot somewhere around its edge. Find a narrow-blade screwdriver and pry off the covers. Then you can add water to the cells the same as you would with any wet-cell battery.

When adding water, make sure the plates are covered and then some. Most batteries have some sort of a split-ring device in the top of each cell to help you get the water level up where it belongs. Don't overfill them; any excess you put in will simply boil out when you charge the battery.

And as far as that old debate about what kind of water to use—distilled or straight from the tap—I'd say that, unless your local water supply is loaded with minerals (that is, "hard" water), you will do just fine with tap water. If the water has a hardness measure of three grains or more (call your water company or the town's water department for the specification), you should probably buy a bottle of distilled water.

The whole water issue is sort of a tempest in a

teapot. The important thing to remember vis-à-vis water in batteries is to make sure there's enough of it. Enough said.

MOTHBALLING

You are in the home stretch! It's always a good idea to remove all valuable gear from your boat for the winter. The compass and electronic equipment are much safer back home in the garage than on board the boat. Clean the connectors and terminals with an ink eraser and, if any of them are broken or getting tired, make a note on your springtime commissioning checklist to fix them.

If your boat's bilge has a drain plug, remove it and leave it in a spot that you'll remember next season. I routinely put the drain plug in the galley sink, but anyplace that works for you is fine. *Warning:* Don't forget to replace this plug before launching your boat in the spring! A launching followed by a sinking is no way to start a new boating season.

There are two types of drain plugs: the rubber turn-tight style and the threaded bronze pipe plug. If your boat has the pipe plug type, remember to put a smear of pipe dope or a few wraps of Teflon tape on the threads before you wind it in next spring.

Depending on how your boat is blocked, there might be areas in the bilges that have trapped water or antifreeze left over from winterizing. Sponge these areas bone dry now. If there are any spots in the bilge that have collected water in the past—usually from condensation or deck leaks—put a couple of cups of nontoxic propylene glycol antifreeze there in anticipation of that happening again.

I like to sprinkle a handful of rock salt in the bilge around the drain. If any water collects here from condensation over the winter, the rock salt will keep it from freezing. Keep this stuff away from metal hardware and remember to sweep it up when you commission the boat next season.

Mildew Never Sleeps

Open all the lockers, bins, and drawers, and sponge out any collected water you find. Wherever possible, it's best to leave these bins and lockers wide open so you don't find a mildew farm next spring when you open the boat up. Bilge access openings in the cabin sole should also be left open, but be careful if you go down below during the lay-up season; you don't want to fall down into the bilges. It might be wise to hang a warning sign in the companionway to remind you that the floorboards are up.

Wipe all of the smooth surfaces in your boat with a dilute mixture of Clorox and water or, for a fresh, sweet smell, apple cider vinegar. Either of these will kill the mildew spores that are colonizing the surfaces, give the boat a clean smell, and keep mildew at bay for the cold and dry winter months (when it doesn't grow that much anyway).

Remove the bunk cushions and all bedding, towels, and linens. Bring all this stuff home for storage in a dry place. If necessary, pull the foam out of the cushions and send the covers out to be dry-cleaned while the boat is laid up. If you can't store them at home, by all means tip the cushions up on their sides so that air can circulate around them and in the lockers underneath.

Check the food storage lockers and the refrigerator. They should be completely empty and clean. Wipe the inside of the fridge with a dilute mixture of water and Clorox and leave its door wide open.

Caring for Hardware

Polished metal hardware always suffers when a boat is stored, but there's an easy way to arrest this degradation. After you've cleaned the boat, rinsed it off well with fresh water, and dried the hardware, apply a heavy coat of any kind of wax you have on hand to the metal hardware.

Next spring, take a soft cloth and buff the wax. Presto! Hardware that looks as good as new. No green spots or discoloration from off-season corrosion.

Tarp Tips

OK. All the gear has been lubricated, stabilized, winterized, or removed for safe storage. Everything inside is opened. All that's left is the winter cover.

I'm not going to give you blow-by-blow instructions for winter covering, but I am going to share a few of my strong opinions on the subject.

The first of these is that shrink-wrapping a boat is dumb. I think boats are better off being covered yet allowed to breathe. I suppose if your boat is shrink-wrapped on a really dry day and it's effectively sealed, it might stay pretty dry inside. But that's a lot of ifs and maybes.

I'm also no fan of the blue plastic tarps that lots of people use. They don't allow a boat to breathe very much either. If you do decide to use one, at least make sure you leave the ends open enough to allow some air circulation over the winter.

So no shrink-wrapping and no blue plastic tarps. What does that leave? Canvas tarps. That's right, good old-fashioned canvas tarps. They have a number of advantages. For starters, they breathe. That means your boat will stay drier and sweeter inside.

The second big plus to a canvas tarp is that it weighs enough to stay on your boat all winter. Don't laugh! By my reckoning, a blue plastic tarp is about twice as likely to blow off your boat over the winter. If you ignore my suggestions and use a plastic tarp, at least make sure you tie it on securely and visit the boat once in a while to make sure the tarp is still in place and doing its job. (An especially good time to visit the boat is when a big snowstorm is forecast.)

No matter whether you go with the blue plastic or a canvas tarp, you're going to have to build a frame to support it. There are four things to remember.

1. Make sure you put the "rafters" of your frame close enough to each other so the tarp won't sag between them. If it does, the tarp won't shed snow. Then, when a warm day comes, the trapped snow will melt into a huge and heavy puddle. Once this happens, it's just a matter of time before the tarp and the frame collapse. Then your boat has no cover (and you've got a big mess to clean up).
2. Pitch the frame steep enough so that snow, ice, and water are shed by the cover. The reasons for doing this are the same as the reasons for putting rafters on close centers.
3. Leave the ends of the tarp open bow and stern to provide good air circulation underneath. This helps keep your boat sweet and mildew-free over the lay-up season.
4. Make sure you pad any sharp spots on your frame with carpet before you drag the tarp over and tie it down. I usually find plenty of suitable padding material in the dumpster behind my local floor covering shop. Use a utility knife to cut the carpet remnants you find into 4-by-6-inch pieces. Use an industrial-strength staple gun, such as a Swingline T-50, to staple the padding on the ends of the rafters and any other sharp spots on the frame. (If your frame is made of metal, secure the padding with fiberglass-reinforced strapping tape.)

That's it; you're done winterizing, you've gotten to know your boat much better as a consequence, and you have the satisfaction of having done it yourself. Congratulations! See you next spring (next chapter) when we undo all of your labors and put the boat back into service for another season.

Questions and Answers

Question: I own a 28-foot cruiser powered by twin sterndrives. I keep it in the water, in a covered slip, over the winter. This is in Texas and I like to use the boat year-round. We do get several nights that go below freezing in a typical winter. What's the best way to winterize the boat so I can immediately use it without having to drain water, etc.? Should I be afraid to use heaters in the engine compartment?

Answer: I used to work in a boatyard in Connecticut, which gets plenty of nights that go below zero in a typical winter. There, we had a small icebreaker powered with a freshwater-cooled inboard engine. Needless to say, it stayed in the water (or ice) all winter. We kept it from freezing by draining the raw-water strainer and pointing a heat lamp in a clamp-on holder at the heat exchanger. But that's a freshwater-cooled engine.

You don't specify, but I assume your sterndrives are raw-water cooled. This is a tricky question. There are several things you could do that would probably work, but if they failed, your boat could sink.

For example, you could install a proper engine-block heater, such as a Kim Hotstarts. You might have to import one from New England because chandlers in Texas might not even know what one of these is. But if you have a power failure that coincides with cold weather, your boat's engine would be unprotected. Depending on what froze, you risk not only some engine damage but also the possibility of—gulp—sinking your boat.

Don't get a coil dipstick heater, either. A proper engine-block heater should be installed inline in one of your cooling hoses. It's designed to circulate heat through the water in the system. But because your application is different from the closed loop of a car's system (or a freshwater-cooled marine engine for that matter), it won't be that effective. It should, though, be enough to prevent damage under the relatively mild conditions that prevail in your area.

If you do install an inline coolant heater, it should go in the line between the circulating pump and the thermostat housing. Alternatively, if your engine has a water heater bypass loop, it could go in a short length of hose connected to those two fittings. (Obviously, the freshwater system and heads should be winterized and properly prepared for the winter; forget about keeping these in commission.)

Or, you could open the petcocks and drain down the block after using the engine, close the petcocks, stick the inlet hose into a bucket of nontoxic antifreeze, run the engine until the bucket is nearly emptied, and replace the hose.

None of these scenarios will protect the exhaust housing and sterndrive. If your boat is subjected to cold weather and wave action, ice can build up inside there, freeze, and damage the gearcase.

Then, of course, there are heat lamps. You might try a couple of these. Just don't point them toward any fuel system components. The short answer is that you're taking a chance if you try to keep your boat commissioned in the water.

It's risky business, especially when no one is there to keep an eye on things for you. By the way, if you have standard marine insurance, your boat is probably not covered under these circumstances.

Question: How can you tell without pulling the engine if the freeze plug is out or the block is cracked?
Answer: You look for the new cooling water exhaust—the one in the engine room. Engines pump a lot of water. If your freeze plug is gone or there's a crack in the block leading to the outside, you will definitely find a noticeable water leak.

Most of the engine blocks used in popular sterndrives have a couple of big freeze plugs on the aft end of the block casting. If one of these leaks, water will flood out of the bottom of the bell housing.

An engine block can also be cracked internally, in which case the water will enter the crankcase. This is easy to check for by pulling the dipstick. If you've run the engine, the oil will probably be "moose milk"; if you haven't, there will be water droplets clinging to the dipstick.

Question: My wife and I own a 1992 Chaparral 1900 SCL Sport with a MerCruiser 4.3LX engine. We have been avid boaters for the last four years. Two months ago, we had our first baby, so we don't expect to do much boating in the next three or four years, until our daughter is old enough to be safely on board.

We are currently assessing whether to sell the boat or keep it in storage. Is there any reason beyond the purely financial equation whether to keep or sell the boat? If we do keep it, is there any preventive maintenance I should do differently than the standard winterizing tasks, given that I might not use the boat for several years? Is there any benefit to starting it up every year and running it for several hours?
Answer: If you like the boat, and you can afford to hang onto it, then by all means do so. Don't worry; it can wait while your daughter grows up a bit.

If you can find a clean, dry place to store the boat indoors, great. Here are some pointers for mothballing it so it doesn't deteriorate during the lay-up period.

Winterize the boat in the conventional way. Make sure this includes changing the oil and thoroughly fogging out the engine. Top off and stabilize the fuel. After sitting the length of time you envision, this gasoline will have degraded totally. When you finally commission the boat, you'll have to pump it out, purge the system, and refill it with fresh fuel. Don't even think about running your engine on this fuel.

Spray all the metal surfaces and parts with WD-40 or a similar product, but keep it away from the hoses, plug wires, and other rubber parts. Grease the cable linkages at both ends and remove the batteries for storage outside the boat.

You'll have to monitor the electrolyte level in the batteries and periodically charge them, though they will probably be all but due for replacement by the time you take the boat out of mothballs.

Clean the boat thoroughly. Get all of the water out of it and leave the bilge drain plug out. Open all of the lockers and bilge access openings; leave everything you can wide open. If the seat cushions are easily removed, do so. Store them in an extra-dry spot, so mildew doesn't gain a foothold.

Sprinkle a handful of rock salt in the bilge near the hull drain (try not to let the salt touch any metal hardware if you can help it) and make sure the boat is properly leveled when you block it up so that any water that condenses will reach the drain.

You can keep your boat's deck hardware looking good by applying a coat of wax or liberally smearing it with Vaseline. When you put the boat back in commission, wipe off this protective coating. The hardware will look as good as the day you laid the boat up.

You'll want to cover the boat with a clear plastic sheet so birds and bugs don't make a mess of it. Before you pull on this snood, hang one of Star brite's MDG Mildew Control Bags in the boat.

As you'll discover, there are three stages of child development: rug rats, curtain climbers, and yard apes. In my experience, the younger kids are, the easier it is to take them places, including out in a boat. When they graduate from curtain climbers to yard apes (typically at about four years), the fun really begins.

Question: I understand that there is an aftermarket attachment for MerCruiser sterndrives that will allow flushing the engine with fresh water without having to attach the "ear muffs" to the outdrive. If so, where can they be purchased? Do you recommend them?

I have a Sea Ray 270 DA with twin 4.3 LX MerCruisers that I keep in salt water. Hanging out from the swim platform to attach the flush adapter takes more gymnastic ability than I possess.

Answer: There is a device on the market called the FlushPro. It's a product of Perko, Inc. (16490 NW 13th Ave., Miami, FL 33169-5707; 305-621-5707; www.perko.com/flushpro). It's made in three sizes to fit the plumbing systems of various engines; the middle-sized one sells for $77.

This unit is an improvement from other similar products that have been marketed in the past because it's fully automatic. The other units used a valve that—if left in the wrong position—could allow your boat's engine to overheat the next time you used it.

One other consideration. If you're not a good plumber, I would have the FlushPro installed by a professional marine mechanic; you don't want to sink your boat or cause cooling system leaks.

Question: This year my mechanic is recommending that I store my 1988 Grady White with a 175-horsepower Johnson outboard with the gas tanks as empty as possible. This is a 180-degree turnaround from his previous advice.

Apparently, he is concerned that the oxygenated gasoline mandated in our area during the fall and winter season does not store well, even when stabilizer is added. He said that both Mercury and OMC have had complaints of major engine damage in the spring from using oxygenated gasoline that was stored over the winter.

Is this a recognized problem? If I empty the tanks, how do I keep condensation from deteriorating their insides?

Answer: Yes, indeed, OMC has introduced a dramatic change in their lay-up recommendations for gasoline-fueled marine engines, outboards and sterndrives alike.

They now recommend that the tank be drained down to less than half full. Then the remaining fuel in the tank should be treated with a stabilizer such as OMC's 2+4. Before the engine is started in the spring, OMC says the tank must be refilled to the top with fresh gasoline, preferably premium grade.

MerCruiser's official position is that if there's little or no alcohol in the fuel, you should leave the tanks topped off with stabilizer added. If the alcohol content of the fuel is 10 percent or more, they recommend a procedure similar to OMC's.

The Volvo-Penta technician I spoke with said that fuel tanks should be left topped off and stabilizer added.

Personally, I don't like the idea of leaving gasoline tanks any less than chock-full. Any airspace left in a tank is a condensation factory. All else being equal, the more airspace, the more condensation. Who needs it? Furthermore, a partly full tank is an explosion hazard. Strangely enough, a full one is not.

The problem that OMC is trying to avoid is major engine damage at springtime start-up. They say this is caused by a dramatic drop in octane over the lay-up season.

Here's my take on this issue. Top off the fuel tanks, with premium grade gasoline if it's available. Then add the necessary fuel stabilizer. In the springtime, if you are worried about engine-damaging octane drop, make this deal with your boatyard: They can have the gas from the tank for their boom truck or whatever. It's theirs free, if they'll pump it out.

Either that, or run the engine gently until the old fuel is used up. Once you've emptied half the tank, top it off with fresh premium grade gasoline again to get the octane back up closer to what the engine expects.

Just "soft-pedal" it with the throttle for this period. Once the old fuel has been cycled out of the system, you can resume normal operation without worrying about engine damage.

8 COMMISSIONING

It's human nature that, once a new boating season starts, our brains shift gears. We stop thinking about getting the boat ready, checking things out, overhauling marginal equipment, and performing routine service. Instead, all we want to do is put the groceries on board, drop the docklines, and go. Even the most dedicated boater has a hard time doing any more than giving the engine room a sniff for gasoline fumes and checking the engine oil before getting under way.

Hold your horses. Commissioning time is your last chance to make things right before you start a new season. I can't emphasize this point strongly enough. So now, before the pressure is on to have fun, fun, fun, do your homework. If any systems or equipment are "looking for better weather," it's safe to assume that they're not going to get any better with use. So square them away now.

As with winterizing, commissioning is a chore that's best approached with a handful of lists. It has one other thing in common with winterizing—there's an on-land component and an in-water component. This chapter includes a list that spells out all the necessary operations, both before and after launching.

Your mind-set is also an important commissioning tool. Avoid the mental trap of saying to yourself, "The seacocks (or whatever) worked fine last season, why bother taking them apart and wasting my time servicing them now?"

On-Land Commissioning

This is mostly an inspection operation. You'll need some basic hand tools such as screwdrivers, wrenches, and the like. You should also have a mechanic's inspection mirror and a flashlight with fresh batteries. Since you're going to be working in the engine room, make sure the flashlight is an explosion-proof model (it must be so labeled).

Wear clothes that don't have much sentimental value because you're going to be wriggling around in the nooks and crannies of your boat's engine room and bilges and, even if you keep these spaces fastidiously clean, you're going to get messy.

On-Land Commissioning: Blow by Blow

I like to start by installing the bilge drain plug, if the boat has one. It's an item you don't want to forget, especially if you're not going to be on hand when the boat is launched. If you followed my advice, it's sitting in the galley sink. Retrieve it now, wire brush the threads clean, and apply a smear of pipe dope to the threads. Either Permatex or Teflon thread paste work well, though the Teflon stuff is much easier to clean off your hands and is a little more lubricious, making it easier to wind the plug in place.

I avoid Teflon thread tape, but if you have some on hand, that will work OK. If you elect to use this stuff, put three or four wraps on the threads, applying it in a clockwise direction (viewed from the threaded end of the plug).

Wind the plug in by hand then tighten it tightly with a wrench. This fitting has a pipe thread. As you know, these make their seal by virtue of a smear of pipe dope and a thorough tightening of their tapered threads.

Seacocks, Strainers, Hoses, and Clamps

I assume you disassembled, cleaned, greased, and reassembled the seacocks last fall. If you didn't, refer to chapter 7 and do so now.

Exercise the seacocks to make sure they work smoothly and effectively. When you're satisfied that they're operating properly, leave them in the "closed" position (with the actuating handle 90 degrees or across the direction of flow through the seacock). After the boat has been launched, you can open these one by one as you do the in-water part of your commissioning routine.

If you didn't service your boat's raw-water strainers last fall, you'll need to do that now. See the preceding chapter for instructions.

If you've ever had to replace a length of marine hose, you know that these specialized hoses cost a fortune. But the price is worth it. Your life can depend on the integrity of a length of hose. That's why you should give these hoses a more-than-cursory going over. Remove the clamps from the ends and inspect the layers of hose to make sure that there's no degradation or delamination taking place inside where you can't see it.

CHORES TO ACCOMPLISH BEFORE THE BOAT IS LAUNCHED

- Install bilge drain plug
- Inspect seacocks (serviced in the fall, right?)
- Close seacocks
- Inspect raw-water strainers
- Inspect hoses and hose clamps (double clamps where required?)
- Inspect engine drive belts
- Adjust drive belt tension, if necessary
- Check pulley alignment
- Inspect flexible impeller pumps
- Service pumps as needed
- Inspect engine zincs
- Replace zincs as necessary
- Disconnect, clean, and reattach battery leads at engine and vapor-proof switch
- Check engine wiring harnesses
- Wash batteries, inspect, top off cells, and charge as needed
- Install batteries (see Bring on the Batteries on page 127)
- Check battery hold-down hardware
- Check control cables, especially the end fittings
- Grease controls at both ends of cables
- Spray WD-40 or oil on throttle linkage at carburetor
- Check function of controls and start in neutral safety switch
- Secure control cable ends with ty-wraps or safety wire
- Check fluids (lube oil, trans fluid, power steering, and coolant)
- Check steering gear fluid level in reservoir at helm
- Check steering gear for leaks and loose hardware
- Inspect trim tab equipment and fluid level
- Inspect all bilge wiring
- Check fitness of bonding system wiring
- Renew any damaged components and clean ends as needed
- Inspect wiring at distribution panel
- Clean corroded terminals
- Seal terminal wiring with Liquid Electric Tape
- Check pumps and float switches for function
- Check lights—especially running lights—for function
- Check spares kit for completeness and fitness of parts
- Inspect stuffing box hose (replace at least every five years)
- Pack stuffing boxes (propshaft and rudder)
- Check drive train hardware (coupling, strut, stern bearing)
- Paint bottom and pull off masking tape
- Renew zinc anodes on running gear
- Set extra paint and supplies aside for yard crew

Ozone, engine room heat, and the passage of time all take their toll on hoses. Even a hose that's been inspected with a fine-tooth comb can fail. For that reason, it's a good idea to replace all the critical hoses on your boat every five years or so.

By my definition, critical hoses include fuel lines, exhaust hoses, and any others that run below the waterline anywhere in their travels. One of the most critical and often neglected hoses on a boat is the one that connects the stuffing box to the shaft log on an inboard-powered boat. Many boatowners aren't even aware that there is such a hose. It's a real chore to replace, but nonetheless it's very important. I'll tell you how to do it beginning on page 132.

While you're disconnecting the hoses, inspect the hose clamps. If they don't run smoothly and seal positively, replace them. Make sure they don't have any corrosion. Good marine-grade hose clamps are all stainless steel, but it's not unusual to wind up with some that have low-grade stainless or even regular steel parts. Check any clamps you're considering buying with a magnet. If the magnet is attracted to any part of them, pass them over for nonmagnetic stainless ones.

Remember the rule for double clamps: All hoses that run below the waterline *anywhere along their route* must have double hose clamps at both ends.

Belts and Accessory Drives

While we're on the topic of rubber parts that can degrade unnoticed and cause lots of aggravation when they fail, let's not forget the drive belts on the engine. Here's how to inspect them.

Check each belt by twisting it on its side so you can critically examine the running surface (the underside). Look for excessive shininess here. A shiny belt can't do its job of transmitting power properly. Look also for cracking in either the top or the bottom. This is a function of heat and aging. When a belt starts to show any of these symptoms, it's time to replace it.

Drive belt construction has come a long way. Ten years ago, belts were routinely replaced every season no matter how many hours of service they had seen. Because of the critical nature of marine service (remember, you can't walk home) I suggest that you replace drive belts every other season and carry spares and the necessary tools to replace one if it does fail.

Accessory drive belt tension is critical: Too loose and the accessories won't work; too tight and they'll be damaged.

If you carry replacement belts in your boat's spares kit, as you should, it's best to rotate your stock at belt replacement time. That is, install the ones from the spares kit on the engine and put the factory-fresh ones in the spares kit. That way you'll have fairly fresh belts in your spares kit if you ever need them.

Drive belt tension is critical too. Overly loose belts don't transmit power properly and, if they're loose enough, they can even ride off the drive pulleys at high rpm and fly off the engine. On the other hand, drive belts that are adjusted too tight can damage the bearings and bushings in the accessories—alternators and pumps—that they drive.

If the belt has the correct tension, you should be

able to deflect the belt no more than 3/8 inch midway between pulleys when you push it with about ten pounds of pressure.

While you're servicing and inspecting your engine's accessory drive belts, make sure that the pulleys are properly aligned by sighting them from straight overhead and from the side. If they're not aligned, the belts will have an even rougher life.

Mystery Zincs

In addition to sacrificial zinc anodes that protect the underwater hardware, some marine engines—especially freshwater-cooled models—have small zincs installed in the cooling system plumbing. If you remember our earlier discussion of electrolysis (chapter 5), you know that the cooling system has metal components that are in contact with seawater or 50/50 coolant mixture. The zincs are installed because they are less noble than the copper and brass components, such as the heat exchanger, that they protect.

If your engine has any of these zincs, it behooves you to know where they are and how to replace them. Most often they take the form of what's called a zinc "pencil." Though it's a bit larger in diameter than a pencil, it has much the same shape. One end has a male thread cut into it, which is screwed into a specially machined pipe plug. To make these easy to locate, the special pipe plug is often painted a different color from the rest of the engine. Their locations are spelled out in your engine owner's manual.

The pencils themselves come in a standard length and often have to be cut down a bit on the nonthreaded end with a hacksaw before installation so they fit in where they belong.

As with all zinc anodes, these are electrical components and depend on clean attachment points. To replace one, remove the pipe plug with a wrench and loosen what's left of the old one by grabbing it with a pair of Vise-Grips.

Use the male portion of your battery post–terminal cleaning tool to clean out the female threads inside the pipe plug, then wind the new zinc pencil in. Check it for fit in the cavity and, if necessary, cut it down to the correct length.

Once it's been trimmed to the right size, tighten it into the pipe plug with your Vise-Grips. Wire brush the threads on the outside of the pipe plug, smear on a bit of Permatex or Teflon thread paste, and tighten it in place with a wrench. This is a pipe thread, so it needs to be tightened securely to make an effective seal. Don't overdo it, though, and crack the threaded boss it's installed in.

Wiring: Out of Sight, Out of Mind?

Many boaters don't pay any attention to their engine room wiring until the engine won't start or one of the gauges dies. That's no way to run a boat. There's not really that much wiring in the engine room, and it's easy to access and inspect. Five minutes spent on a "look-see" at the beginning of the season can save a lot of aggravation later.

At the least, you should undo and clean the heavy-gauge battery lead connections because they are prone to corrosion. Most folks are pretty good about cleaning the battery end of these cables, but the connections at the engine's end and vapor-proof switch are often neglected for years. If corrosion rears its ugly head here, you can wind up hearing the dreaded "click, click, click" when you turn the ignition key. So now, before you install the batteries, take a few minutes to perform this simple service. (By doing it with the batteries out, you won't have to worry about sparks, short circuits, and exploding batteries.)

The positive terminal is a ring lug at the end of the red cable that leads from the battery switch. It's attached to the starter solenoid. Even if the connection looks OK from the outside, you should disassemble it, clean it with a wire brush, reconnect it securely, and apply a coat of Liquid Electric Tape. If you're not already familiar with this product, you should be. It's sold by Star brite in a gooey brush-on liquid formulation. When it dries, it cures into a flexible neoprene coat that excludes water and forestalls corrosion better than anything else I've come across. It's easier to use than heat-shrink tubing and, since it goes on as a liquid, it can conform to terminals or connections of any shape.

While you've got the Liquid Electric Tape out, I

suggest that you disconnect each of the other engine wiring terminals one at a time, clean them with a wire brush, retighten them, and seal them. These terminals include the ones on the sending units that relay coolant temperature and oil pressure information to the gauges and/or idiot lights at the helm and the low-voltage wires at the ignition coil.

In the course of inspecting and weatherproofing these connections you should also subject them to what I call the "torture test." Tug on the wire terminal with a couple of pounds of force. If the wire pulls out of the ring lug, that connection was either improperly made or is beginning to corrode. Refer to chapter 5 for tips on making connections, providing adequate strain relief, and neatly bundling wiring into a businesslike harness.

Most likely your engine also has a big, multipin connector that connects the engine wiring to the harness that runs to the helm. It's a good idea to open this connection and check inside to make sure there's no greenish corrosion starting to grow in here. A little spritz of WD-40 in the female socket half of this connector is a good idea, too.

Bring on the Batteries

When it's time to pull the batteries out of their secure winter storage, follow the instructions in the preceding chapter for washing, inspecting, topping off the cells, and charging them before you bring them on board the boat. Give the terminals and posts a good cleaning with your wire brush battery post–terminal cleaning tool.

The ends of the battery cables often take a beating. Repeated flexing and corrosion can make the bitter end of the cable (where it goes into the connector) brittle. Eventually, it can break and leave you stranded. While time is on your side, look at this critical link in your boat's electrical system. If you do have to swage new ring lugs on the ends of the cables, do yourself a favor and get a hefty piece of heat-shrink tubing to go over the completed connection.

If you've never used heat-shrink tubing, you should make its acquaintance. Not only does it seal out corrosion but, especially for connections like these, it makes an effective strain relief, eliminating the flexing that fatigues and ultimately breaks battery cable ends.

You probably don't have the large, special crimping tools to secure ring lugs on the end of battery cables anyway. If you remove the cable and take it to your marine mechanic, it should be simple and inexpensive to have the ends redone. Don't forget to ask for the heat-shrink tubing end treatment; it can't be put on after the connection is crimped.

When you've done all these chores, it's time to put the batteries back in their boxes. Make sure to install the positive terminal first (a good habit) and always use a wrench that's too short to touch both terminals at once. That will eliminate the hazard of a short-circuited battery exploding.

Before you close the boxes for the season, there are two more things you need to do. First, spray the made-up terminal connections with a coat of Krylon battery terminal protectant or a similar product. This stuff does a great job sealing battery connections. Well-sealed terminals forestall the growth of the powdery deposits and corrosion that make for poor connections and poor performance. The tops of the batteries stay cleaner and you're much less likely to hear a click instead of a crank when you turn the key.

Some mechanics smear Vaseline on the battery cable ends at the battery terminal posts to keep corrosion at bay. This works well, but it's such a mess that I prefer the spray stuff I mentioned. Which product you use is up to you, but do use something.

Second, check the battery box hold-down hardware. If the clips or the screws securing the boxes are not sound and strong, replace or refasten them as necessary. You don't want your batteries drifting around the engine room secured only by their cables.

Control Freaks Take Note

If there's one thing most boaters take for granted, it's their engine controls and cables. Provided no one ever steps on them when climbing into the engine room, they often last for the life of the boat. Just the same, for positive control and reliable performance, a little inspection and an occasional dab of grease is in order.

Have a helper operate the controls at the helm while you observe the cable and linkage operation in the engine room. Make sure there's no binding and that the cables, and especially their ends, are not bent or kinked. Check the hardware that secures the cable jacket ends to make sure it's tight. Inspect the clevis and cotter pins in the bitter ends of the cables and also give some attention to the cable release hardware.

I like to bind the quick-disconnect release hardware fittings with a nylon ty-wrap or a few tight turns of Monel seizing wire. They hardly ever pop out unprovoked but, with the attendant loss of engine control, if it ever does happen, once is enough for anybody.

You should apply some good-quality marine grease to the cable ends where they emerge from the cable jacket. You might have to pull a rubber dust jacket out of the way and have a helper exercise the shift and throttle controls to make sure the grease works back inside where it can do some good.

Both ends of the cable—engine and helm—should get the inspection and lubrication treatment. If you had to slide the dust jacket out of the way, make sure you return it to its proper position after greasing. There are two more control components to lubricate in the engine room.

Put a dab of grease on the start-in-neutral safety switch mechanism on the shift control cable. This is a small interlock switch mounted near the end of the shift cable that keeps the engine from starting unless you've selected "neutral" at the control. The carburetor also has some small linkage components associated with the throttle cable. Give these a spritz of WD-40 or some similar product.

Checking Vital Fluids

Though you changed the engine lube oil and filter at the end of last season, I think it's a good idea to check its level now. There are also some other fluid reservoirs in the engine room that need to be checked before you put the boat into service for another season.

Most sterndrive power plants have power steering with an on-engine reservoir. This should be checked with the engine shut off and the steering set to dead ahead. There are marks on the stick for warm and cold fluid.

If your boat has a hydraulic steerer, check the level of fluid in the reservoir at the helm. See your owner's manual for the recommended fluid if it needs topping off. Inspect the hydraulic steerer hoses for telltale wetness. This can be hard to spot; it pays to bring a flashlight in with you and wipe the end fittings with a rag to help spot any leaks.

Inboard engines and some sterndrives have a transmission inside the boat. If yours does, you will need to check the transmission fluid level.

Owners of freshwater-cooled engines must make sure that the coolant in the expansion tank is up to the proper level. If the system uses a remote coolant recovery bottle, check the level in there. With the engine cold, make sure the coolant is at the lower mark. If you need to top off the coolant in a freshwater-cooled engine, use the coolant recommended by the engine manufacturer. This is usually a 50/50 mixture of ethylene glycol antifreeze and water. Remember that this product is highly toxic and tasty to pets. Don't leave any of it sitting around in an open container.

If your boat has trim tabs or an outboard with power trim and tilt, check your owner's manual for the recommended fluid and the proper method for checking its level.

No matter what kind of steering system your boat has, you should visually inspect its mechanical components for wear or damage before each new season begins. Look for loose hardware especially inside the transom where the cables impart motion to the sterndrive or the rudders and quadrants on inboard-powered boats.

Bilge Wiring

You couldn't design a worse environment for wiring than your boat's bilges. It's always moist, sometimes hot, and subjected to vibration and fumes from the engine and other equipment. Just an all-around nasty place. That's why, whenever possible, boatbuilders avoid running wiring down low in a boat's bilges. But some wiring—for bilge pumps and bonding systems, for example—must be located down there.

You can take the following steps to improve this wiring's lot in life.

Besides moisture and corrosion, another enemy of bilge pump wiring is mechanical strain on the connections. The good news is that there are a host of handy clips and ty-wraps with screw holes that allow you to properly secure this wiring so it isn't subjected to strain.

All bilge pump wiring connections should be made up high, well above the level of any potential water. Even though they won't be getting bathed in bilge water, they will still be subjected to wetness from condensation and the generally moist environment that they inhabit. So if you have to renew any of your bilge pump wiring connections, slip a piece of heat-shrink tubing onto one of the wire ends before you crimp the terminals.

When properly sized to the terminal being sealed and heated with a cigarette lighter or heat gun (make sure there are no gasoline fumes present before you do this) this tubing shrinks down and makes a gas-tight seal around the connector. If you cut a long enough piece of the tubing to reach an inch or so beyond each end of the connector, heat-shrink tubing also makes a very effective strain relief.

Bilge wiring should be solidly secured with ty-wraps and nylon clips fastened with short, self-tapping stainless steel screws. It should be routed out of harm's way so that you're not likely to step on it when you climb through a cabin or cockpit sole hatch.

In addition to bilge pump connections, there is one other very important system down here—the bonding wiring. That's the heavy-gauge wiring that connects all the through-hull fittings to ground. These cables are often the poor stepchildren of the boat wiring world. They're neglected, corroded, and often broken clean off. Since they were put down there to keep all the underwater hardware at the same electrical potential, they have an important job of preventing electrolysis.

Check them and renew any broken wires or loose attachments now. Make sure the ends are clean and bright so they can effectively conduct stray current. They're usually stripped bare, doubled over, and grubbed against the metal hardware with a hose clamp. In more elegant installations, they're secured under a screwhead with a ring lug. No matter how the connection is made, make sure the attachment sites are clean and bright so these important cables can do their job.

A Terminal Case

Your boat's terminal blocks and its distribution panel are the nerve center of the electrical system. Because of their location—up high in the living spaces of the boat—they're not usually subjected to corrosion. Just the same, these deserve a quick inspection to make sure they are raring to go.

In most boats, the AC and DC wiring panels are right next to each other. For your safety, make sure you know which system you're working on. Also, before working here, be sure to disable the generator (tag the control so no one turns it on) and make sure the shore-power system is not plugged in.

I like to satisfy myself that the connections are clean by unhooking them one at a time and cleaning them with a small brass bristle brush. (Make sure the battery switch is off before you do this.) Then I remake the connections, tighten them snugly, and paint on a coat of Liquid Electric Tape. If you give them this treatment, you might never have to attend to them again.

Testing, One, Two, Three

Finish your electrical system inspection by checking everything to see that it's functioning properly.

I like to start with the bilge blowers, one of the most important pieces of electrical equipment on a boat. Flip on the switch, but don't be satisfied if you hear the blower motor running.

Put your hand over the outlet ventilator to make sure that there's a good flow of air blasting out. Duct hoses can get squished or fall off the blower. You can only be sure all systems are go by feeling for the rushing flow of air.

Next, test the bilge pumps for manual and automatic operation. Perform the manual test by flipping on the switch; the pump should run when you do this. To check the automatic function, turn the bilge pump switch to automatic. The pump should run when you lift the arm of the float switch and shut off when you lower it.

Lights are next on the list. Start by switching on each of the 12-volt cabin lights to make sure they work. When it comes to navigation lights, I'm not satisfied to merely make sure the lamps burn when I turn on the switch. Instead, before testing them I like to open up each of the fixtures, clean the lamps and the lamp holder contacts with an ink eraser or small brass bristle brush, reinstall the lamps, and check the O-ring seals (if the fixtures are fitted with O-rings). Any O-rings should also be lightly smeared with white Teflon grease before reassembly.

Then I button things up, flip on the switch, and make sure that all the lights function properly. At this point it's also a good idea to make sure you have spare lamps for all running lights in your spares kit.

Speaking of the spares kit, this is a good time to make sure that yours is in order and that all of its contents are well organized and in usable condition. Replace anything that is corroded, broken, or weathered. See the next chapter for information on assembling a spares kit.

This is also a good time to give the ship's first-aid kit a similar inspection. Shortages, outdated medicines, and shopworn supplies should be brought up to snuff before the season begins.

Stuffing Boxes

If there was ever a piece of marine hardware that was out of sight and out of mind, it's the lowly stuffing box. Lots of boaters seem to be afraid to open this perceived can of worms that lurks down in the bilges of inboard-powered boats. Don't be! Stuffing box maintenance is not really that scary. And it is necessary.

If you have an inboard-powered boat, you'll find a stuffing box for each propshaft and one for each rudder. They allow these shafts to exit the hull, turn as they must with a minimum of friction, and leak only a little bit. The rudderpost stuffing box shouldn't leak at all; see the following instructions for particulars.

If your boat's stuffing boxes are packed in the traditional way, they will have three to five rings of beeswax-impregnated, braided flax packing. (Avoid the graphite-impregnated stuff if you come across it; it can cause electrolysis problems.)

I mention the traditional way because there's a packing that's been on the market for a decade or so that provides a tighter seal with less friction than the old-fashioned stuff that's been in use for the last century or so. It's called Drip-Free Packing. It's a highly lubricious packing material that contains Teflon. The Drip-Free Packing kit includes enough packing for a typical stuffing box, plus the Teflon grease that's used with this material. The neat thing about using Drip-Free is that you tighten the stuffing box so that it doesn't drip at all. To order Drip-Free Packing, or to get more information about the product, contact Waterline Marine, 159 Blue Hill Rd., Surry, ME 04684; 800-747-1939; www.machineworksatessex.com/Marine/watrline.htm.

To repack your boat's stuffing box, you'll need two pipe wrenches large enough to fit the big nuts on this piece of hardware. Some stuffing boxes have a packing gland and locknut that are loosened with a hammer and punch; if yours doesn't have flats for a wrench, it's the hammer-and-punch type. You'll also need a sharp knife to cut the packing, a cheap corkscrew, a pair of Vise-Grip locking pliers, some marine grease, and the packing itself. It takes about a foot and a half of packing to repack a typical stuffing box. This material is inexpensive and it's sold by the foot at most well-stocked chandleries.

Start by loosening the locknut and packing gland. Use one wrench to hold the packing gland in the tightening direction while you use the other one to unlock the locknut from it. Once these parts are separated, spin off the gland and slide it forward on the propshaft so that you can gain access to the inside of the stuffing box. Dig out the old packing that lies between the shaft and the inside of the stuffing box. The first couple of rings usually come out pretty easily.

If you have difficulties getting all of the old packing rings out, I've found that you can make a handy tool by cannibalizing a cheap corkscrew. Make this tool by breaking the corkscrew apart to separate the screw portion. That's the tool you'll use in the next step. Wind the screw part into the packing and then use a pair of Vise-Grips to tug the old packing out. Keep removing packing until you are sure you've gotten it all out.

When all the packing is removed, you will feel only metal if you probe the recess with a thin-bladed screwdriver. The only way you'll be able to look in here is with a mechanic's inspection mirror. (Otherwise, the shaft blocks your view.)

Count the number of rings of packing that you removed. Packing is available in a host of different sizes. Select the size that measures one half of the difference between the diameter of the shaft and the inside diameter of the stuffing box. For example, if your boat has a $1\frac{1}{4}$-inch shaft and the inside of the stuffing box has a diameter of $1\frac{3}{4}$ inches, $\frac{1}{4}$-inch packing is what you need.

Before you buy the new packing, there's one other piece down here that needs a careful look. Just abaft the stuffing box you will find a short length of very heavy duty hose with four hose clamps. It connects the stuffing box to the shaft log. (The shaft log is the fiberglass tube in which the shaft exits the boat's hull.)

This hose is of extra-special, heavy-duty, four-ply construction and it's called, logically enough, stuffing box hose. It comes precut to a standard length, depending on the size of the stuffing box. Four inches is typical for the smaller diameters; larger sizes run somewhat longer. The price is between $10 and $20. Your boat's watertight integrity is riding on this hose, but some boaters have been known to forestall replacement for as long as a decade. Good thing it's well-made stuff, eh?

If this hose isn't in tip-top condition, you should replace it. The only unpleasant wrinkle is that, in order to replace it, you have to back the shaft out of the engine coupling. Most boaters don't have the necessary tools for this job, but I've provided an overview of what this task entails on the next page.

Once you've brought the new packing down to the boat, you need to determine how long to cut the new rings you will install. The easiest way I've found to do this is to wrap the new packing snugly around the shaft and mark it so the cut ends will meet in a perfect butt joint. (Don't use a pencil; even small amounts of graphite can cause electrolysis damage to propshafts and rudderposts.)

After cutting the first ring of packing, test-fit it around the shaft. If it's just right, go ahead and cut the necessary number of rings to the same dimension. Use a sharp X-Acto knife or a fresh, single-edge razor blade and make the cuts square and neat.

To pack the stuffing box, put a smear of grease on the first ring of packing, wrap it around the shaft, and slide it into the stuffing box. You can use the packing gland as a "pusher" tool to shove the ring of packing home. Now you can put the succeeding rings of packing in. Make sure you stagger the joints opposite each other on each succeeding ring as you slide it in place. Be careful not to let them get cockeyed when you insert them.

Keep adding rings of packing until you've put in as many as you took out earlier—it's usually between three and five. Grease the threads of the stuffing box lightly, but make sure to keep the grease away from the rubber hose.

Reinstall the packing gland. Make sure the gland is well caught with at least five turns of thread engaged. If it won't go on that far, you've probably got too many rings of packing inside.

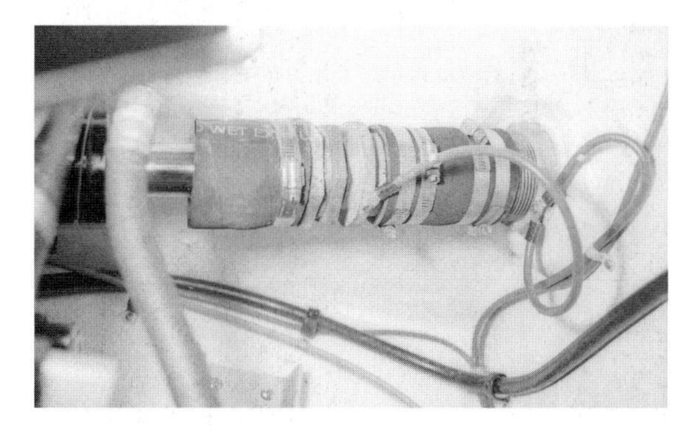

A businesslike stuffing box installation. The hose at right is the stuffing box hose and is secured with double clamps. The wire is a bonding wire attached to the stuffing box proper. The short length of rubber hose at left is designed to keep spraying and dripping water from making a mess in this portion of the engine room.

Finish by winding the gland down by hand until it's snug and giving it another turn or so with a wrench. Spin the locknut forward against it, and lock the gland and locknut together with a pair of wrenches. After the boat is launched and the engine is commissioned, you will adjust the stuffing box. (See pages 139–40 for instructions on adjusting the stuffing box.) At this point you've tightened it up enough so it shouldn't leak on launch day.

Just the same, I'd ask the yard crew to take a gander down there when they launch the boat to make sure there are no leaks. (Don't worry; if you tell them you repacked your own stuffing box, they'll be sure to have a look. Yard crews hate it when boats sink in the Travelift well.)

If the rudder stuffing box hasn't been packed in a few years, you should attend to it as well. The procedure is the same as for the propshaft one, though there's no hose on this one.

Replacing the Stuffing Box Hose

The first step in this job is to cut the safety wire and remove the setscrew(s) in the sides of the coupling. Note that these don't actually hold the shaft in there; provided everything is properly done, the shaft to the coupling is a hammer-in fit. The setscrews are a safety device.

You'll use a slide hammer to extract the shaft. To attach this tool to the aft end of the shaft, the propeller has to be removed. This calls for another special tool—a prop puller. Once the prop is off, the slide hammer is attached and the shaft is backed out of the coupling by the rearward action of the sliding weight.

The shaft doesn't have to be removed all the way—it just needs to be backed out of the coupling and the stuffing box into the shaft log. When it's free of the coupling, use a hammer and punch to remove the key from the keyway (unless it stayed in the coupling).

When you remove the hose clamps attaching the hose to the shaft log, you'll be able to pull off the stuffing box and hose together as an assembly. Once these are off, you can undo the other two hose clamps.

No matter how good the hose clamps look, I always replace them with new, all stainless steel ones. Check them with a magnet to be sure the magnet doesn't stick. Push the new hose onto the shaft log and secure it with new clamps. It's a good practice to stagger the hose clamps so their screws are on opposite sides of the hose and space them out evenly. Also, make sure they're both bearing solidly on the shaft log inside, not on empty hose.

Now you can slip the other two hose clamps over the hose and push the stuffing box assembly back in place. Tighten these clamps securely, observing the same rules as for the other two.

Smear a fingerful of grease around inside the rings of packing so the end of the shaft won't mess them up. You're ready to have your helper outside the boat slowly push the shaft back in. It will be necessary to hammer it into the coupling from outside the boat with a sledgehammer and a block of wood (to protect the end of the shaft). Before allowing the shaft to enter the coupling, make sure the key in the shaft and the keyway in the coupling are properly lined up.

The helper should give gentle taps to drive the shaft home while you look in the setscrew holes with a flashlight. Look for the dimple marks on the shaft to come into view. When they're perfectly centered in the holes, tell your helper to stop hammering. (If it goes too far, you'll have to switch back to the slide hammer to back out the shaft a bit and try again.)

Replace the setscrews, tighten them securely, seize them in place with Monel safety wire, and reinstall the propeller. I use a block of wood braced between a propeller blade and the hull to hold things steady while I tighten the propeller nut, then the locknut, then finally lock the two together.

Now that the stuffing boxes and hoses are in good shape, you should give the other underwater hardware an inspection before you get set for bottom painting. I assume that last fall you performed the thorough running gear inspection outlined in chapter 7 (stern bearing, propeller, rudders, etc.). If not, jump back to those pages and take care of it now.

Bottom Painting

This is the last job you have to do before you tell the boatyard office that the boat is ready to be launched. Chapter 2 gives you step-by-step instructions for bottom painting. So put on some old—very old—clothes and prepare to paint your boat's bottom.

Last Warning!

Before giving the yard office the go-ahead to launch the boat, you should give the bilges and engine room one last look. Make sure you've closed all the seacocks and that all the hoses are back on their fittings and secure. Did you remove any sink or scupper drains last fall? If so, square these away now, so you don't forget later.

Check any and all hoses that you've disturbed to ensure that you properly tightened the hose clamps. Oh, and make sure that you are absolutely positive that you reinstalled the bilge drain plug and tightened it securely.

I don't mean to sound pedantic, but it's such a bummer to have your boat sink on launch day.

As soon as the boat is in the water, the first thing you want to do is examine the stuffing boxes to make sure they're not leaking. If you tightened them up as instructed, they shouldn't be. When you're sure the boat is in no danger of sinking, get your boat's compass and electronics out of storage and reinstall them. Make sure all the power, signal, and antenna connections are clean and bright. If they aren't, use an ink eraser to gently clean them.

Now apply power and check out the function of this gear—but don't expect the depth-sounder to give reliable readings if the boat was just put in the water. It usually takes several hours of "wetting" for the transducer to properly couple with the water and give good data.

Make sure the VHF radio works and test the transmitter portion by making a radio test call. By the way, don't call the coast guard for this; they don't appreciate this type of unimportant radio traffic. Test the transmitter on low power first, then on high.

POSTLAUNCHING: THE REST OF COMMISSIONING

Chores to Accomplish after Launching

- Check stuffing boxes
- Install compass and electronic gear
- Apply power and check function of electronics
- Test radio (don't call the coast guard)
- Service fuel filter
- Tune up engine (use parts from spares kit and renew)
- Clean carburetor
- Make final stuffing box adjustment
- Open seacocks and commission head
- Commission freshwater system
- Inspect shore-power cord and receptacles
- Plug in shore-power cord and test all receptacles with circuit checker
- Check GFCIs by exercising self-test function

Servicing Fuel Filters

Most boats have two filters in their fuel systems. The first, and most important, is the primary fuel filter–water separator, which has a replaceable fuel filter element and a sediment bowl. The bowl is designed to allow water and heavy particles of rust or trash to settle out before the fuel is filtered.

The other filter is a small trash filter that's part of the engine. On sterndrives and inboards that have this secondary filter, it's usually installed inside the carburetor inlet fitting where the steel fuel line from the fuel pump enters the carburetor body.

Most outboards have a small plastic secondary trash filter underneath the cowl in the fuel line. You'll find details on servicing these in chapter 4.

By themselves, these secondary filters are virtually useless. And, if you have a proper primary filter-separator, nothing should make it into the secondary filter anyway. If you don't have a primary filter-separator, get one now—they are a must-have item. If you're not good at plumbing, have your yard or engine dealer's mechanic install it for you, but do be sure you've got one. A proper filter-separator has much more capacity to filter out trash and water than the tiny secondary filter. If you have one and inspect it regularly for water, you never have to get stranded by dirty or water-laden fuel.

First, make sure that the battery switches are shut off and that there's no source of flame or ignition anywhere on the boat. For the duration of this job and the leak-checking operation that follows, the smoking lamp is not lit.

Second, shut off the fuel valve at the tank. This is important: If the tank is higher than the filter, the tank's contents might siphon out into the bilge as you work. By shutting off the valve, the most fuel that can siphon out is what's in the lines. (In most cases, even this won't siphon out because the vacuum created by the shut valve will make the fuel stay put.) Always position a loaf pan or other container under any fittings you undo.

There are several types of primary filters on the market. They have a lot in common with each other, so my instructions are going to be a bit generic.

Many of these filters take the form of a cast metal "header" portion, which is fastened to a bulkhead in the boat. The inlet and outlet connections are made to fittings that are screwed into the header. The filter itself (and the water separator bowl if the filter has one) attach underneath the header.

Most of today's filters use a disposable spin-on filter element that combines the filter cartridge and sediment bowl in one part. These do a good job, but they have one drawback: To find out if the filter has trapped any water, you must remove the filter element, dump the fuel out of it into a disposable aluminum meatloaf pan, and visually inspect it for telltale "balls" of water rolling around in the bottom.

The best filters, such as the popular ones made by Racor, have a separate sediment bowl with a replaceable filter cartridge inside. Some of them have a clear plastic bowl that allows you to make a visual inspection for water each time you use your boat. At a glance, you can tell if the filter has trapped any water and do the necessary water removal operation at the tank before it becomes a problem. The plastic bowls are only legal for diesel and outboard-powered boats, however. Owners of gasoline sterndrive or inboard-powered boats must have primary filters with metal sediment bowls to meet coast guard regulations.

Spin-on type primary fuel filter. These work well, but you must remove and drain them to check for the presence of water.

If you have the simple, spin-on type of filter, wipe the fuel filter header and the replaceable element clean with a lint-free rag. Then put your disposable loaf pan under the filter, spin the old element off, drain the fuel into the loaf pan, and inspect it. If there's any water in it, follow the directions on pages 94–95 for removing it. If it's clean, you can safely dispose of the fuel by pouring it through a filter funnel right back into your boat's deck filler. Make sure you dump it in the one marked "fuel," not "water" or "waste."

Replacing the filter is easy; these spin-on elements are installed the same as an oil filter. Inspect the neoprene gasket on the base of the new filter, make sure the gasket from the old element isn't still stuck to the header, and simply screw on the element by hand. Once the gasket has made contact, hand-tighten the filter as tight as you can. That's it; you're done. When you start the engine later, the very first thing you will do is check the new filter for leaks. After the engine has run for a minute or two, check it again using the leak-hunting tips on page 136.

If your boat's primary filter is not the spin-on kind, you've got a bit more work to do to replace it.

The next most popular type of filter is the AC style. It consists of a spin-on fuel bowl with a replaceable fuel filter element inside. Start by wiping the outside of the filter with a clean, lint-free rag. Get your loaf pan ready and spin off the canister. Drain the bowl and filter element contents into the loaf pan and inspect for water and trash as outlined above.

Wipe out the inside of the metal bowl with a clean rag and make sure no corrosion has started in there. If the bowl gasket didn't come out attached to the top of the bowl, you will find it inside the groove in the header. Carefully remove it and discard it. (The new filter element will come with a fresh gasket.)

Install the new filter element and, if there was a spring or any other parts in there, replace them in the same orientation. Now put the gasket in the groove in the header and tighten the bowl in place. Snug it up tightly, but don't rip off the header of the bulkhead in the process. As with the spin-on filter, leak checking will be your first mission when you start the engine up later.

Most of the fanciest filter-separators (popular brands are Fram and Racor) have a central stud that runs from the top of the filter assembly and holds the whole assembly together. Most, but not all. Some of these have a ring of machine screws that hold the whole thing together. When you inspect yours, it should be obvious how it is to be disassembled.

No matter what type of fuel filter you're servicing, you should wipe the entire unit down with a clean, lint-free rag before you start the disassembly procedure.

Next, put a loaf pan underneath the filter to catch any fuel drips. Hold the filter bowl as you loosen the fastener(s) on top that allow it to drop free. Once it's loose, carefully pour the fuel from the bowl into your loaf pan and inspect for water in the gas.

Wipe out the inside of the bowl with a clean, lint-free rag and check the condition of the gasket or O-ring that seals the bowl to the header. If this part is distorted, squished, cut, or chewed up in any way, get a replacement before you reassemble the filter with the new element.

In most cases the new filter element is simply dropped into the bowl before it's reattached to the header. Make sure you put it in right-side up and, if there are any gaskets on top, make sure the old one came out with the filter element that you removed. Two gaskets are *not* better than one.

Finally, snug up the fastener(s) on top. To help the O-ring seat properly, spin the lower portion back and forth a bit as you snug things up. As with all fuel filter reassembly, do not overtighten the fasteners. That won't help seal leaks; in fact, it's more likely to cause them by distorting the O-ring. Plan on checking for leaks when you start the engine.

Engine Safety Check

Before tuning up the engine, I like to start it up for the season and let it burn out all traces of the fogging oil. Then, when I install fresh spark plugs I know they won't be subjected to fouling. This practice also lets me check for fuel, oil, and coolant leaks and draws my attention to any problems that need to be squared away. Before you proceed, wash your hands thoroughly to eliminate any traces of gasoline on them.

Open the seacock or ball valve on the raw-water inlet, turn on the fuel shutoff valve on the top of the tank, and turn on the battery switch. Run the blower for ten minutes and then give the engine room a sniff test for gasoline vapors.

The fuel lines are empty, so it might take a bit of cranking to start up your engine. Be patient, but don't crank the starter motor for more than fifteen seconds without giving it a two-minute rest. Once you get the engine running, bring the rpm up to a fast idle, say 1,500 rpm. Check the oil pressure gauge to make sure it comes up to where you expect. When you are satisfied that the engine is running properly (not necessarily well—it has oily spark plugs), move to the engine room and do some leak checking.

Be careful. The engine is running, so you must make sure you don't get your body or your clothing caught in any of the accessories, drive belts, or other moving parts.

Start by checking the fuel filter that you serviced. With clean hands, run your fingertips or a clean rag around the mating surfaces of the filter. Use this rag to blot around one area at a time and, before going to the next one, sniff the rag. If you smell any gasoline, the last spot you checked has a leak. Stop the engine immediately and correct the problem. Once your fuel filter servicing work has passed muster, move on to the rest of the fuel system. Carefully check the fuel pump, the carburetor, and the hard steel fuel line that connects these two components for leaks.

When you're satisfied that there are no fuel leaks, move on to the oil filter. Check the base to make sure it's not leaking. Again, if it is, shut the engine off immediately and square away the problem.

Check the cooling system for leaks, especially the hoses, the raw-water strainer, the heat exchanger (on freshwater-cooled engines), and all the connections. Don't forget to look at the exhaust system and its connections while you're doing this. Once you're sure the engine has no leaks, shut it off. You are ready to move on to the next step.

Tune-Up Time

If you are like most boaters, you probably tune up your boat's engine only once a year. You might have done it in the fall after you hauled the boat, but even if you did, it will still be necessary to adjust the timing and test run the engine now that the boat is back in the water.

Newer marine engines, with electronic ignition systems, don't have any points or condensers to replace. If your engine isn't one of these, you'll have to start by replacing these components. Here's how.

1. Access the inside of the distributor by loosening the screws (or releasing the clips) that secure the distributor cap, lifting it off the distributor, and moving it off to the side. You won't be able to move it far without disconnecting the high-tension leads to the spark plugs. In the interest of not scrambling things up, leave the wires attached to the cap.
2. Remove the gasket under the cap and inspect the cap for burned or pitted contacts, or carbon tracking inside. If the cap or the rotor show any signs of these faults, replace them.
3. Remove the rotor by simply pulling it up sharply; it will come right off the top of the distributor's shaft.
4. Use a wrench to loosen—but don't remove—the nut at the side that has two wires secured under it. Get it just loose enough to free the wire ends. Needlenose pliers are great for pulling out the wire leads.
5. Remove the screw that secures the condenser (the silver metal can lying on its side). *Warning:* Don't drop the screw into the distributor. Lift the condenser out of the distributor and replace it with the new one. If its wire lead is too long, you can get rid of the excess length by pigtailing it. Using a pencil as a form, wrap the lead around and around. Slide the pencil out and voilà!—a shorter wire. Secure the new condenser with the old screw and push its terminal end underneath the screw you loosened at the beginning of this operation.
6. The breaker point assembly has two screws. One is a hold-down screw that secures the point set to the breaker plate. The other acts as a cam that, when you turn it, opens and closes the point set and adjusts the gap setting. Remove the hold-down screw and remove the breaker point assembly from the distributor. Again, don't drop the screw inside the distributor.
7. Install the new breaker points and make the hold-down screw snug. (Don't tighten it too

much; it has to be loose to allow you to set the point gap.) Bend the electrical lead from the point set back and forth like a piece of ribbon candy so that its end winds up right at the terminal nut. Put it under the nut with the condenser lead and use a wrench to tighten this electrical connection securely.

8. To adjust the breaker point gap setting, you will need a screwdriver, a set of feeler gauges, and the recommended factory gap setting. This specification should be in your engine owner's manual or on the tune-up specs sticker affixed to the engine.

   The first step is to get the breaker point cam follower on one of the high points of the distributor shaft cam. If your engine is a V-8, this cam will have four high points. Unless you have a remote starter button to crank the engine, the easiest way to do this is to have your helper crank the engine from the helm.

   Stay clear of the drive belts, engine accessories, and other moving parts during this operation. Don't be satisfied until you've got the cam follower right on the high point of the cam; this is critical to get the points properly adjusted. It might take a few short taps of the key to crank the engine around until the cam is on this high point.

   Open and close the point setting by turning the adjuster screw back and forth until the appropriate feeler gauge smoothly slides in between the point contacts. When it's just right, the feeler gauge will not spread the points open, but there shouldn't be any excess room either.

   Tighten the hold-down screw on the point set and recheck the gap setting. Don't be surprised if it's no longer right. This setting often changes when the hold-down screw is tightened. If it has changed, loosen the hold-down screw a bit and readjust as needed. After you're done, make sure you tighten the hold-down screw securely. Then recheck the gap.

Replacing the Cap and Rotor

It's almost time to button up the distributor. Make sure everything looks businesslike so you can install the new rotor, which is simply pressed onto the top of the distributor shaft. It only goes on one way because it and the shaft are keyed. Some rotors have a stamped piece of metal that fits inside the hole on the bottom. This piece might be drifting around in the box. If you find one, press it back in place, then line up the notch and key on the two parts and press the rotor all the way home on the top of the shaft.

The new distributor cap should have come with a fresh gasket. Make sure you've removed all traces of the old one, then smear a thin film of silicone sealant on the new one, and put it in place on the underside of the new cap. Install the cap on the distributor, orienting it properly. It has a notch, like the rotor, and can only go on one way.

Tighten the hold-down screws securely or snap the clips that secure the cap, if your boat's distributor uses that system.

Bring the old cap with the wires still attached adjacent to the distributor and move the wires onto the new cap one at a time. Make sure the wires go on the new cap in the same positions as they were on the old one. *Hint:* Use the screws or the mounting clip recesses to orient the cap. If you get these wires wrong, the engine will run poorly, if at all.

Renewing Spark Plugs

The last ignition system components to be replaced are arguably the most important ones: fresh spark plugs. To replace them, you'll need the new set of plugs, a spark plug wrench, a spark plug gapping tool, a pair of pliers, and a clean rag.

To avoid scrambling the ignition wires, it's best to replace one spark plug at a time rather than using an assembly line technique. However, you can prepare the new plugs for installation assembly line–style.

Start by unwrapping the fresh plugs and tightening the top contact screws securely with a pair of pliers. Then consult your owner's manual for the correct spark plug gap setting. Using the appropriate gauge from your gapping tool, check the gap specification on the first spark plug. (You're checking the air gap between the side electrode and the center one.)

If the gap is too wide, gently rap the bottom of

the plug on a hard surface and recheck it. If the gauge won't fit, indicating that the gap is too small, use the bending tool on your gapping tool to gently bend the side electrode out a bit. Then recheck the gap. If you overdid it, rap the bottom of the plug on the engine block to close the gap a bit and try again. Make sure that, when you're done setting the gap, the adjustable electrode is still square relative to the center one. If it's bent to one side, the spark plug won't perform properly.

Spin the spark plugs in by hand then give them a good "oomph" with your spark plug wrench. Now you can reinstall the high-tension leads. It's good to put a bit of grease inside each of the boots and twist them as you push them onto the plugs.

Timing Is Everything

To set the ignition timing you will need the following tools: a wrench to loosen the bolt underneath the distributor, a timing light, and some white chalk or a white battery marking pen to highlight the timing marks and make them easier to see.

1. Look up the timing setting in your owner's manual if it's not on a sticker on the engine. It will be expressed as so many degrees *before top dead center*, sometimes abbreviated BTDC.
2. Find the timing tab on the front of the engine adjacent to the crankshaft pulley. Use your chalk or white marking pen to highlight the appropriate mark and give the index mark on the pulley the same treatment. When the timing is set correctly, your timing light is hooked up, and the engine is running, the timing light will flash at the exact instant the number-one spark plug fires. If the engine is at idle rpm and the flash occurs when the marks are lined up, the timing is set correctly.

   By moving the distributor clockwise or counterclockwise, you will change the position of the index mark when the light flashes. That's how you set the timing. It's best to only loosen the clamp bolt a little bit so the distributor moves stiffly. A small movement of the distributor translates into a big change of the timing setting. Now you are ready to hook up the timing light and start the engine.
3. Run the bilge blower for ten minutes, then get in there and give it a sniff test to be sure there are no explosive gasoline vapors in the engine room. Hook up the timing light's positive and negative leads to the battery or to the positive and negative terminals of the ignition coil (these are marked).
4. Clamp your timing light's inductive pickup over the number-one spark plug lead. (That's the front cylinder on an inline engine, or the left front one on a V-6 or V-8.) If the inductive pickup clamp has an arrow molded into it, the arrow should point toward the spark plug end of the high-tension lead. Make sure the power and pickup leads are nowhere near the belts and pulleys on the engine, then use your wrench to loosen the distributor clamp bolt. Retighten the bolt so you can just barely budge the distributor.
5. Make sure the raw-water inlet and fuel shutoff are open and start the engine. Let it run at a fast idle (1,500 rpm or so) for five minutes so that it can warm up somewhat.

   Throttle it back to idle rpm and again, making sure the wires won't get caught in the belts and pulleys, point the timing light toward the timing tab and press the trigger on the light.

   Note where the timing light's stroboscopic flashes appear to "freeze" the marks in place. If the index mark and the mark that corresponds to the desired setting are lined up, the timing is perfect. Tighten the bolt and recheck it. (Like the breaker point gap setting, this often moves when you tighten the hold-down bolt.) If it has moved, loosen the bolt a bit and try again.

   If the marks don't line up, you will have to move the distributor. As you do so, you'll see the index mark appear to move. Move it until it lines up with the mark you highlighted and lock up the bolt. Again recheck it.

   If you move it too far either way the engine will stall from having its timing too advanced or retarded. If this happens, move the distributor back toward where it was when it was still running, restart the engine, and try it again. Relax; you'll get it.

6. Before shutting off the engine, have your helper advance the throttle and make sure the timing moves away from the mark. This is the advance function of the distributor. When the engine rpm increases, the timing should automatically advance. If it doesn't, there are a few possible causes. The mechanical advance weights may be seized up, a vacuum hose might be faulty (if your engine's distributor uses that system), or—in the case of a distributor with an electronic advance system—the control module might be defective. Now you can shut off the engine and unhook the timing light.

Certain distributors, such as Delco's EST, use a different timing procedure. If you have one of these, you might have to move a plug to a different position to set the timing or attach a special timing fixture that you will have to buy. You can find out about this procedure by consulting a shop manual or asking your engine manufacturer or mechanic.

If you neglect to do this, the distributor won't respond properly and you won't be able to set the timing. If your engine has one of these systems, don't forget to return things to normal when you're done setting the timing.

Cleaning the Carburetor

Before you start this procedure—the last step in tuning the engine—let me offer two important warnings. First, you will need to use carburetor cleaner, which is a strong and dangerous chemical. You don't have to worry too much about breathing the vapors because you will use it with the engine running and it sucks them in. But you do have to worry about absorbing it through your skin. Work with care, wear disposable gloves, and wash your hands well after you finish.

Second, you have to do this job with the engine running. To clean the carb, you must run the engine *with the flame arrester removed.* This is a potentially dangerous situation because, if the engine backfires, there's no flame arrester to contain it and prevent a carburetor fire. To minimize the hazard, follow the procedure I outline here and do it after setting the timing correctly and with the engine still warm (so it will run smoothly and be less likely to backfire).

1. With the engine shut off, remove the nut on top of the center of the carburetor. Put the nut in a safe spot like your pocket. If your engine's carburetor has a plastic rainhat, remove it. Don't lift off the flame arrester yet. Make sure your clothing and body are clear of any moving parts, then start the engine and bring the speed up to about 1,500 rpm. Once the engine is running smoothly, pull off the crankcase ventilation hoses and lift off the flame arrester.
2. Inspect the top deck of the carburetor, the throttle plates, and the inside of the carburetor bores for sooty carbon and brownish deposits. Wherever you find this grime, blast a spray of carburetor cleaner. Do it just a little bit at a time so the engine can ingest the cleaner and crud without stalling. Let the engine recover and then give another short spritz of the cleaner. Continue this procedure until the carburetor is clean as a whistle.
3. Shut off the engine and reinstall the flame arrester, crankcase vent hoses, and the rainhat. If there was a washer sandwich under the top nut (metal and rubber), put the rubber side down against the rainhat. Put the top nut on and secure it with your wrench.

Final Adjustments to the Stuffing Box

If you recall, we left the stuffing box tightened enough to ensure that it wouldn't leak when the boat was launched. That's great, except that if you're using conventional packing, you *want* the stuffing box to leak—but just a little bit, mind you, and only when the propshaft is turning. Here's how to get this adjustment just right.

A properly adjusted stuffing box with conventional packing should drip about three or four drips per minute with the engine idling *in gear.* When the propshaft is not turning, the dripping should cease. Since you have to check this rate of leakage with the engine idling in gear, remove any loose clothing and jewelry. And just in case you're in the habit of wearing a necktie when working on your engine, forget it.

Start the engine and allow it to run at idle in gear. Stay clear of the moving machinery and get down by the stuffing box with a flashlight. Any drips? If there are none, or the rate of leakage is more or less than four drips per minute, put the engine in neutral and shut it off.

If the drips were too few, undo the locknut and loosen the packing gland; tighten it if there were too many. Just make a small adjustment. Then lock the nut and packing gland back together with your two wrenches and restart the engine. Put it back in gear at an idle and, staying away from the moving parts, shinny in there and check it again.

Repeat this procedure, shutting the engine off for each adjustment session, until you get the leakage rate into the target range of three to four drips per minute with the engine idling in gear. Lock it up again with your wrenches and double-check to make sure the drips haven't changed in frequency.

A rudder stuffing box doesn't have to drip at all. It should be snugged up a bit tighter than the point at which it stops leaking. Make sure the locknut and packing gland are locked together and periodically check both rudder and propshaft stuffing boxes during the season. After repacking and running the boat for a while, the stuffing boxes might loosen and need to be readjusted. You're done in the engine room.

Juice It Up

Now you can open up the seacocks for the head system. Pump each head and make sure that water enters and exits the bowl. Check the head and all its associated plumbing for leaks. Leave the system with the Y-valves in the proper position for use.

Next, check the freshwater system. If you left the water heater isolated last fall when you winterized, now is the time to remove the bypass connection and restore the original connections. (Throw the bypass plumbing pieces in your toolbox. They'll come in handy for winterizing the system at the end of the season.)

Fill the water tanks with fresh water until they're about a third full, then turn on the breaker at the panel, open the faucets, and start running the water out of the system. You will have to do this a few times to flush out the antifreeze.

When all the antifreeze is out of the system, fill the tanks for the season. If you are in the habit of using any water conditioners or microbe preventatives, such as Sudbury's Aqua-Fresh, add it now.

Well, how about that? You've just commissioned your own boat. I hope in the process you've learned your way around its dark recesses and gained a better appreciation of what marine mechanics face daily. I also hope you will agree there's a certain satisfaction to be gained from doing the job yourself.

Questions and Answers

Question: My wife and I plan to take delivery of a new 225 Aquasport Explorer Walkaround next spring. The boat is powered by a Johnson 200 hp Ocean Runner engine.

After owning several "previously owned" boats, I'm giving a lot of thought to how best to break in this new engine. People at the boatyard said to add extra oil to the fuel tank just to be sure. I've never had a VRO-type engine before and can't afford to buy another if this unit fails prematurely. Any recommendations?

Answer: For starters, you should indeed mix extra oil—in the traditional 50:1 ratio—in with the fuel. The VRO system won't know it's in there and the engine will get an extra dose of oil. Do this for at least the first ten hours of operation on the new engine.

OMC recommends the following break-in procedure:

1. For the first ten minutes of operation, run the engine in gear at a fast idle, say 1,800 to 2,000 rpm.
2. For the rest of the first hour (fifty minutes), do not run above half throttle or, in any case, above 3,500 rpm. Vary the engine's speed during this interval.

3. When the engine starts on its second hour of operation, run it at full throttle until the boat is on plane, then throttle it back to a midrange speed that keeps the boat on plane. During this hour you can also run it at full throttle for one-minute intervals, then return to three-quarter throttle or so. Again, vary the engine's speed.
4. For the next eight hours of operation, avoid continuous full throttle operation, vary your speed, don't bring a bunch of people on board, or go waterskiing or boogie boarding.
5. After this first ten hours is over, take the boat to the dealer to have the cylinder heads retorqued.
6. After twenty hours of operation, the engine has to go back to the dealer once again for its twenty-hour check. They will drain and refill the gearcase, check the ignition and fuel systems, retorque the cylinder heads again, and check the engine for leaks and other faults.

A prudent break-in procedure will pay big dividends in long, trouble-free engine life.

9 TOOLS, SPARES, AND EMERGENCY PREPAREDNESS

Tools

There's nothing quite so frustrating as finding something on the boat that needs tightening, adjusting, or replacing and not having the tools on hand to deal with it.

Lots of boaters use the same tool kit to work on their boat that they use around the house. Up to a point, that's fine. After all, many of the tools are the same. But just as in real estate, the three most important features of a set of tools are location, location, location. Put another way, all the fancy tools in the world won't do you any good if they're back home on a shelf in the garage and you're five miles offshore with a fouled set of spark plugs.

That's why I strongly urge you to put together a set of boat tools; that is, boat-only tools. The only time this toolbox should come home is in the winter, when you empty the boat for the lay-up season. If you make this your policy, you'll never be caught short, wishing the wrench set was here instead of there.

This doesn't have to be a big deal tool kit. It should, however, have a well-rounded selection of fastener tools, troubleshooting tools, and simple hand tools that will enable you to tackle the most common repair and replacement operations that are likely to crop up on your boat.

Here's a list of the tools that I've found handy to have on board for routine alongshore cruising.

Tool-Buying Tips

If you can't assemble a complete kit of tools for the boat from the various toolboxes you've got kicking around the house, it's time to go tool shopping.

The first order of business is to buy the highest-quality tools you can afford. In the long run, cheap tools are no bargain. At worst they will let you down; at best they make any job you tackle more work than it needs to be. Better to have a modest selection of good tools than an overstuffed box full of junk.

Fastener Tools

Wrenches

Hand wrenches should be drop-forged. A drop-forged wrench won't spread its jaws when you put on the pressure. You will want to start with a set of hand wrenches. I like the so-called combination wrenches. Each one of these has an open-end and a box-end wrench (one on each end) in one size. They're less costly to buy if you get a complete set at one time. A typical set comprises thirteen wrenches and takes you from $1/4$ to 1 inch in $1/16$-inch increments.

Adjustable wrenches are also useful. Buy brand-name ones with precisely machined mechanisms. These have a minimum of free play. The sloppy brand X models open and slip when you use them. All you wind up with is bleeding knuckles and rounded bolt heads.

RECOMMENDED TOOL KIT

Fastener Tools

Wrenches

- set of combination wrenches (1⁄4 inch through 1 inch)
- 3⁄8-inch drive socket wrench set (including a spark plug socket)
- 10-inch adjustable wrench
- Allen wrench set
- line wrenches (necessary for fuel line fittings)
- oil filter wrench

Pliers

- conventional pliers
- slip-joint pliers (optional)
- baby Vise-Grips
- needlenose pliers
- electrical crimping pliers

Screwdrivers

- slotted and Phillips conventional screwdrivers
- slotted and Phillips stubby screwdrivers
- slotted and Phillips right-angle screwdrivers
- Torx screwdrivers (to fit any Torx fasteners on your boat)

Power Tools

- battery-powered drill motor (or)
- line-powered drill motor

Troubleshooting Tools

- air-gap spark checker
- digital multimeter (or $15 RadioShack analog model)
- solid-state AC circuit checker (Hubbell or Marinco)
- induction-type timing light
- compression tester
- antifreeze checker (only needed if your engine is freshwater-cooled)

Miscellaneous

- pocketknife
- hacksaw
- drill bits
- gasket scraper
- spark plug gapping tool
- mechanic's inspection mirror
- small magnet
- flashlight(s) (must be explosion proof)
- parts grabber
- snake (fishtape)
- clamp-type battery carrier (for batteries without handles)
- battery cleaning tool
- battery marking pen
- work gloves
- large steel-bristle wire brush
- small brass-bristle wire brush
- ink eraser
- hammer

Even the best adjustable wrenches are not so good. Whenever you can, use a size-specific wrench for loosening and tightening fasteners.

Socket wrenches are indispensable for getting on inaccessible bolt heads that can't be approached with a conventional wrench. Again they're best purchased in a set. I bought an S•K (my favorite brand) set of 3⁄8-inch drive socket wrenches that included a ratchet handle, 3- and 6-inch extensions, and metric and U.S. shallow and deep sockets in the most common sizes for around $110. Purchased separately, these tools would sell for over $300. (S•K Hand Tool Corp., 9500 W. 55th St., Ste. B, McCook, IL 60525; 800-U-CALL-SK [800-822-5575]; www.skhandtool.com.)

Speaking of sockets, there's a handy, special-purpose socket made for spark plugs. It has a rubber gripping insert that holds the plug in place when you

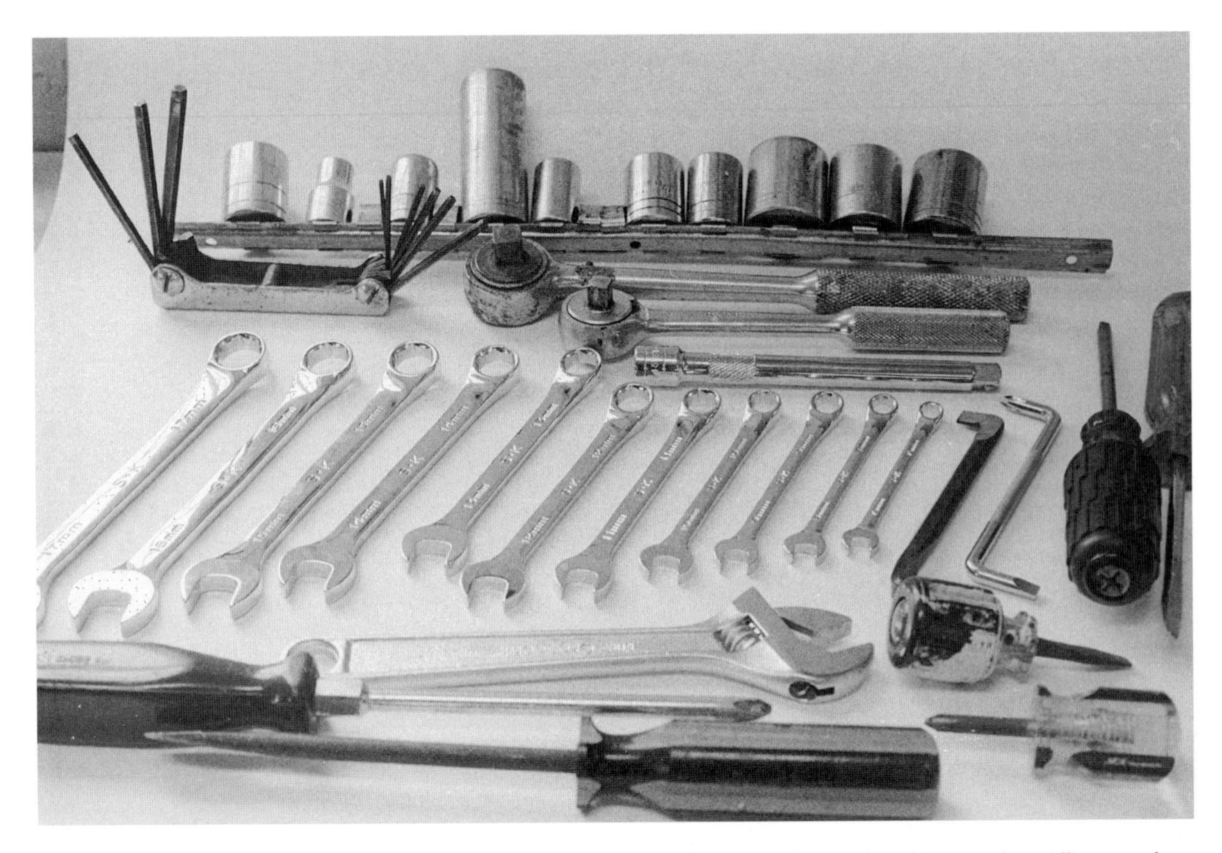

Fastener tools for working on engines and other equipment, from top to bottom: sockets and ratchet wrenches, Allen wrench set in a folding handle, combination wrenches, adjustable wrench, and screwdrivers.

extract it. Spark plugs come in two sizes (5⁄8 inch and 13⁄16 inch), so make sure you get the correct spark plug socket for the ones in your boat's engine.

If you ever have occasion to undo fuel system connections, you must have line wrenches. A line wrench looks like a box-end wrench with a slot that allows it to slip over the tubing. Line wrenches get a much better grip on the super-tight plumbing connections in a boat's fuel system. If you manage to undo one of these connections with an open-end wrench and don't mess up the fittings for good in the process, consider yourself lucky.

Don't forget Allen wrenches. If the one you need is always missing from that little vinyl pouch, buy a set in which all the wrenches fold out of a handle like a pocketknife. Eklind (Eklind Tool Co., 11040 King St., Franklin Park, IL 60131; 800-EKLIND-1 [800-355-4631]; www.eklindtool.com) makes them and they're modestly priced. You might need to buy two sets to get all the sizes you'll need for working on your boat, but you'll never lose another one again.

Pliers

Pliers are sort of the Rodney Dangerfield of the tool world—they don't get any respect. But they do have their uses. It's just that they're job-specific, so you'll need a few different ones to handle your boat maintenance duties.

Start with a pair of good-quality, drop-forged pliers of the conventional pattern. Make sure they have a smooth-acting, strong joint. Of course, since these are slip-joint pliers, there has to be a certain amount of play—but you want to avoid excessive wobbliness. If you can afford them, buy a pair of the conventional pliers' big brother: slip-joint water-pump pliers.

Then there are Vise-Grip locking pliers, arguably the handiest tool yet devised. If you only equip your tool kit with one pair of them, I would opt for the baby ones: the 5-inch model with curved jaws. These have all sorts of conventional (and unconventional) uses on board a boat, including doing yeoman's duty as temporary emergency handles in all sorts of shipboard applications. As a bonus, Vise-Grips also have a good cutter that can be used for snipping all kinds of wire and other types of stock. If your budget is bottomless, buy the 10-inch Vise-Grips, too. No matter what you do, make sure you buy genuine Vise-Grip brand locking pliers. In my opinion, the generic locking pliers on the market can't hold a candle to the real McCoy.

Needlenose pliers are handy for working on delicate linkages, cotter pins, and the like. If you're a tool nut, you might want to consider a pair of bent-nosed ones in addition to the conventional straight-nosed style. These should have rubber-dipped cushion grip handles. S•K is the brand I usually reach for.

Finally, there are the ubiquitous electrical crimping pliers. If you like to do your own low-voltage wiring on the boat, you should arm yourself with a good pair of these and a small box of miscellaneous connectors. You can get a cheap pair of crimping pliers for $6, though if you really plan to use them, I'd advise against it. Good ones cost $20 or more, but the better ones make a pronged crimp that really makes your connectors bite the wire and hang on like grim death. The better ones also have much more comfortable handles, which are handy if you have to make several connections.

Screwdrivers

When it comes to screwdrivers, again, stay away from the cheapies. If you go stock up with an assortment of the 69¢ ones in the paper bucket by the cash register at the hardware store, you'll be all set for opening paint cans, but little else. High-quality screwdrivers are made of good steel with precisely ground tips. There's a world of difference; opt for the good ones.

Does your boat have any Torx fasteners? These are the screws with the unusual looking splined heads that are starting to appear on cars and other consumer goods. If so, make sure you get the appropriately sized Torx screwdrivers for them. Nothing else will work.

Power Tools

If you like to do projects on the boat, you're going to need a drill motor. Unless your projects include cutting large-diameter holes in fiberglass with hole-saws, you will do just fine with one of the newer, more powerful, battery-powered drill motors.

When it comes to boat work, these are the best thing since sliced bread. They're safer than a conventional corded drill since there's no AC power. Best of all, since they aren't tied down to a power cord, they're easy to use. This item doesn't actually have to be kept in your boat's tool kit since you will be using it for projects, not emergencies.

Troubleshooting Tools

Your eyes and ears are important troubleshooting tools when it comes to diagnosing malfunctions. But human senses have some limitations. For example, no one wants to hold onto a spark plug lead while they crank the engine to check for spark. Fortunately an air-gap spark checker is happy to do the job. Not only will it tell you whether a spark is present, it will also give you an idea how hot that spark is.

The Stevens Instrument Company (see contact information on page 34) makes a nice four-lead model (S-48H); cost is $39.13 plus shipping. This is a handy tool for troubleshooting all kinds of engines—lawnmowers, boats, and cars. Yeah, I know, your boat's engine has more than four cylinders. No matter; you can check for spark on four cylinders at a time with this tester, which is just fine. (The Stevens Company also makes an eight-cylinder model, if you don't mind spending more money.)

A word of warning on spark checking with an air-gap checker: This is an explosion hazard. Unless you're absolutely sure there are no explosive gasoline vapors in the engine room, it's safer to use a timing light to perform this test. See chapter 3 for details.

A multimeter is a must-have item. You can get by with a simple $15 analog one from RadioShack, but if you can afford it, I'd urge you to buy one of the fancier digital multimeters (DMMs) such as the ones made by Fluke. These cost more, but they're far more versatile and rugged than the old-fashioned analog types. They're also hard to misuse. For example, if you set a conventional meter to the ohmmeter function and hook it into a circuit that has power in it, bye-bye meter. Perform this stunt with a DMM, though, and it will just flash its digits at you and wait for you to figure out what you're doing wrong. Learn how to use a multimeter and you'll be a troubleshooting whiz kid. (See chapter 5 for detailed instructions on using this tool.)

If your boat has a shore-power system, you should have a solid-state circuit checker. Hubbell and Marinco both make nice ones. These allow you to check your boat's AC wiring for faults. More important, when you go cruising, you can use one of these checkers to give the dock wiring a test before you hook up your shore cord.

These testers have three LEDs. Using one is simple. Plug it in the outlet being tested, note which LEDs are lighted, and consult the chart attached to the unit. This tester will detect open grounds, reversed hot and neutral leads, and a host of other potentially dangerous wiring faults.

A timing light is not really a troubleshooting tool and, if you don't do your own engine tune-ups, you don't even need to own one. Even if you like to do your own tune-ups, you'll only use this tool once a year, so it might be something you want to borrow from a friend.

If you do decide to buy one, make sure you select an inductive pickup timing light. These are the easiest to use. There's a new wrinkle in the timing light world: the self-powered, inductive pickup timing light. It's powered by a set of D-cell flashlight batteries, so the only wire you have to hook up to use it is the pickup lead. I consider this tool a welcome development because the fewer wires a timing light has, the less likely you are to get one of them tangled in the drive belts on the front of the engine.

I'm including a compression gauge in this list of troubleshooting tools because when an engine won't go, the problem is fuel, spark, or compression. However, it's almost always one of the first two. (Compression is something that usually diminishes over time as an engine wears out—unless a head gasket blows.)

A compression tester, however, has another use. At the end of each season, it's useful to take readings on each of your engine's cylinders. By doing so, you will be taking stock of the condition of the engine's moving parts and gaining insight into how much of a toll wear and tear is taking on its internal parts.

If your engine has freshwater-cooling (the so-called closed-cooling system), you'll need an antifreeze checker to measure the freeze-protection level of the coolant when you winterize. This is an inexpensive tester that gets its reading by measuring the specific gravity of the coolant. Thus, strictly speaking, it's a hydrometer. You can find a serviceable one at any auto parts store for less than $10.

Miscellaneous Tools

First, some indispensable cutting tools: a pocketknife, a hacksaw, and an assortment of drill bits. Here are some other "nice-to-have" tools.

- A gasket scraper is handy when you have to rebuild flexible impeller pumps and other assemblies. If you use it on bronze or aluminum castings, be very careful not to scratch and gouge the soft, finely machined surfaces.
- If you do your own tune-ups, you should have a spark plug gapping tool in your bag of tricks. The simple round one that fits on a keyring is OK, though the wire type is better. You'll find the recommended spark plug gap setting in your engine owner's manual or on a sticker affixed to the engine.
- A magnet of any sort is handy. Use it to test hose clamps and other hardware bits and pieces to make sure they're made of high-quality (nonmagnetic) stainless steel. A telescoping magnetic probe is

handy for retrieving tools and parts that you drop down in your boat's bilges.

- You can't do much mechanical work on board a boat without a flashlight. No matter what brand you choose for your main flashlight it must be explosion proof and should have a halogen bulb.

When it comes to flashlights, I don't think you can beat the ones from Pelican. They are bright, explosion proof, rugged, and easy to use. They aren't particularly cheap, but when you need a solid, reliable light on board, they fill the bill nicely. A penlight is handy for shedding some light in the nooks and crannies of your boat's engine room. If you ever have to read an identification plate from your engine's distributor you'll find the penlight indispensable. Pelican makes an explosion-proof one, which is safe in an engine room.

I've found that a headlamp is incredibly handy for mechanical work in a boat. I have yet to find one that's rated explosion proof though. (Strictly speaking, you'd probably be safe if you turned it on before you entered an explosive atmosphere, but I just don't use mine if there are any gasoline fumes about.)

- A mechanic's inspection mirror really comes in handy for several chores. It's a small mirror on a telescoping, swivel-jointed handle. There are times when you simply can't fit your head where it needs to be to see something important. That is, unless you have one of these mirrors. You can find one at any auto parts store.
- A parts grabber is another handy gadget. It's a flexible probe with a plunger at one end. When you push the plunger, three (or four) spring-loaded fingers extend from the business end of this tool. You won't need it very often, but when you do, nothing else will do the trick. There are big ones, which are handy for retrieving wrenches that you've dropped in the bilge, and small ones that are great for starting screws where your fingers can't fit.
- If you like to install your own accessories, you'll find a fishtape indispensable for snaking wires. You unreel enough of the flat steel tape to probe through the area the wire must run, attach the wire to the end when it sticks out, then pull the wire back through to make your connections. (See chapter 5 for pointers on using this tool.)
- If your boat has batteries that don't have carrying handles, you'll need a clamp-type battery carrier. Don't trust the ones that grab the battery by the terminal posts—they don't always hold. And for heaven's sake, don't overtighten the clamp-type battery carrier either; it's strong enough to break a battery and doesn't need to be that tight to work.
- Speaking of batteries, you must have a battery post and terminal cleaning tool. This is a small female wire brush that you push down on the battery posts and spin. It cleans the posts in a jiffy. Then you undo the bayonet cover and expose the male wire brush inside, which cleans out the inside of the terminal ends on the cables. When it comes to cleaning battery terminals and posts, nothing works nearly as well as one of these. Incidentally, this maintenance should be done regularly—corrosion never sleeps.
- If your boatyard is going to store your batteries over the winter, buy a battery-marking pen to write your boat's name on them before you hand them over. This tool is also handy for highlighting the timing marks on your engine if you do your own tune-ups.
- Include a stout pair of leather work gloves in your boat's toolbox. A couple of pairs of disposable plastic gloves are a good idea as well. They cost next to nothing and keep your hands and skin protected when you have to use dangerous chemicals such as carburetor cleaner.
- Wire brushes are handy. I like to have two: a small, brass-bristle one for delicate jobs and a large, steel-bristle one for heavy-duty wire brushing duties.
- There's one other abrasive tool that comes in handy for working on electrics and electronics—an ink eraser. You can either buy one at the local stationery store or use one of the free ones that come on sweepstakes pens that show up in the junk mail from time to time. This tool is just the ticket for cleaning terminals and connectors to make your boat's electrical connections reliable.
- Lastly, the ubiquitous hammer. Don't reach for this tool lightly. Use it only when you're making an

adjustment that really requires it, or when you're trying to free up a seized assembly. I do not subscribe to the school of thought that says if something doesn't move, wallop it with a hammer.

THE SPARE PARTS KIT

This is just as important as your tool kit—maybe even more so. In a pinch, you might be able to improvise tools (as we all know, a butter knife makes a pretty serviceable screwdriver). On the other hand, if you try to improvise a water-pump impeller with a couple of blades missing, you'll find out about the meaning of the word futility.

Essential Spares List

- propeller
- bulbs for all lamps (especially running lights)
- any necessary fuses (most modern boats use magnetic breakers)
- engine drive belts*
- hoses*
- assortment of hose clamps
- spark plugs*
- cap and rotor*
- points and condenser (if your engine has a conventional ignition system)*
- replacement fuel filter elements (carry at least two)*
- other engine parts recommended by your mechanic*
- flexible impeller pump parts or a complete spare pump*
- duct tape
- electrical tape
- electrical connectors
- nylon ty-wraps (assortment)
- Monel seizing wire

*Rotate your stock of these items; use your spare ones at tune-up time and replace them with fresh ones.

Many of the items in your boat's spare parts kit are somewhat perishable—rubber parts like drive belts are a prime example—so you don't want to leave them down in that dank engine room for ten years. Therefore, I like to rotate my stock of periodically replaced parts by using the one in the spares kit when I'm performing routine maintenance. Then I restock the kit with a fresh one.

Some engine manufacturers package spare parts kits with a good supply of replacement parts to help you get home. That's a good start but, if you can't get hold of a kit, you can certainly make a nice do-it-yourself equivalent. The manufacturer-packaged kits don't have everything you need anyway. If you're using one of them, read on to see what else you should be carrying.

- A spare propeller is a good place to start. Regardless of whether your boat is powered by an inboard, a sterndrive, or an outboard, a spare prop can save the weekend if you have a minor case of what I euphemistically call "cockpit error."
- Carry a full complement of spare lamps for your running lights. If one of them burns out, it's nice to be able to replace it immediately without hunting for a replacement. Spare lamps for your other light fixtures are in the nice-to-have category. It's not a matter of life or death if you can't replace one of your cabin or cockpit lights.
- Although most modern boats use magnetic circuit breakers to protect the electrical circuits against overloads, you might still find old-fashioned fuses in the back panels of electronic devices. Find out what sizes you need to service your equipment and stash a box of each in the spares kit. Label them as to what gear they fit.
- If you replace drive belts regularly, chances are you'll never have one of them fail. But for my peace of mind, I carry spares in my kit. If none ever break, just cycle them onto the engine at replacement time and put the fresh ones in your spares kit.
- It's impractical to carry spares for every hose on your boat. (You'd have to dedicate one of your hanging lockers just to hold them.) But, even so, a few lengths of hose in the most popular sizes can come in handy.
- You'd be crazy to go offshore without a good complement of hose clamps. A bad hose clamp on

one of your boat's hoses can make trouble at the damnedest time, and nothing else will really do the job. Make sure the clamps you stock in your kit are constructed completely from high-grade (nonmagnetic) stainless steel.

- If I had an outboard-powered boat and could only bring one spare part and one tool, it would be a set of spark plugs and a plug wrench. Nine times out of ten, when an outboard craps out or runs poorly, the plugs are fouled. A fresh set of plugs will get you on your way in two shakes of a lamb's tail. (Don't cross-thread or overtighten spark plugs in an outboard's aluminum cylinder heads.) Sterndrive- and inboard-powered boats rarely need unscheduled spark plug replacements, but why take a chance? If you never need them, they will be waiting for you at tune-up time. (Chapters 4 and 8 include directions for installing spark plugs in outboard motors and inboard/sterndrive engines, respectively.)
- If your sterndrive or inboard engine has an old-fashioned ignition system—conventional battery and coil with breaker points—you should carry a cap and rotor, a set of breaker points, and a condenser. If it's equipped with electronic ignition, you'll just need the cap and rotor.
- Marine engines don't have air filters, but they do have some sort of fuel filter. And do they ever work for a living. If you get a load of dirty or water-laden gasoline, you will have to replace the fuel filter after you clean the water or junk out of the tank. I'd suggest you carry two replacement elements at a minimum.
- Some engines have special parts that might fail at untimely moments—fusible links, for example. When you collect your other engine spares, ask the shop foreman or mechanic if there are any other critical parts that fail from time to time on your particular engine. Add these to your list.
- I like to stock a small fishing-lure box with a good selection of electrical connectors. Make sure you include butt connectors, ring lugs, spade lugs, and bullet connectors, both male and female.
- That fishing-lure box also makes a sensible home for some precut lengths of heat-shrink tubing. If you cut them in 3-inch lengths they will fit in the box and be long enough to cover any connections you might need to make.
- A few nylon wire clips and the short stainless steel panhead screws that are used to secure them will come in handy as well. Stocking your spares box with these articles will let it do double duty. It can serve as a spares box and a source for parts when you do small electrical installation jobs on the boat.
- Though they probably won't fit in a lure box, you should make sure your spares kit has some nylon ty-wraps in it, too. Stock a few sizes and make sure you include some of the handy ones that have a screw hole. (These take the same small stainless screws that you are carrying for the wire clips.)
- Finally, your spares kit should include a spool of 0.031-inch Monel seizing wire. This can be used to secure control cable ends, anchor chain shackles, driveshaft coupling setscrews, and all sorts of other hardware bits that you want to proof against loosening caused by vibration. When you twist this wire, do it tightly and be careful not to poke the sharp ends into your hands or fingers. Bend the twisted ends down against the hardware to lessen the danger.

Sticky Stuff

- Some boaters claim that duct tape makes the world go round. I'm not sure if I would ascribe such powers to it, but just the same, it is pretty handy stuff. The only downside to using duct tape is that it makes a gooey mess of whatever you stick it to. Throw a roll in the spares kit anyway.
- Electrical tape also comes in handy. I don't use it for permanent wrappings because eventually it starts to come unwrapped. Think of it as a stopgap measure. Buy the best quality you can find because the cheap stuff is truly junk.

Pumps in the Dumps

Most engines have flexible impeller pumps. If they ingest a load of sandy or silty water, they can get scuffed up and lose their effectiveness. You can either carry a rebuild kit and the necessary tools to replace the affected parts, or you can go the super easy route and just carry a complete replacement pump and the tools needed to perform a pump transplant.

If your pump sheds some impeller blades, you will have to track down the missing pieces inside the engine before you try to put it back in service. (In the case of the circulating pump in a freshwater-cooled engine, the heat exchanger is the most popular destination for loose impeller bits.)

If you are carrying only a replacement impeller, and the pump's cover plate is scuffed up as well, here's a useful trick that will get you home. Flip the cover plate over and put the lettered side toward the impeller. Of course, some of those letters are the pump's model number. Given time and wear they might become indecipherable. Write them down on a slip of paper before you do this.

Speaking of slips of paper, if you can't track down a gasket for that cover plate, you can make one from a thin strong piece of paper; typing paper works well. Cut it accurately to match the housing and the screw holes, smear a thin film of grease on both sides, and reassemble the pump. Again, this is a get-home measure only. When you get back in port, collect the necessary parts and rebuild the pump properly.

Emergency Preparedness

The first line of defense when it comes to preparedness is actively avoiding emergencies. This includes making sure the fuel tank is full before heading out, listening carefully to the weather radio and changing your plans if bad weather threatens, and checking things out carefully in the engine room (any water in the fuel filter–water separator?) before you undo the docklines. Most of this is simple common sense, which, as one wag once observed, is not nearly as common as it ought to be.

Besides common sense, there are three things that make any boat and crew more capable of dealing with unexpected calamities and breakdowns: an intimate knowledge of the boat, the ability to stay calm and keep everyone on board calm as well, and having a good complement of safety gear and knowing how to use it effectively. It's the skipper's responsibility, of course, to make sure that each of the above safety measures are met. Although they should be part of your normal routine, they are especially important when you take friends and kids out on your boat. You shouldn't take this responsibility lightly.

Know Your Boat, Inside and Out

As the skipper, you should know your boat cold. This is a broad edict that includes knowing how it behaves in differing conditions, where every through-hull fitting and seacock is, what the boat's weaknesses are, and a hundred and one other details.

Learning where everything is can be doubly important if you are not in the habit of doing your own boat maintenance. When an emergency crops up, your mechanic won't be there to tell you where the through-hull fitting and shutoff are for the engine's raw-water inlet. It's up to you to know.

You might want to use a label maker to mark locker doors that provide access to important fittings and shutoffs. When you stow gear in these spaces, make sure that heavy articles, such as spare anchors, can't shift and damage fittings and hoses. Also make sure your stowed gear doesn't impede access to your boat's mechanicals.

Of course, you should know where the first-aid supplies are stowed and how to use them.

Staying Calm

Keeping your wits about you when someone finds water swirling around above the floorboards is one of the hallmarks of a good skipper. Ideally, you should consider in advance how you would cope with various shipboard emergencies. For example, if I found the floorboards floating around, I would appoint one of the adults to get everyone in their PFDs and another crewmember to get on the VHF and begin to radio a Mayday message to the coast guard. At the same time, I would get to work stanching the leak and getting the water pumped out of the boat.

An educated crew is another important component of a safe ship. Each member should know where the safety gear is stowed, how to use the radio, what the procedure is for transmitting a Mayday call, how to get position information from the GPS or loran for that Mayday transmission, and so forth.

Don't put yourself in the position of being the only person on board who knows anything about safe boating. Encourage your spouse and children to take safe-boating courses. Apart from this formal training, you can (and should) share the mysteries of navigation and route-finding with them.

Don't adopt a macho "Only I can do that" attitude. It's more relaxing to cruise with a competent crew. It's also safer in case, heaven forbid, something should happen to you.

Crew education should also include first-aid training. When was the last time you took a first-aid course? First-aid recommendations are continually changing. Also, memory gets hazy. It's best to renew your first-aid training every couple of years to keep abreast of new developments and keep the procedures fresh in your mind.

Safety Gear

It's true that necessity is the mother of invention. And invention is an important component when it comes to dealing with onboard emergencies and incidents. But it's not all you want in your bag of tricks.

A sensible inventory of safety gear that's tailored to the *type of boating you do* can be indispensable. If you confine your boating to the shores of a small lake, it would be silly to carry a six-person raft, an emergency supply of food and water, and an EPIRB. If, on the other hand, you make extended passages in the Caribbean or other less-traveled waterways, the equipment mentioned above would make perfect sense.

Of course, at a minimum there are certain items that you are required to carry. The U.S. Coast Guard booklet *Federal Requirements and Safety Tips for Recreational Boats* lists these. You should be able to find a copy of this booklet at your local ship's store, from the Coast Guard Auxiliary, or at the coast guard booth at a boat show. You can also read it on-line at www.uscgboating.org/safety/fed_reqs/landing.htm. The emphasis here is on the word *minimum*; consider the contents of the government's booklet to be a skeleton list.

The size of your vessel dictates what gear you are required to carry. For most boats less than 65 feet, you must carry an approved (type 1, 2, 3, or 5) PFD for each person on board; a type 4 (throwable) PFD; at least one type B-1 fire extinguisher; day and night visual distress signals; a bell, whistle, or other efficient sound-producing device; ventilation ducting and blower; and a flame arrester on the carburetor of any gasoline-fueled engine or genset mounted in an enclosed space.

You can probably see why I call that a skeleton list; it's the product of legislative compromise. On a typical boat, I would make sure that I had at least two, preferably three, strategically located fire extinguishers. I'd have one in the galley, for example, but not where I would have to reach through a galley fire to get to it. The cockpit is a good spot for the second fire extinguisher. If your dinghy has an outboard, you should carry one there, too.

Flares: Alert, Then Locate

There are two types of flares with two types of functions: alert and locate. The first is the aerial type, which is designed to alert potential rescuers to a distress situation. The second type are the handheld ones that allow your would-be rescuers to home in on your position; the so-called locate function.

I'm amazed at the number of boats that carry a basic flare kit. You know, the orange drum that satisfies the coast guard requirements. You call those flares?

If you want to acquaint yourself with real flares, take a look at Pains-Wessex or Schermuly parachute flares. If you ever find yourself on the bridge of a ship, these flares are what you'll find in the safety gear locker. In fact, by international agreement they're required to be carried on these vessels. But a ship in distress should be easier to notice than a relatively small pleasure boat. So, even if you don't own a ship, there's no reason you can't carry these superior flares.

Their light output is 30,000 candlepower. They fly higher than other aerial flares—300 meters or better versus 110 meters for the gun-launched 25-millimeter flares that most boaters carry. This makes them visible from as far off as twenty miles—a circle covering nearly 1,300 square miles. These flares are harder to overlook or ignore than lesser models. Also, since they descend by parachute, they light up the sky for forty seconds or so instead of the eight seconds that the 25-millimeter ones stay aloft.

Admittedly they don't come cheap. In fact, you might want to make sure you're sitting before you continue to read—these flares cost around $40 apiece. (That's for the red ones; the white sell for $62 a piece.) Considering what's at stake, though, these are the only flares I carry. If something goes drastically wrong, you won't think twice about shooting off $120 worth of flares. Invest in these and the chances that your message will be received are much better.

OK, now that you've gotten their attention, what's next? It's time to help them locate you. Here's where fluorescent orange day markers, signal mirrors, handheld flares and strobes, or even a good bright flashlight come into their own.

If it's daytime, the day marker, that big orange flag in your safety kit, can be seen for quite a distance. Mount it as high as you can as soon as you've sent up your big flares. Don't start burning your handheld flares until you see a potential rescuer (aircraft or vessel) approaching.

A mirror can be quite conspicuous and visible for a surprising distance. Put it to work if the sun is in the right part of the sky to bounce its rays toward a would-be rescuer.

At night, handheld flares are the name of the game. It's good to have several on hand. Before you light them, get up as high on board your boat as you safely can to increase their visibility. I stick with Pains-Wessex or Schermuly for these as well. They sell for $12.95 a piece.

A small strobe, such as the ones from A.C.R., is very effective at night. They run for a long time on the small battery inside, so this is an item to put into operation as soon as you've stabilized things and launched the rockets. Don't discount a strobe for daytime use either; they're actually quite visible even on a sunny day.

Your safety bag should also include a good, bright flashlight and spare batteries. You can't do better than one of the corrosion-proof, explosion-proof, waterproof ones manufactured by Pelican.

Dye markers aren't taken very seriously, but perhaps they should be. By day they help make a boat in distress much more visible to searchers in aircraft.

All of the serious safety gear I've mentioned, including the A.C.R. strobes, are sold by Landfall Navigation. If you don't have a copy of their extensive catalog, which lists paper charts and navigation publications for the entire world, electronic and celestial navigation supplies and equipment, and the most extensive selection of safety gear I've found anywhere, contact them and ask for one (Landfall Navigation, 151 Harvard Ave., Stamford, CT 06902; 800-941-2219; www.landfallnavigation.com).

It's not a bad idea to keep your boat's safety gear together in a watertight case or a kayaker's drybag—you'll keep the individual items together, clean, and dry. This strategy is also handy if you have to abandon ship, because everything you will need—except food, water, a handheld VHF (and/or EPIRB), and PFDs—is together in one container.

Having the necessary safety gear on board is not the whole story. It must be stowed in a location that everyone knows and it must be regularly inspected.

Inspection is a simple enough operation. Check flares at the beginning of each season so you can be sure that they won't go past their expiration dates before the boating season ends. When they do go past their dates, they no longer satisfy coast guard regulations. If you have the standard flares, consider donating expired ones to the local Coast Guard Auxiliary for practice purposes.

If you carry the Schermuly or Pains-Wessex SOLAS-grade flares, you can follow a different procedure with outdated ones because these brands are likely to remain perfectly functional long after their expiration dates have passed. Add new ones to keep you within the letter of the law and retain the old ones for backups. (I've successfully launched SOLAS flares that were five years out of date.)

The VHF: Sometimes It's All You Need

Almost all the readers of this book have VHF radios installed on their boats. Practically all of our coastal waters are served by a network of repeater stations and antennas, which means you should be able to raise the coast guard from almost anywhere you can go with your boat. Failing that, if you transmit your Mayday with all the pertinent information, it can be relayed by another vessel that's within range of rescue authorities.

The key to radioing a Mayday message is furnishing all the necessary information. You should use a standard format in which you transmit the following information in this order:

- Name of the vessel and the radio call sign
- Your location in either absolute coordinates (latitude and longitude), or in range (nautical miles) and bearing (true, not magnetic), from a clearly defined landmark or geographical point
- Nature of the emergency
- Type of assistance you are requesting
- Number of persons aboard and condition of any injured crewmembers
- Condition of your vessel (its seaworthiness)
- Description of the vessel (length, type, and hull and superstructure colors)
- What radio frequency you will be monitoring

For more particulars on Mayday messages and other radio usage hints, refer to the radio section of the invaluable *Eldridge Tide and Pilot Book*. This bright yellow book, published annually since 1875, should be carried on every boat that plies the waters of the eastern seaboard of the United States. It sells for a modest $11.95 and contains much too much information to detail here. If you can't find one at your local chandlery, contact the publisher: Robert E. White Instruments, 711 Atlantic Ave., Boston, MA 02111; 800-992-3045; www.robertwhite.com.

Thomas Reed Publications has recently published a new edition of *Reed's Nautical Companion*, a mighty handy reference book to have on any boat. Almost every chapter has been updated/revised/rewritten, including the very thorough one on communications. It sells for $24.95 and is available at chandleries or from Thomas Reed Publications, 398 Columbus Ave., #302, Boston, MA 02116; 800-995-4995; www.reedsalmanac.com.

Your best bet for position information is either GPS or loran. If you can't furnish coordinates or range and bearing to a landmark, provide your position according to dead reckoning. Include your last known position, course, and the time since you were there. This is important—if the rescuers know where to begin looking, they can lend you aid more quickly.

If your boat's electrical system is disabled or you have to abandon ship, a handheld VHF provides a good backup communications system. Its range is much less than a fixed-mount model, but many lives have been saved by these small radios. Keep in mind that, in a pinch, even a cellular phone can provide communications.

EPIRBs

An Emergency Position-Indicating Radio Beacon (EPIRB) is an emergency radio that, when switched on, broadcasts a signal that allows rescuers to locate a boat in distress. There are two main types of EPIRBs. The more expensive ones are the 406 MHz models. Their signals are picked up by a network of rescue satellites and relayed to search and rescue organizations. They work anywhere on the globe. These are really expensive—expect to pay between $650 and $1,000. The more costly ones have a built-in GPS receiver that transmits your position with the Mayday request. Midrange models interface with your handheld GPS and store your position when you abandon ship.

For as little as one quarter of that figure, you can get a class B EPIRB. These work well enough in coastal waters and they save many lives each year. The signals they transmit are monitored to some extent by the same SARSAT satellites that the 406 types communicate with, and also by ships and aircraft. They transmit on a frequency of 121.5 MHZ and sell for about $130.

One problem with EPIRBs is that they're easily turned on and there are too many false alarms—many more than actual emergencies. Therefore, the coast guard is not too keen on having them come into more widespread use. But they do save lives, day in and day out. Consider carrying one.

Hull Plugs

Some people make fun of these tapered wooden plugs, claiming that only sailboaters rely on them. Not so. For my money, there's nothing better if you have a failed hose on an inlet that either has no seacock or has one that won't close. (Of course, that won't happen to you if you follow the seacock maintenance tips found in this book.)

To work effectively, a wooden plug should fit the opening *properly*. If the conditions allow you to do so safely, install an emergency plug from the *outside* of the boat. Because of the pressure of the incoming water, it's hard to insert one from the inside of a boat. It has to be hammered in firmly and doing so could crack the tailpiece of the through-hull fitting. Then you'd have to scramble overboard to rap the plug into place and you'd have to know where the offending through-hull fitting was located. (This is one of the times when it's handy to know your boat like the back of your hand.) Some safety-conscious boaters even mark the toerail of their boat adjacent to every through-hull fitting—not a bad idea, if you think about it.

Manset Marine (50 New County Rd., Rockland, ME 04841; 207-596-6464; www.mansetmarine.com) sells hull plugs under their Seven Seas brand name. A bag of ten assorted sizes that cover most normal-sized through-hulls sells for around $10. If you're handy with a bandsaw and a belt sander, you can even make your own. However, since a bag of ready-made ones is so cheap, it's probably not worth your time to do so.

It's human nature to turn a blind eye toward the possibility of anything going wrong. Popular boating magazines often like to soft-pedal any discussion of emergency preparedness. Some editors think it makes people nervous to read about disasters at sea.

I think we're all grown-ups and that it's possible for us to mentally rehearse what we'd need to do in the event of an onboard emergency. In fact, I think that the more prepared we are for an emergency, the less likely it is that one will ever befall our boat or our crew.

Index

Numbers in **bold** refer to pages with illustrations

D

E